The
DIAMONDBACKS
Collection

50 OF THE GREATEST CARDS IN
SPORTS COLLECTING HISTORY

Other books in the series by these authors:

The T206 Collection: The Players & Their Stories (2010)

The Cracker Jack Collection: Baseball's Prized Players (2013)

The 100 Greatest Baseball Autographs (2016)

Legendary Lumber: The Top 100 Player Bats in Baseball History (2017)

An All-Star's Cardboard Memories (2018)

Baseball & Bubble Gum: The 1952 Topps Collection (2020)

The DIAMONDBACKS Collection

50 OF THE GREATEST CARDS IN SPORTS COLLECTING HISTORY

Tom Zappala & Ellen Zappala

with John Molori

FOREWORD & CONTRIBUTIONS BY JOE ORLANDO

Peter E. Randall Publisher

Portsmouth, New Hampshire

2022

© 2022 by Tom Zappala and Ellen Zappala

ISBN: 978-1-942155-44-7

Library of Congress Control Number: 2021924633

Produced by Peter E. Randall Publisher

Portsmouth, New Hampshire 03801

www.perpublisher.com

Book design: Grace Peirce

Photography credit: Chrissie Good

Player card images provided by the Ken Kendrick Diamondback Collection.

Additional memorabilia and images provided by The Mike Heffner Collection, Heritage Auctions, The Brian Seigel Collection, SCP Auctions, sports artist James Fiorentino, and Professional Sports Authenticator (PSA).

Additional copies available from: TomZappalaMedia.com and Amazon.com

Printed in Canada

To the great athletes we have written about over the years.

1952 Roy Campanella game-used jersey, Campanella game-used bat circa 1955, Jackie Robinson milk glass and fan club pin circa 1950, and Brooklyn Dodgers team-signed baseball, 1949. *The Mike Heffner Collection.*

Contents

Foreword

IN THE WORLD OF COLLECTIBLES, from trading cards to comic books to coins, there is one thing that rings true with hobbyists of all types.

It's all about **The List**.

If you're a collector like me, then you know exactly what I mean.

We start with an idea, a theme...or a list before we begin our journey. Sometimes, that list is predetermined, one that is created by the manufacturer. Other times, it is one dreamed up by the collector. It can be anything you want it to be, and why not? After all, it's your collection and your money.

Then, and only then, the hunt begins. One by one, collectors seek to check items off the list by finding the items they want and in the grade they desire. Their work is not done until the collection is complete in content and completely satisfying in quality. It is the exercise of bringing items together that, in the eyes of the collector, should be together.

So, why is developing *The List* such an important first step?

By establishing *The List*, you are setting the goal. In collecting and in life, goals are important. They help keep us focused on the task at hand. They help keep us disciplined, especially when it comes to buying. It's not about how lofty those goals are, as we all have different budgets and tastes...it's the exercise of setting those goals that matters. A large part of collector enjoyment is attributed to the act of working

towards something, or better stated, checking everything off that list.

As collectors evolve, gain more experience, and become more informed about what they're buying, they get better at it. The process itself gets easier as we fine tune our collections over time. As we get older, we have a better understanding of what we like. To be clear, not everyone goes through this process, and it tends to show. If you have been a lifelong hobbyist like me, then you have probably gone through periods where you felt your collection was going off the rails. You buy and buy but wake up one day to realize there is no real rhyme or reason to what you've built.

The List approach isn't for everyone, but having one makes for an improved collecting experience.

Now, to the collection, and the man, of the hour.

I can think of no better example of a collector who committed to this concept more than Ken Kendrick, owner of one of the most prestigious pound-for-pound card collections in the world, one that has been proudly displayed in venues such as the hallowed halls of Cooperstown. While Ken does collect other things, such as the classic 1952 Topps baseball set, which is currently second on the PSA Set Registry's All-Time Finest rankings, the core of his collection is centered around 50 of the greatest sports cards ever made.

Original artwork © James Fiorentino

WILLIE MAYS

If we were putting together a book of the top 50 sports cards in existence today, from a literal standpoint, opinions would naturally differ from one hobbyist to another. There would be strong arguments both for and against the merit of each card considered for inclusion. In today's market, there is no question that plenty of surefire candidates for a hypothetical *Top 50* remain, those that are not found in this book, from cards like the 1957 Topps Bill Russell to the 1965 Topps Joe Namath to the 1979 O-Pee-Chee Wayne Gretzky. It would also be ludicrous to ignore the rise of contemporary icons like Tom Brady and LeBron James, or the increased demand for certain rarities featuring Michael Jordan or Mike Trout. The only question would be which of these cards should be admitted to the exclusive club.

That, however, is *not* what this book is about.

To be clear, the 50 cards that make up the anchor of Ken's amazing collection were hand selected by him after years of not only studying the marketplace and doing intense research, but also identifying the 50 cards he personally wanted to buy. This book is a celebration of those 50 cards, which are amongst the most desirable cardboard treasures in the hobby. When you peruse the pages of this book, there will be no doubt about that.

Once upon a time, Ken started with a goal of 20 cards after being inspired by a published list in the late-2000s. As time passed, Ken kept the original 20 intact but expanded his list to 50 so he could build upon the tremendous foundation already in place. A collector in motion stays in motion, and Ken enjoyed the process so much that he wanted to further his vision. Ken's collection is built on the unquestioned legends, and cardboard, from different sports.

The Mount Rushmores of the diamond are all here. *The Georgia Peach*, *The Sultan of Swat*, *The Iron Horse*, Jackie, Mickey, Willie, Roberto, *Hammerin' Hank*, *Teddy Ballgame*, and more. While there is no mistaking Ken's love for baseball as it dominates his collection, some of the hobby pillars from the worlds of basketball and football are also represented. From the 1935 National Chicle Bronko Nagurski to the 1948 Bowman George Mikan to the most important sports card of the entire post-1980 era—the 1986 Fleer Michael Jordan.

They are all here in an amassment that Ken has appropriately dubbed the Diamondbacks Collection. The pedigree connects his involvement in the sports world as the managing general partner of the Arizona Diamondbacks directly to his other passion.

Like Ken, passion is what drives most collectors. It is also what separates this hobby, and asset class, from so many others. There is a sentimental and nostalgic element present here. This element takes it from being an activity that merely helps pass the time, or a traditional investment, to another level of participation altogether. Sports connects people, it excites people, and from all walks of life. Sports, and sports collecting, have the ability to get individuals emotionally invested in a way that so many other endeavors cannot. There is a story behind every collectible.

That is why we are all here waiting to turn the pages of this book, and that is why Ken started down this road years ago. With persistence, patience, and a ton of focused desire, Ken took on his own list and won.

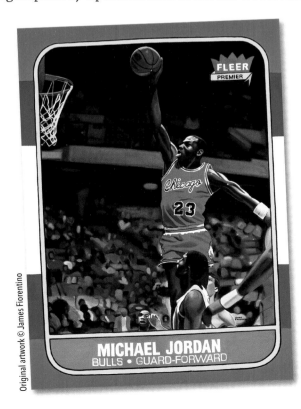

Acknowledgments

BEHIND MOST AUTHORS IS A TEAM of professionals that help make our work much easier. This book is no exception. We have been blessed to work with some of the most gifted and talented individuals in both the publishing and collectibles world.

Special thanks to our dear friend and hobby expert, Joe Orlando, who has contributed insightful card, memorabilia, and market analysis for all our books. Thank you, Joe, for sharing your knowledge and expertise with us.

Many thanks to our friend and colleague, John Molori, who has collaborated with us on five of our books. John's colorful and folksy writing style always makes for a fun and entertaining read.

Original artwork © James Fiorentino

COBB, DETROIT

A special shout out to Mike Heffner, president and CEO of Lelands Auctions, for allowing us to photograph memorabilia from his personal collection, to private collector Brian Seigel for the memorabilia used on the book cover, and to David Kohler of SCP Auctions for additional memorabilia.

We also thank Chris Ivy, Mike Provenzale, and Derek Grady of Heritage Auctions for providing many amazing and rare photo images of players for use in this book.

The exceptional original art featured on pages viii–xi is the work of talented, award-winning sports artist, James Fiorentino. Thank you, James, for allowing us to display your work.

The amazing sports memorabilia photographs in this book and on the cover are the work of Chrissie Good, senior photographer for Collectors Universe. This is our third book project with Chrissie, and we appreciate her special ability to bring our ideas to life through her photography.

Special thanks to Jackie Curiel, PSA Chief of Staff, for her painstaking efforts on fine-tuning card images and working with her staff to produce flawless results. Jackie has been an integral part of all our book projects, and we appreciate everything she has done to make them successful. Kudos also to Luis De Alba, PSA Imaging Processor, for his fine work, and thank you to Professional Sports Authenticator (PSA) for providing card images for the last chapter.

Thank you to Kevin Struss, one of the most respected and knowledgeable trading card experts in the hobby, who provided excellent input and perspective throughout this project.

Many thanks to Nicki Adair, executive assistant to the managing general partner and EVP/CFO of the Arizona Diamondbacks, for imaging the cards in the Diamondbacks Collection for use in this book.

This is our seventh book with Peter E. Randall Publisher, and like our six previous award-winning books, we are extremely proud of this one. Deidre Randall and staff have produced another beautiful and exciting book. Many thanks to Deidre for her unwavering pursuit of excellence, to Grace Peirce for her expertise and creative designs, to Zak Johnson for his careful editing, and to Kael Randall for his assistance with this project.

Thank you to former major-league pitcher, Tom Candiotti for sharing his vast knowledge of and contributions to the hobby. His interview was both fun and informative.

Very special thanks to the guy who made this book possible. Ken Kendrick, managing partner of the Arizona Diamondbacks, always made time in his extremely busy schedule to work with us. Whether it was to make a suggestion or to provide a key piece of information on a particular card, Ken has always been great to work with.

Lastly, thank you to collectors and sports fans. We appreciate your support!

Introduction

WHEN I WAS A KID IN THE EARLY 1960s, my pal Wayne and I liked to walk down the street to the local neighborhood store, Eddies Variety. We were in there so often, that we became good friends with the owner, a wonderful older gentleman, Mr. Abdul. Every Friday afternoon, Wayne and I would go to the store with twenty-five cents each, enough to buy a few packs of baseball cards. Mr. Abdul gave us a tip. He told us the best time to buy packs was on Friday mornings because that was when his new inventory came in. We couldn't wait to get our new packs each week and we would immediately sit on the sidewalk outside Mr. Abdul's store to open those packs. Then, Wayne and I would begin our weekly routine. "Got him." "Got him." "Need him." "Got him." "Need him." "Need him."

We would go back and forth trading cards until every card was examined. By the time we were done, we would typically swap about three or four cards. Personally, I was trying to put together a collection of my favorite Red Sox players. For Wayne, it was a collection of the current stars of the day. Most kids at the time loved to put together collections—any type of collection. It could be your favorite team, stars, player by position, whatever you desired.

This book is about a collection, not just any collection, but arguably the greatest 50 cards in any private collection on the planet. Owning the Diamondbacks Collection would be the dream of every kid or, for that matter, every grownup in the collectibles world. This collection represents the majority of the highest graded and certainly the most desirable sports cards in the world. From the famous Honus Wagner card to the iconic 1952 Mickey Mantle, to the more recent 1986 Michael Jordon rookie card, the Diamondbacks Collection has been curated by a guy who not only loves the hobby but who has made our National Pastime his life. Ken Kendrick, managing general partner of the National League Arizona Diamondbacks, has been a passionate collector since childhood.

Although the Diamondbacks Collection focuses heavily on baseball, it includes cards from other sports that are simply beautiful. The 1935 National Chicle Bronko Nagurski, as well as the 1916 Famous & Barr Co. Jim Thorpe, and the 1948 Bowman George Mikan represent the greatest cards in those sports. This magnificent, one-of-a-kind collection takes us on a journey through an unprecedented time in the history of American sports...from the early 1900s through the

Original artwork © James Fiorentino

Roaring Twenties and the Great Depression to the fabulous Golden Age of Baseball and beyond. The stories about the players featured on these fabulous sports cards discuss their professional and personal lives, and their impact on the game. In addition, longtime collector and hobby expert, Joe Orlando discusses the unique features of each card in this superb collection and gives us a look at the evolving hobby.

Each one of these cards is a piece of art. Ruth, Cobb, Robinson, Aaron, Williams, DiMaggio, and the rest of the superb athletes featured in this book are brought to life on these tiny pieces of cardboard.

Enjoy!

Tom Zappala

1969 Hank Aaron signed game-used bat, 1969 signed game-used jersey, and Aaron signed game-used cap circa 1969. *The Mike Heffner Collection.*

The Story Behind the Collection

★ ★ ★ ★ ★ ★ ★ ★ ★ ★ ★ ★ ★ ★ ★

Behind every great collection is an astute collector. Behind this extraordinary collection, there are two.

In the next pages, you will get a peek behind the curtain at the backgrounds of both the managing general partner of the Arizona Diamondbacks, Ken Kendrick, and former major-league pitcher Tom Candiotti. You will learn how their passion for the hobby evolved into Tom first laying the foundation, and Ken building on it to compile one of the greatest personal collections ever assembled.

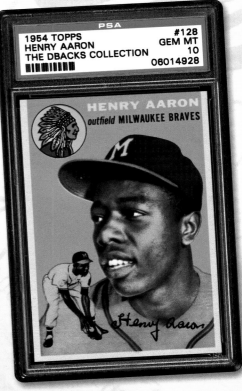

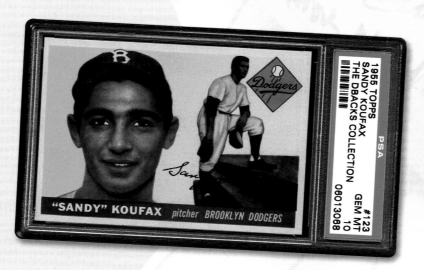

Profile of an Elite Collector

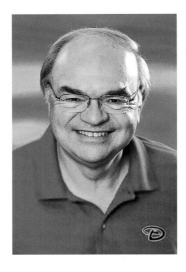

THE OWNER OF ONE OF the most elite sports card collections in the hobby, Ken Kendrick is proud to share his superb collection with sports fans and collectors. The Diamondbacks Collection includes some of the rarest and most valuable cards of notable sports pioneers and legends that span a significant part of sports history. Viewed as particularly important in the collecting world, the cards included in this collection and showcased in this book have been exhibited in the Baseball Hall of Fame in Cooperstown, New York, the Phoenix Art Museum, and other venues. Select cards from the collection were included in the Baseball Hall of Fame's "We Are Baseball" touring exhibit. What follows is the story of Kendrick's road to assembling the Diamondbacks Collection, a road that started when he was a young boy.

A native of Princeton, West Virginia, Kendrick has always been passionate about sports. As a kid, he played Little League and first started collecting in 1952, when he was eight years old. Like other kids across the country, young Ken and his buddies would walk to the local store for a pack of cards, rip it open, and go through the cards looking for their favorite stars while chewing the flat piece of pink gum. He was thrilled if he found the card of a player from one of his favorite teams, the Brooklyn Dodgers, or the Cincinnati Reds. The vibrant and now famous 1952 Topps set had just been released and that piqued Kendrick's interest in card collecting as a youngster.

A three-sport athlete in high school, Kendrick then moved on to West Virginia University where he earned his business administration degree in 1965. He landed in the computer industry during the days of big mainframe computers, working for IBM in Baltimore, Maryland, for his first three years after college. Kendrick saw opportunity in the emerging software side of the business and left IBM to start a successful software company. Datatel, Inc. developed computer software used by colleges and universities for infrastructure technology management. Kendrick's company rapidly became a leader in the industry. After more than 20

years at the helm of Datatel, Kendrick relinquished the day-to-day operation of his company to his management team and moved to Arizona in 1990 to take on new challenges. Once there, he also renewed his interest in both sports and sports card collecting.

In Arizona, Kendrick invested in a few companies, one of which was the Phoenix Suns basketball team. It was about this time that Kendrick reconnected with his childhood baseball card collection while visiting his mother. Yes, she was one of the few mothers in America who did not throw out her son's card collection. Once Kendrick got back to Arizona with those cards, he started to catalog his childhood treasures and to look the cards up in price guides. With the recent explosion of the card collecting hobby, there were more resources available to collectors and Kendrick quickly determined that some of his cards had significant value. Inspired, he began to work on completing the many Topps and Bowman sets in his boyhood collection.

The Diamondbacks Collection includes some of the rarest and most valuable cards of notable sports pioneers and legends that span a significant part of sports history.

Another investment opportunity soon arose for Kendrick when the managing partner of the Phoenix Suns approached him about becoming part of an ownership group of a potential Major League Baseball franchise in Phoenix. Baseball fans in Arizona were thrilled when Major League Baseball awarded one of the two available expansion franchises to Phoenix in 1995. Right out of the gate in 1998, the Arizona Diamondbacks team was successful on the field, winning several division championships and the 2001 World Series. However, there were financial pressures on the team, and Kendrick decided to take on a greater role to sort them out. He assumed the position of managing general partner of the Diamondbacks in 2004, and under his leadership, team finances were restructured to eliminate significant debt and a lucrative deal was struck with Fox Sports Arizona.

Throughout all of this, Kendrick continued to work on his collection. He completed his multiple boyhood sets from the early 1950s through the late 1970s before turning his sights on putting together an elite collection. When retired knuckleballer Tom Candiotti joined the Diamondbacks as a game broadcaster in 2006, he and Kendrick realized they were both passionate about sports card collecting—specifically, about collecting a grouping of the most elite, sought-after cards in the hobby, in the highest grade available. Candiotti had been working on this for some time and had already compiled an impressive collection. When Kendrick saw Candiotti's cards, he realized they were exactly what he was looking for. They could be the core of the elite collection he had dreamed of. Eventually, Kendrick acquired several of Candiotti's cards and they became the base of his Diamondbacks Collection.

An avid, competitive, and still active collector, Kendrick began adding to his elite collection by acquiring the top cards referenced in *Collecting Sports Legends: The Ultimate Hobby Guide*, a book authored by Joe Orlando. Although the book includes sports memorabilia such as autographs and game-used bats, Kendrick focused on the Top 20 cards list, which details some of the most important and most prized cards in the hobby. He had acquired all of them except for the top card on the list, the "Mona Lisa" of trading cards—the elusive Honus Wagner T206 card, long considered the ultimate card in the hobby. It was a proud day when Kendrick acquired the Wayne Gretzky Honus Wagner T206 card to complete his elite grouping of the hobby's Top 20 cards.

Interestingly, for Kendrick, collecting is not just about acquiring the best card at the best grade, it is also about the player featured on the card. Some of the cards in his collection are of players that he knew personally or who he

met at one time. Others are cards of players who were his boyhood baseball heroes, and others are cards of players who were trailblazers, who had a significant impact on the history of their sport and on our culture. For example, Kendrick was a Brooklyn Dodgers fan as a kid, and one of his favorite cards in the collection is the 1955 Topps Sandy Koufax rookie card. Just looking at it brings back happy memories of listening to ballgames on the radio with his dad.

Ken Kendrick

The 1957 Topps Brooks Robinson rookie card also has sentimental value for Kendrick, reminding him of his years working for IBM in Baltimore. Kendrick and his dad attended the 1966 World Series games in Baltimore to witness the legendary third sacker help the Orioles beat the defending champion Los Angeles Dodgers for the 1966 World Series title—the franchise's first championship win. The Joe DiMaggio cards in the collection remind Kendrick of the time he conversed with the great slugger at a California bar in 1983 during DiMaggio's Mr. Coffee spokesperson days. For historical and cultural significance, Kendrick's favorite is his 1948 Jackie Robinson rookie card. Another Brooklyn Dodgers boyhood hero of Kendrick's, Robinson broke baseball's color barrier in 1947, and proceeded to propel "Dem Bums" to six National League pennants and the 1955 World Series championship—the franchise's only championship as a Brooklyn team.

Today, in addition to collecting, Ken Kendrick continues his active role in the day-to-day operations of the Arizona Diamondbacks as managing general partner, and he is the chairman of the Arizona Diamondbacks Foundation. He is involved in numerous philanthropic endeavors and has served on the boards of many charitable organizations. Because "his knowledge of the game and dedication to the sport will help guide the mission to preserve history, honor excellence, and connect generations," Kendrick was appointed to the board of directors of the Baseball Hall of Fame in 2020.

From Notable Knuckler to Crafty Collector
A Conversation with Tom Candiotti

THERE ARE CERTAIN ELITE CLUBS akin to baseball—Yankee center fielders, Red Sox left fielders, Dodgers starting pitchers. The brotherhood of knuckleball pitchers is larger, but no less unique.

One of the most consistent and respected members of this club is Tom Candiotti. The California native played 16 MLB seasons (1983–1999) and compiled 151 wins while baffling batters with his often-unhittable flutter ball. Candiotti was an innings eater, logging over 200 innings pitched in nine seasons. He played for Milwaukee, Cleveland, Toronto, the Dodgers, and Oakland, and led the American League in complete games in 1986 with 17. Candiotti's durability and reliability made him a valuable commodity until his retirement from the game at age 41.

Throughout his career and through to today, Candiotti has also distinguished himself in another area of baseball—collecting. What started as the typical youthful pastime of heading to the local card shop to score the latest Don Drysdale or Carl Yastrzemski card eventually evolved into one of the foremost sports card collections in the world. In 2006, Candiotti was hired by the Arizona Diamondbacks as a broadcaster. This new career led to a friendship and shared loved of collecting with Ken Kendrick, the Diamondbacks managing general partner, and that ultimately led to Kendrick's creation of his storied Diamondbacks Collection.

Candiotti's development as a collector and hobbyist started in childhood. "Growing up, I was always intrigued by baseball and statistics," says Candiotti. "In Little League, we all got a free snow cone after games. I would trade mine for a pack of baseball cards." While in college, Candiotti made his first foray into the financial potential of collecting. He offers, "While I was at Saint Mary's, I went to my first card show and bought a Willie Mays card. 'This is great,' I thought to myself. It only cost me $5.00. When I got back to school, another student offered me $20.00 for it. I made the deal and told the guys I would buy the beer that night."

A few years later, Candiotti's collecting would move from six packs to six figures. "In 1986, I was with Cleveland, and we were playing in Texas against the Rangers. I heard there was some kind of national sports convention in town. I walked over there, and it was unreal. It was the first time I attended The National [National Sports Collectors Convention]. Slowly but surely, I moved into buying cards," Candiotti continues. "As I started making more money in baseball, I could afford to buy better cards." Playing for several MLB teams gave Candiotti the opportunity to span the nation in search of his baseball treasures. "As I traveled with my teams, I would find a card shop in a given town and just hang out there and kill time before a game. I also went to a lot of big card shows where I was signing autographs. When I wasn't signing, I would take time to walk around and see the different tables and cards. I was making more money in the big leagues, and cards that I read about I now could own.

I got to know a lot of collectors in different parts of the country and really immersed myself in the hobby."

As the industry became more sophisticated, Candiotti took advantage of new sources of information. "I subscribed to *Sports Collectors Digest*," explains Candiotti. "Sometimes I would see an ad for a card on sale, and I would buy it. To be honest, I still love getting those big thick catalogs from the auction houses." Technology also took Candiotti's collection to another level. He relates, "The Internet made it easy to view offerings from a number of auction houses. It provided more options and more cards to be seen, and it was easier for me to not only buy cards, but also to research them. I really did my homework." In addition to publications and websites, Candiotti sought guidance from Marshall Fogel, the Denver-based attorney and collecting icon. "Marshall and I had many phone conversations," says Candiotti. "He would give me a lot of history and background on the cards I was interested in buying. He was an astute collector, and he directed me toward intelligent collecting."

Indeed, Candiotti took a different approach to his passion. He explains, "Everyone was out there collecting sets, but I looked at collecting more like real estate. I wanted to buy the best cards of the best players that were in the best condition. Marshall and I worked on a list, and he knew the people who had the cards available to purchase. I methodically went about the business of getting the best cards. At one point, I had 20 of the top 25 cards in the industry."

Concern over the security of his collection is what eventually led Candiotti to sell most of his cards—that and connecting with Ken Kendrick, the equally passionate collector who would purchase most of the treasure trove. Says Candiotti, "As I continued to acquire high-end cards, I wasn't comfortable keeping them in my house. I kept them in a safety deposit box, but there was no real fun in that." When he joined the Diamondbacks, Candiotti bonded with Kendrick. "I met Ken when I was hired by the Diamondbacks as their game broadcaster in 2006.

"We really just started talking about baseball and comparing the cards he had with mine. When he finally saw my collection, he was like a little kid."

Candiotti agreed to sell Kendrick most of his collection, but not without a slight shred of seller's remorse. "There was a little bit of hesitation," Candiotti recalls. "It took me so long to acquire all of the cards. The great thing is that Ken was going to buy the entire collection. I wanted to keep it together and not sell the cards individually." Candiotti and Kendrick share more than just a professional connection. They are, at the very heart of the matter, passionate collectors. "For me, a big part of the joy of collecting is the thrill of the chase," says Candiotti. "Figuring out which cards you want to purchase and finding out where you can get those cards. You get more joy from collecting when you really have to search out an item."

Even more of a thrill for Candiotti is passing on his love of collecting to sons Casey, Brett, and Clark. "I do a lot of collecting with my kids," he relates. "Sometimes, they tell me they are interested in a particular player, and we'll go out in search of certain cards. They really like a lot of the young players in the game. Collecting today is different from when I first started. There are so many different types of cards and companies. So much has changed, but the fun of doing it is the same. I am so glad that my kids share that joy and are really into collecting."

1958 Mickey Mantle signed game-used jersey; 1946 Joe DiMaggio
signed game-used jersey. *SCP Auctions*

The Best of the Best

★ ★ ★ ★ ★ ★ ★ ★ ★ ★ ★ ★ ★ ★ ★

The first ten cards showcased in this book represent arguably the greatest pieces of cardboard art in existence today.

From the famous and controversial T206 Honus Wagner card, to the highest-ranking example of the elusive T206 Eddie Plank, to the iconic 1952 Topps Mickey Mantle, to the only known 1951 Bowman Mickey Mantle to achieve the highest grade of PSA 10, to the amazing 1933 Goudey Babe Ruth cards and 1934 Goudey Lou Gehrig cards, these pieces of cardboard are the crème de la crème in the hobby.

THE 1909-1911 T206 HONUS WAGNER is *THE* card to own without any doubt. For over a century, this tiny treasure has taken on all comers, and it still is regarded as the Holy Grail or *Mona Lisa* of all trading cards. The popularity of the set, the elite status of the featured player, and the lore behind its scarcity combine to give the card an allure like no other. That said, as much as this card checks all the relevant boxes when it comes to appeal, this is a great example of an object being worth more than the sum of its parts. After decades as the hobby's most cherished jewel, this card has taken on a life of its own. Its legend is now more important than its reality. The specific card pictured in this book has been the subject of much debate and controversy over the years.

Wagner, who is still regarded as one of the best, if not the best, shortstops in the history of the game, lies at the center of a set that many consider the most popular baseball card issue ever released. Wagner might not have been the era's most revered player as he battled with Ty Cobb for that honor, nor is the card the set's greatest rarity, but the T206 Wagner is its most important and desirable component. Renowned photographer Carl Horner took the classic portrait used to create this card, and the regal quality of the image gives the Wagner an appearance that beautifully matches its reputation. It seems fitting that the king of all cards, the epitome of hobby royalty, looks the part.

The card, which is believed to fall within the 50–75 known examples range, has been the subject of many debates over the years. Was the card pulled from production at Wagner's insistence because he didn't want his image associated with the product or was the halt in printing simply a result of a contractual dispute over money? The collecting public might never know the full story, but...at this point...the reason behind the rarity is arguably a nonfactor as it pertains to interest or value. Today, the mere sight of the Wagner generates the kind of reaction that goes far beyond baseball cards. Although Wagner, the player, was very real, the card itself is more akin to a mythological figure in the eyes of collectors.

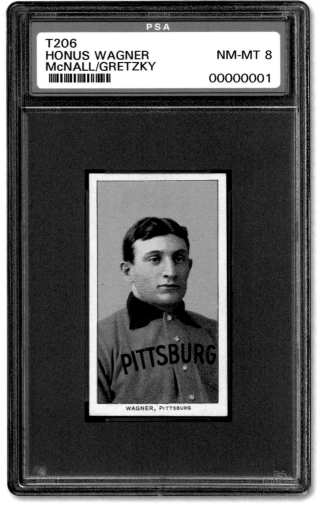

This card is the sole example to reach the PSA NM-MT 8 grading tier with none higher in the PSA Population Report.

The Flying Dutchman

Whenever the conversation about Honus Wagner comes up, the first thing usually mentioned is *THE CARD*. Taking that iconic piece of cardboard and putting it aside for a moment, let's talk about Honus Wagner the man—one of the greatest shortstops who ever played the game. The age-old assertion that it is difficult to compare players from different eras does hold weight, but if you look at Wagner's whole career, the argument to consider him at the top of the list is compelling.

Born in 1874 in Chartiers, Pennsylvania, Johannes Peter "Honus" Wagner began playing baseball with his brothers and friends at an early age. His brother, Albert, who played professionally for the Steubenville, Ohio, team of the Inter-State League, asked his manager to give his younger brother a look-see because Honus had all the tools needed to become an incredibly good ballplayer. Wagner wound up freelancing for five different teams that first year, becoming an offensive force for all of them. The owner of one of those teams, Ed Barrow, was so impressed with the young player's ability that he brought Wagner to New Jersey to play for his Atlantic League team, the Paterson Silk Weavers. Because Wagner was extremely successful at torturing pitchers in the league, Barrow asked the National League's Louisville Colonels to take a look at the young infielder. Neither club President Barney Dreyfuss nor team manager Fred Clarke were terribly impressed. Wagner's awkward appearance and stocky build led them to believe that the young prospect would not have the necessary agility to play in the big leagues. However, they decided to take a chance on Wagner and the rest is history.

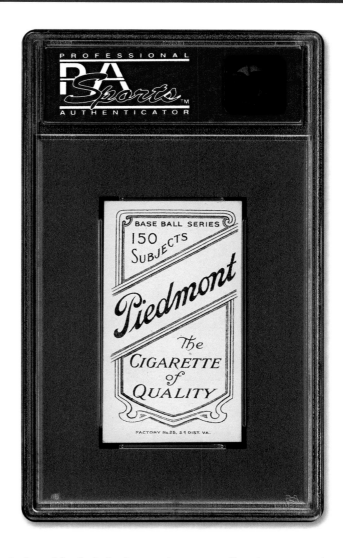

Wagner immediately became one of the best hitters in the league, batting .335 in 62 games in 1897. He had power with his heavy 40-ounce bat, speed, defense, and yes, agility. After the 1899 season, the Colonels were one of four teams that were disbanded in order to make the league smaller and more competitive. Dreyfuss became part-owner of the National League's Pittsburgh Pirates and Wagner, with several of his Colonels teammates, joined the Pirates soon after. In 1900, his first season with the Pirates, Wagner dominated the league both offensively and defensively. He could play any infield position except catcher, and wherever he played he was the best at that position. That season, Wagner batted a whopping .381, led the league in doubles and triples, and banged out 201 hits. The years 1901 through 1903 proved to be remarkably successful for the Pirates, with Wagner leading the team to three straight titles. The 1901 and 1902 teams dominated the National League, but the World Series had not yet been established. In 1903, the Pirates won the National League title again and faced the upstart American League's Boston Americans in the first-ever World Series. Unfortunately, the Pirates lost to the Americans in an eight-game contest with Wagner batting a paltry .222. It took him years to get over how poorly he played in that Series.

Wagner settled into his permanent position of shortstop in 1904 and continued to decimate National League pitching through 1909. He never batted less than .339 during that

period, and he led the league in many offensive categories. Wagner was considered the best defensive shortstop in the game. His tremendous speed on the basepaths was a lethal weapon against the opposition. Over the course of his career, Wagner stole over 700 bases to earn the nickname "The Flying Dutchman." By the middle of the first decade of the twentieth century, Honus Wagner had become a bona fide superstar. He endorsed products, made appearances, and he was one of the highest-paid players in the game. Pirates fans could not get enough of him. Off the field, Wagner was cordial to fans but on the field, he was a tough, hard-nosed player who was never afraid to mix it up with an opposing player. From 1900 to 1909, Pittsburgh dominated the league behind the bat of Wagner. During that period, he won seven batting titles and five stolen bases titles while leading the league multiple times in RBI, triples, doubles, hits, and runs scored. After posting a 110–42–2 record in 1909, the best record in franchise history, Wagner and

Honus Wagner

active in business ventures, most notably a sporting goods store that continued in operation for 93 years. "The Flying Dutchman" was elected to the inaugural class of the Baseball Hall of Fame in 1936, along with fellow legends Ty Cobb, Babe Ruth, Walter Johnson, and Christy Mathewson. Cobb received the most votes, with Wagner and Ruth tying for second place. At the 1944 All-Star Game, Wagner was the honorary coach for the National League team. Honus Wagner passed away in Carnegie, Pennsylvania, on December 6, 1955, at the age of 81.

Wagner finished his stellar career with 3,420 hits and a .328 lifetime batting average. An eight-time batting champ, four-time RBI leader, five-time National League stolen base leader, and seven-time doubles leader, Honus Wagner was named starting shortstop of the All-Time MLB team and named to the MLB All-Century team. His bronze statue sits outside of PNC Park, home of the Pirates.

the Pirates redeemed themselves in the World Series, vanquishing the American League Detroit Tigers and their 22-year-old brash superstar Ty Cobb. The 35-year-old Wagner had an excellent Series, batting .333. On the other hand, Cobb did not fare as well, batting only .231.

As Wagner got older, his numbers waned, but he averaged .334 to win the batting title in 1911, not so bad for a 37-year-old player. After 21 years in

the big leagues, Wagner called it quits in 1917 at age 43. He played semi-pro ball after his professional playing days ended, enjoying the game that brought him so much success. Wagner then worked for the Pirates organization in various capacities for more than twenty years. He spent most of his time as a hitting instructor, mentoring some notable players including future Hall of Famers Pie Traynor and Ralph Kiner. He also coached at what today is Carnegie Melon University. Wagner was

Jeter, Banks, Ripken, and the rest certainly deserve their accolades, but when you look at the numbers, Honus Wagner gets our vote as the best shortstop in baseball history, even though he played over 100 years ago. By the way, that little piece of cardboard with his image on it happens to be the most famous sports card of all time. Pretty cool.

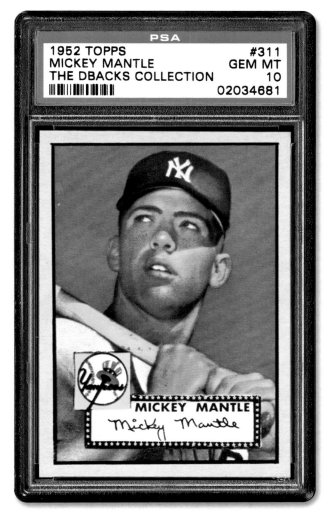

OF ALL THE ICONIC ISSUES found in this book, and in the entire hobby for that matter, no other card possesses more symbolic power than this piece of pop culture art. While the T206 Honus Wagner is widely regarded as the Holy Grail of all trading cards, the 1952 Mickey Mantle is the card world's more sentimental poster child. The hobby transformed forever in the 1980s, as our niche pastime blossomed into a nationwide phenomenon. That metamorphosis was driven by baby boomers and no figure loomed larger to that generation than Mantle. He was the idol of all idols, and this card is the centerpiece of the most important baseball card set of the post-WWII era.

Even though it is not his true rookie, the 1952 Topps Mantle is *THE* card to own of the Yankees legend. In 1952, after issuing a handful of smaller sets the previous year, Topps decided to launch its first major baseball effort at 407 total cards. In an attempt to compete with Bowman, the reigning card manufacturing king, Topps produced and heavily marketed a larger design. This format allows the collector to enjoy the images in a superior way, and it is so fitting considering the striking appearance of the Mantle card specifically. The card's aesthetics provide a virtual perfect storm of eye appeal, from the rich blue and yellow colors to his fable-like name, which is complemented by his facsimile signature on the front.

This PSA Gem Mint 10 is one of three examples to reach PSA's highest grading tier.

Unbeknownst to some collectors, there are two slightly different versions of this double-printed card, although no difference in value has been assigned by the market to either at the time of this writing. Furthermore, they are believed to have been produced in equal quantities. One version possesses a white print dot near the left border, a partially filled black box surrounding the Yankees logo, an "E" that finishes downward in Mantle's facsimile signature, and stitches that point to the right on the reverse. The other version features no white print dot, a solid black box around the Yankees logo, an "E" that finishes upward in Mantle's facsimile signature, and stitches pointing to the left on the reverse.

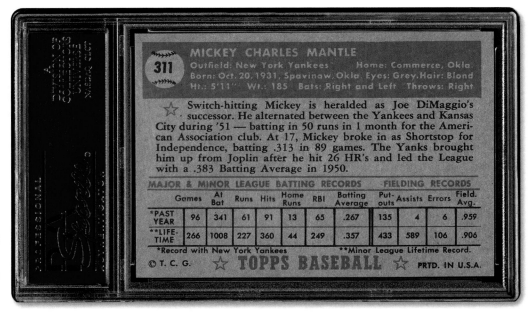

The card can be found with wide variances in color and centering, which can impact eye appeal depending on the severity. Thankfully, for collectors seeking high-grade specimens, the Mantle card was part of one of the greatest finds in hobby history. In 1986, about 5,500 uncirculated 1952 Topps cards were unearthed by recognized hobby figure Alan Rosen. Approximately 75 Mantles were found within the immense group, which was largely comprised of cards from the high-number series. While the centering varied from card-to-card, the fresh appearance was consistent throughout since the cards were stashed away for decades.

The version on the left possesses a white print dot near the left border, a partially filled black box surrounding the Yankees logo, an "E" that finishes downward in Mantle's facsimile signature, and stitches that point to the right on the reverse. The version on the right features no white print dot, a solid black box around the Yankees logo, an "E" that finishes upward in Mantle's facsimile signature, and stitches pointing to the left on the reverse.

The Commerce Comet

Collectors and fans alike speak about Mickey Mantle with almost a sense of reverence. Many consider the 1950s and 1960s as the Golden Age of Baseball. Because of the invention of television, greats like Mays, Clemente, Williams, Berra, Aaron, Banks, and Spahn came to life in homes around the country. The young Mickey Mantle was part of this phenomenon, and he soon became larger than life.

Although the iconic 1952 Mantle card is not his true rookie card, it epitomizes everything that Mantle was about, so it is an appropriate starting point to the discussion of his career and his launch to superstardom. The discussion will continue on page 33, where the 1951 Bowman Mantle card is showcased, and cover the glory years, the later stages of his career, and the demons that plagued him.

Although Mantle's .298 lifetime batting average and 536 career home runs are not the highest on record, and his 2,415 hits were surpassed by many, one needs to take a closer look at his storied career. With his combination of pure talent, power, speed, and the ability to hit balls out of the park, Mickey Mantle mesmerized fans with every at-bat. Mickey Mantle was that good. "The Commerce Comet" or simply "The Mick," was one of the greatest stars in the history of our National Pastime.

Mickey Charles Mantle was born in Spavinaw, Oklahoma on October 20, 1931, and moved to Commerce, Oklahoma, when he was three years old. He was named after Hall of Fame catcher Mickey Cochrane, the favorite player of Mickey's dad, Elvin. From the very start, Elvin "Mutt" Mantle groomed his son to be a ballplayer. He taught the young boy to switch-hit because he thought it was a skill Mickey would need to become a complete ballplayer. As a boy, Mantle regularly played sandlot ball with friends, but he also played football and basketball in high school. It was football that almost derailed his professional career. During a freshman year football practice, Mantle was accidentally kicked in the shin, and after developing a high fever and extreme swelling, he was diagnosed with osteomyelitis, a serious bone disease. At first, doctors seriously considered amputating his leg, but instead they decided to try the new drug, penicillin. His leg was saved, but that injury caused a multitude of leg and knee problems throughout Mantle's career.

After playing on a few local teams, Mantle joined the semi-pro Baxter Springs Whiz Kids, and it was there that New York Yankees scout Tom Greenwade discovered the 16-year-old Mantle kid who could really hit. Greenwade was in Kansas to scout Billy Johnson but instead became enamored with the athletic, switch-hitting Mantle, who slammed two home runs. In 1949, as soon as he completed high school,

With his combination of pure talent, power, speed, and the ability to hit balls out of the park, Mickey Mantle mesmerized fans with every at-bat.

Mickey Mantle

his return to the big club, he wore uniform number "7." In his initial season with the pinstripes, he batted a respectable .267 with 13 home runs and 65 RBI in 96 games. The Yankees won the 1951 World Series against crosstown rivals, the New York Giants, but Mantle had only five at-bats because he tore ligaments in his knee during Game Two. This would be the first of many knee injuries that would dog Mantle throughout his career. During the offseason, the 20-year-old Mantle married his hometown sweetheart, Merlyn Johnson, hoping to start a family.

His father "Mutt" died in May of 1952 of Hodgkin's Disease at 40 years old. Although distraught, the young phenom carried on to have a breakout season, batting .311 with 23 home runs and 87 RBI. That year, Mantle assumed Joe DiMaggio's position in centerfield, which he would patrol for most of his career. He was chosen for the American League All-Star Team but did not play in the game. The Yankees juggernaut continued in 1952, beating the Brooklyn Dodgers in a seven game World Series. Mantle had a brilliant Series, batting .345 with 10 hits. The young superstar was becoming the talk of the baseball world. Even his manager, the irascible Casey Stengel, thought Mantle was, without a doubt, the best player in the American League. In 1953, Mantle batted .295 with 21 home runs, 136 hits, and 92 RBI. Again, the Yankees faced the Brooklyn Dodgers in the World Series, beating them four games to two. Mantle batted a weak .208 in 24 at-bats in the 1953 Series but hit a bomb to deep left field for a grand slam in Game Five.

Mantle signed with the Yankees for $400 and a $1,100 signing bonus. Assigned to their Class D affiliate in Kansas, the Independence Yankees, Mantle's first year in the minors showcased the young slugger's skills. The 17-year-old Mantle batted .313 in his inaugural season. In 1950, Mantle moved up to the Class C Western Association, playing for the Joplin Miners in Missouri. In his second professional season, Mantle batted a magnificent .383 and went yard 26 times.

In 1951, Mantle made his debut with the Yankees. After a slow start, he was sent back to the minors, and he was so disappointed in himself that he nearly quit baseball. After a stern talking to by his dad, Mantle stuck with it and ended up demolishing the pitching at the minor-league level. Upon

Coming out of the 1953 season and their fifth consecutive World Series championship, the Yankees entered 1954 with high expectations. Mantle had another stellar season batting .300, knocking in 102 runs, and smashing 27 home runs. The Yankees won 103 games in 1954, but the Cleveland Indians led by pitching greats Bob Lemon, Early Wynn, and Bob Feller won 111 games and the pennant. However, the baseball world was beginning to understand that this kid from Commerce, Oklahoma, was the real deal. Mickey Mantle's storied career was only beginning, and baseball fans across the country were in for a real treat.

The story continues on page 33.

THIS CARD IS CONSIDERED THE ONLY RECOGNIZED major league rookie issue of the biggest name in baseball history—the figure that is the foundation of our entire hobby. Technically, Babe Ruth is featured on an earlier card, the extremely rare 1914 Baltimore News issue. It pictures him as a minor-league pitching prospect for the Orioles, and yes, the Orioles were a minor-league team in those days, but the M101-5/M101-4 Ruth is widely viewed as his true rookie. The card also offers the kind of symbolic value that is hard to quantify. Pictured as a member of the Boston Red Sox, it was before "The Curse." As an outstanding left-handed pitcher, it was before Ruth transformed into "The Sultan of Swat." The visual represents the calm before the storm.

The M101-5/M101-4 cards, which were distributed by Felix Mendelsohn, feature either a blank back or an ad on the reverse, ranging from the noted publication *The Sporting News* to clothing stores like Herpolsheimer Co. and Famous & Barr Co. Each ad back offers a different level of scarcity and there are several from which to choose. In fact, some advanced collectors have been known to assemble as many back variations of the Ruth rookie as they can, but it comes with a steep price tag. Building a collection of that nature is not for the faint of heart, or the light of wallet. When it comes to condition obstacles to be aware of, the card is commonly found off-center, particularly left-to-right. In addition, dark print defects in the form of specks and lines can impact its eye appeal, especially if it encroaches on Ruth's image.

The M101-5 set was released earlier in 1916 than its slightly updated M101-4 counterpart, but the market has treated the Ruth cards equally when it comes to value. This is one of the rare cases where the set itself has never garnered major attention from collectors, yet the Ruth rookie is able to stand on its own. Interestingly, Ruth is one of the few players to have the same card number in both sets. The issue does offer some other major stars, like Shoeless Joe Jackson and Jim Thorpe, but the combination of the set's difficulty and perhaps its black-and-white design has helped limit the overall interest in compiling the entire set. The Ruth rookie, however, is so historically important and its image so memorable that the card has steadily gained momentum over the last two decades. Today, it has a solid place on any trading card version of Mount Rushmore.

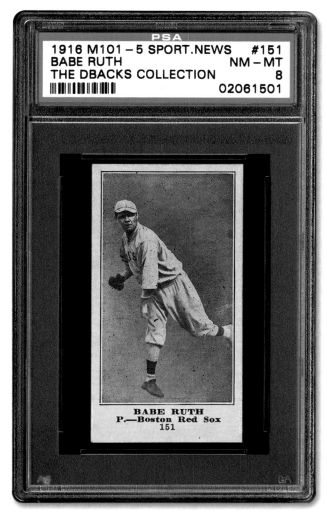

This PSA NM-MT 8 is one of three M101-5 examples graded at that tier with none higher in the PSA Population Report. (Blank back).

The Babe

When the 1916 M101-5 Babe Ruth card was issued, no one in their wildest dreams imagined that the player on this card would become the greatest who ever lived. "The Babe," "Bambino," "The Sultan of Swat" got his big break in February 1914 with Jack Dunn's Baltimore Orioles minor-league team. George Herman Ruth caught Dunn's eye while playing ball for St. Mary's Industrial School for Boys. After watching the young southpaw pitch, Dunn immediately signed him to a contract. Because he kept a close eye on the young, impressionable pitcher, some of the players began referring to Ruth as Dunn's "Babe." The nickname stuck. Jack Dunn had a good relationship with Joseph Lannin,

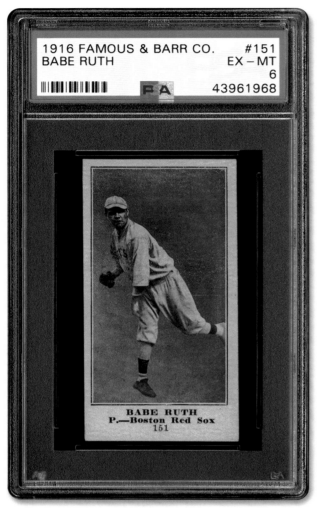

This card is one of two Famous & Barr Co. examples to reach the PSA EX-MT 6 grading tier with none higher in the PSA Population Report.

owner of the Boston Red Sox, and when Dunn needed cash in July 1914, he sold Ruth to Boston. The nineteen-year-old Ruth came up as a pitcher who could hit, which was unusual in the Deadball Era. His first year with the Red Sox was uneventful. As a matter of fact, Ruth shuttled between Boston and Providence, Rhode Island, where he honed his skills with the minor-league Providence Grays and helped them to the 1914 International League pennant.

Ruth appeared in four games with the Red Sox during that first season posting a 2–1 record in 23 innings pitched. In 1915, the young Ruth came up for good and his 18–8 record for the Red Sox was just a sample of things to come. Ruth batted .315 with four home runs in 92 at-bats that year and blasted his first homer on May 6 against his future team, the New York Yankees. After finishing with 101 wins, the 1915

Sox won the World Series, beating the Philadelphia Phillies four games to one. The Sox were loaded with an outstanding pitching staff consisting of Rube Foster, Smokey Joe Wood, Ernie Shore, and Dutch Leonard, and even though Ruth had a good season, he did not pitch in the Series. The Babe started carousing with Leonard and a few others and quickly developed a reputation for burning the candle at both ends. His fiery temper caused problems, too. He had a run-in or two with umpires over the course of the season, and Ruth even broke a toe when he kicked a bench after being intentionally walked in a game. Had he not missed two weeks due to the toe incident, it is likely he would have won 20 games.

The Babe came back with a vengeance in 1916, posting a 23–12 record for Boston and leading the league with his 1.75 earned-run average. He threw nine shutouts, a record for lefties which stood until 1978 when Ron Guidry matched it. In fact, Ruth outdueled the great Walter Johnson in August for one of those shutouts. At 21 years old, Ruth had become the best left-handed pitcher in the major leagues. He also showed talent as a hitter, batting .272 in 136 at-bats. Although Ruth hit only three home runs, the Sox began to see the tremendous potential for his bat. Ruth lobbied for himself, saying he was getting antsy between pitching starts and he could contribute more as a position player. The Red Sox won the American League pennant by two games over the Chicago White Sox and went on to beat the Brooklyn Robins in five games to take the 1916 World Series title. Ruth pitched a masterful Game Two, lasting all 14 innings and giving up only six hits.

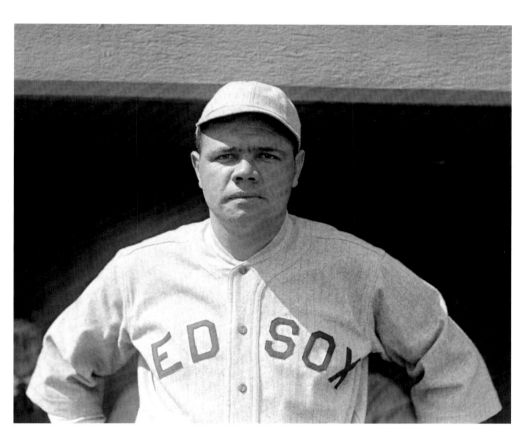

Over the next two seasons, Ruth was a dominant pitcher, and he established himself as a proficient hitter. He went 24–13 with a sparkling 2.01 ERA in 1917, while batting .325 in 123 at-bats with two home runs. Boston finished second to the Chicago White Sox, who became the 1917 World Series Champs. That season, Ruth had a few altercations with opposing players and umpires which launched his reputation as a hothead. In a game against Washington in June 1917, Ruth got into it with umpire Clarence "Brick" Owens in the first inning because he thought Owens was squeezing him on balls and strikes. After rushing home plate and punching Owens in the head, he got tossed from the game and suspended for 10 days. Interestingly, Ruth was relieved by Ernie Shore, who proceeded to pitch a no-hitter.

In May 1918, Ruth, like many other Americans, came down with the Spanish Flu and nearly lost his life. He missed several weeks while he recovered and, in what became a war-shortened season, Ruth went 13–7, batted .300, and led the league with 11 home runs. Boston beat the Chicago Cubs in six games for the 1918 World Series title. The Red Sox struggled in 1919, finishing in sixth place in the American League. Ruth finally got the opportunity to start the transition from pitcher to everyday player and he did not disappoint, batting .322 and shattering the home

run record, going yard 29 times. His pitching record was a respectable 9–5, but with eccentric owner Harry Frazee beginning to sell off players and trade for lesser ones, the Sox took a nosedive. The fans showed up for one reason only, to see the great Babe Ruth.

At 21 years old, Ruth had become the best left-handed pitcher in the major leagues. He also showed talent as a hitter, batting .272 in 136 at-bats. Although Ruth hit only three home runs, the Sox began to see the tremendous potential for his bat.

Clearly understanding that he was the marquee star, Ruth began taking more liberties. He held out for more money and did not abide by team rules. Ruth even jumped the team for a brief period, demanding more money. He figured he

was worth as much as Ty Cobb and demanded an $8,000 raise to $15,000, the same salary that Cobb was making. After some negotiating, Ruth and Frazee settled on a $10,000 salary.

Besides dealing with attendance woes and coughing up more money to Ruth, Frazee was losing money with his New York City theatrical productions. In December 1919, Harry Frazee struck a deal with the New York Yankees that would forever impact the Red Sox, the Yankees, and the game of baseball. Frazee sold Ruth to Jacob Ruppert's Yankees for $100,000 in addition to $300,000 in loans to finance his Broadway

---

In December 1919, Harry Frazee struck a deal with the New York Yankees that would forever impact the Red Sox, the Yankees, and the game of baseball.

---

shows. Ruth was in California at the time and Yankee skipper Miller Huggins flew out to break the news. After a little haggling over salary, Ruth agreed to the $10,000 salary that he was already making, with an additional $21,000 in bonuses to be paid over the 1920 and 1921 seasons. The sale of Babe Ruth to the Yankees started an 86-year World Series drought for the Red Sox. Boston fans celebrated when "The Curse of the Bambino" was finally broken in 2004. The Yanks? They went on to win seven American League pennants and four World Series with Ruth and used that as a springboard to win a total of 40 pennants and an unprecedented 27 World Series titles at the time of this writing.

Red Sox fans have always wondered what it would have been like to have Babe Ruth for his entire career. They can only dream.

The story continues on page 30.

4 1909-1911 T206 Eddie Plank

THE 1909-1911 T206 BASEBALL CARD SET IS
often referred to as "The Monster" due its size, especially
for the period, and for the challenge it poses to those
putting together a complete set. Within the 524 cards
that make up the basic set, there are a handful of rarities
that can frustrate the most seasoned collectors or destroy
hobby budgets if one is so fortunate to acquire them. One
such rarity is the T206 Eddie Plank, a card that doesn't
quite possess the cache of the Honus Wagner, but it
provides a challenge that is more comparable than most
realize. Considering its scarcity, along with the combined
importance of the player and card, one could make the
argument it remains underappreciated.

Incredibly, after a century has passed, there is still no
definitive explanation for its rarity. It is, arguably, the
biggest mystery associated with the T206 issue, and that is
saying something considering all the additional twists the
turns found in the set. The two most frequently espoused
beliefs are that Plank did not give permission to use his
image in the set, which means they were pulled, or that a
defective printing plate prevented a large number of Planks
from ever getting past quality control.

The latter seems highly unlikely since the Plank can be found
in both the 150 and 350 series. It is important to note
that the 150 series Plank generally exhibits richer colors,
a crisper image and is much tougher to find than the 350
series card. As a result, a premium is often paid for the 150
series Plank. Assuming either hypothesis is true, that would
mean hordes of Plank cards were destroyed in the process.
Interestingly enough, a few Plank cards have surfaced over
the years that are missing substantial portions of color. In
addition to its rarity, the Plank card is commonly found with
subpar centering, especially top-to-bottom.

Like Wagner, Plank is a Hall of Famer, so the added star
power gives the card an additional layer of appeal. The
legendary left-handed pitcher got a relatively late start,
beginning his major-league career at the age of 25, but
Plank was able to compile eight 20-win seasons. Plank's
326 career wins remained a record for a lefty until Warren
Spahn eclipsed the mark several decades later. Furthermore,
this portrait pose is Plank's lone appearance in the set, just
like Wagner. Conversely, so many other stars in the set

are featured on anywhere from two to five different cards.
Since obtaining this elusive card is the only opportunity for
collectors to fill the Plank void, the demand for it becomes
even more concentrated.

Gettysburg Eddie

One of the greatest lefties in baseball history, "Gettysburg
Eddie" Plank certainly made his mark on our National
Pastime.

Even though Plank won 326 games, compiled a 2.35 lifetime
earned-run average, and had more complete games and
shutouts than any other lefty, a record that still stands

This card is the sole example to reach the PSA
NM-MT 8 grading tier with none higher in the
PSA Population Report.

today, he actually managed to stay under the radar during his illustrious career.

The famous Eddie Plank T206 card has certainly added to the lore of this great player, but overall Plank has not gotten the respect he deserves. Born on a farm in Gettysburg, Pennsylvania, Plank never played baseball until he was 17 years old. Signed by Connie Mack while pitching for Gettysburg College, he made his major-league debut for the Philadelphia Athletics in 1901, at age 25. In his inaugural season, Plank compiled a 17–13 record with a tidy 3.31 earned-run average. Although not an overpowering pitcher, Plank had an arsenal that included a nasty fastball, an excellent curve, and a crossfire pitching motion which made picking up the ball extremely difficult. The secret weapon of his arsenal, however, was his ability to drive batters crazy.

Besides the nickname "Gettysburg Eddie," in today's terminology, a more appropriate nickname for him would be the "Original Human Rain Delay." Plank talked to himself, adjusted his cap, gave the ball a few extra rubs, shook off his catchers often, and just pretty much fidgeted on the mound. The batters that faced him would sometimes swing just for the sake of swinging. It got to the point that his teammates even got antsy in the outfield, and he frustrated the team's fans. Some of the A's fans would stay away from games in which Plank was pitching because they knew they would never make it home in time for supper. In a 1913 article in the *St. Louis Star*, Louis Lee Arms described a typical Eddie Plank outing this way:

"Receive the ball from the catcher. Then drop it. Rub dust on it. Expectorate upon the glove. Rub the ball vigorously upon the glove. Turn and talk in an animated way to [second baseman] Eddie Collins. Step upon the pitching slab facing the catcher. Nod dissent to several signals. Expectorate again upon the glove. Nod an assent to the signal of the catcher. Back off the pitching slab. Pluck several blades of grass. Walk up to it again. Turn and gaze about the ball field to see that the outfield is properly placed. Wave one outfielder into position. Make a sarcastic remark to the umpire. Make ready to pitch. Consume five seconds in looking steadfastly at the ground. Pitch."

Throughout his career Plank was very consistent, eating up innings and throwing shutouts. Never considered the top pitcher in baseball, he competed with the likes of Walter

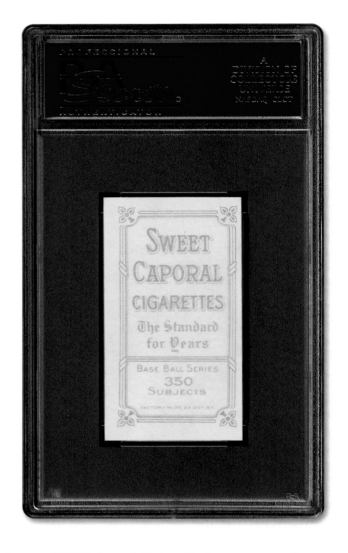

Johnson, Ed Walsh, and Christy Mathewson, as well as teammates Rube Waddell and Chief Bender. However, because of his durability and consistency, Plank was ranked among the top four or five pitchers for most of his career. An eight-time 20-game winner, Plank went 20–15 in 1902, helping the Athletics to the American League pennant. There was no World Series that year because the National League refused to recognize the new American League, but the Athletics became a force in the fledgling league for many years.

In 1903, Plank went 23–16, and in 1904, he compiled a 26–17 record with a 2.17 ERA, but it was the 1905 season that finally paid off for the team. After posting a 24–12 season, Plank faced the great Christy Mathewson and the New York Giants in Game One of the 1905 World Series, dropping a 3–0 decision. He returned to the mound in Game Four to face "Iron Man" Joe McGinnity and lost a heartbreaking 1–0 game. The A's lost that Series but Plank went on to appear

Plank had an arsenal that included a nasty fastball, an excellent curve, and a crossfire pitching motion which made picking up the ball extremely difficult.

in three more Fall Classics. The team made a return trip to the World Series in 1910, beating the Chicago Cubs four games to one for the title. Plank won 16 games that year but was forced to sit out the Series because of a sore arm. The Athletics appeared in both the 1911 and 1913 World Series. Plank posted a 23–8 record in 1911 and was 1–1 in the Fall Classic, helping the A's vanquish the Giants for the championship title. Although he went 26–6 in 1912 with a 2.22 ERA, the Athletics finished third in the league. In 1913, they faced the Giants again, with Plank defeating Christy Mathewson in the deciding fifth game for the championship. Plank's final appearance in the World Series

came in 1914 with the Athletics losing to the Boston Braves in four games.

After that 1914 season, Plank was released when Connie Mack broke up the team. At 39 years old, he jumped to the new upstart Federal League in 1915, won 21 games for the St. Louis Terriers, and notched his 300th career victory. The new league folded after that season and Plank moved on to the St. Louis Browns in the American League. At 41 years old, he decided to wrap up his 17-year career in 1917. The New York Yankees traded for Plank in 1918, but he remained in retirement on his Gettysburg farm and opened a successful Buick dealership and garage.

He also pitched a few games in the Industrial Baseball League that year.

The Battle of Gettysburg was the turning point of the Civil War and the Gettysburg battleground had become a national military park only 22 years before Plank retired from the game. He occasionally gave visiting teammates a tour of the battleground and was also known to give tours to the public. After suffering a stroke, Eddie Plank passed away on February 24, 1926, at the age of 50. If you ever visit Gettysburg, you will find the Eddie Plank Gymnasium at Gettysburg College, Gettysburg Eddie's restaurant, and Plank's Field housing development which is located on part of Plank's original farm. Eddie Plank was elected to the Pennsylvania Sports Hall of Fame in 2012, but his crowning achievement was his election to the Baseball Hall of Fame in 1946.

THE 1933 GOUDEY NAPOLEON LAJOIE has always been considered one of those unattainable cards that most collectors could only dream of owning. Like the T206 Honus Wagner, the lore of the Lajoie card gave it an appeal that exceeded the greatness of the player...and to be perfectly clear and even though this card was made well after his retirement from the game, Lajoie was one of the top players during the first half of the twentieth century. The card, however, became a legend of its own as it represented one of the hobby's "White Whales." Like Moby Dick, the Lajoie eluded most who tried to hunt it down. The combination of its scarcity coupled with its value ensured that it was beyond the reach of the average collector, and it has been since the hobby was born.

The 1933 Goudey set has long been revered by collectors, both for its aesthetic beauty and its vast selection of stars, from Babe Ruth to Lou Gehrig to Jimmie Foxx. Unlike all the other baseball legends that inhabited the set, Lajoie was treated differently, and that treatment resulted in one of our hobby's most noteworthy rarities. The Lajoie card was not included in the set's original release. Consumers kept buying pack after pack, looking for #106. It was a devious but effective plan by Goudey to increase sales. In order to complete the set, collectors had to contact the manufacturer to acquire card #106 the following year as it was printed in 1934. The Lajoie cards were sent through the mail, which is why you will occasionally see impressions or rust stains left by paper clips on the surface. Sometimes, the pressure from affixing the paper clips created what collectors refer to as "spider wrinkles" on the front or back.

The 1933 Goudey set has long been revered by collectors, both for its aesthetic beauty and its vast selection of stars, from Babe Ruth to Lou Gehrig to Jimmie Foxx.

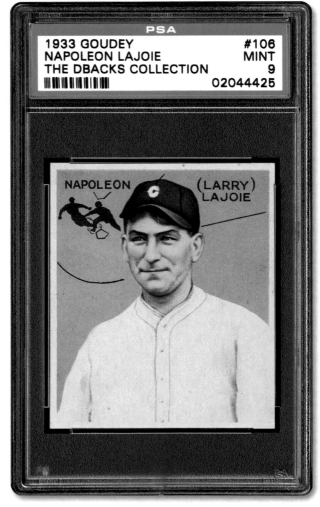

This PSA Mint 9 is one of nine examples graded at that tier, with none higher in the PSA Population Report

Incredibly, considering the overall scarcity of the card, high-grade copies of the Lajoie do exist in reasonable numbers. This is best explained by the fact that these cards were never inserted into packs and avoided much of the traditional handling, especially by young children. The collectors who wanted to pursue the missing card had to make an additional effort. It was, arguably, the hobby's first major chase card. By definition, the people who went the extra mile for the Lajoie were a bit more serious about completing the set and the endeavor altogether. It stands to reason that at least some of these hobbyists preserved the Lajoie over time because they realized how special the card was at the time it was issued. The same can be said of the card today. If one's goal is to assemble the undisputed icons of cardboard, it can't be done without the 1933 Goudey Lajoie.

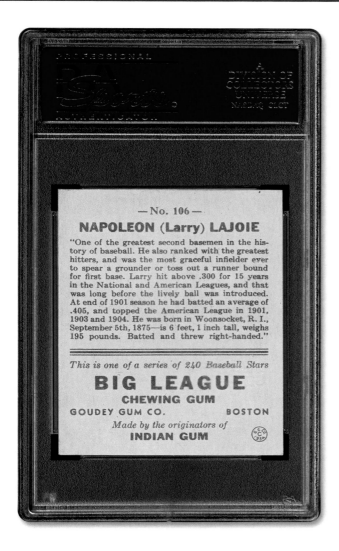

No. 106 —
NAPOLEON (Larry) LAJOIE

"One of the greatest second basemen in the history of baseball. He also ranked with the greatest hitters, and was the most graceful infielder ever to spear a grounder or toss out a runner bound for first base. Larry hit above .300 for 15 years in the National and American Leagues, and that was long before the lively ball was introduced. At end of 1901 season he had batted an average of .405, and topped the American League in 1901, 1903 and 1904. He was born in Woonsocket, R. I., September 5th, 1875—is 6 feet, 1 inch tall, weighs 195 pounds. Batted and threw right-handed."

This is one of a series of 240 Baseball Stars

BIG LEAGUE
CHEWING GUM
GOUDEY GUM CO.   BOSTON
Made by the originators of
INDIAN GUM

The Frenchman

One of the greatest second basemen of all time, Nap Lajoie was a great spray hitter, excellent bunter, had some power, had exceptional defensive skills, and was a leader on the field. Lajoie was so good and so popular when he played for the Cleveland Bronchos that they actually changed their name to the Cleveland Naps.

Napoleon Lajoie, also known as Larry, "The Frenchman," and "Nap," was born in Woonsocket, Rhode Island, where he worked in the textile mills as a child. He briefly patrolled the outfield in the Class B New England League before making a quick jump to the majors. Lajoie was purchased by the Philadelphia Phillies for $1,500 in 1896 at age 21. The Phillies decided to move him to first base and, finally, to second base where Lajoie became the premier guardian of

the keystone sack in the National League and, later, in the American League. A natural athlete, the 6-foot-1, 200-pound Lajoie was blessed with a rifle for an arm, very soft hands, and excellent footwork. Before his career ended, he led the league in putouts five times, assists three times, double plays six times, and fielding percentage six times.

Lajoie never batted below .324 in his five seasons with the Phillies, but after season five he got into a contract dispute. Along with several other players he jumped to the new American League in 1901. His star power brought immediate legitimacy to the junior circuit. Connie Mack signed Lajoie to play for the crosstown Philadelphia Athletics, and he quickly established himself as one of the best hitters in the American League. In his initial season with the A's in 1901, Lajoie's 14 home runs, 125 RBI, and astounding .426 batting average earned him the AL Triple Crown and the AL batting title. He led the league in most offensive categories that year, including hits with 232. Lajoie was so good, that he once was walked intentionally with the bases loaded! A powerful but somewhat undisciplined hitter, he would swing at pitches that were at his feet or in the dirt, but Lajoie usually made contact. He used a specially designed two-knobbed bat with the knobs carefully spaced for better bat control.

The very next year, Mack traded his new star to the Cleveland Bronchos. Why? The Phillies sued Lajoie for jumping to the new league and the court ruled that Lajoie could not play for any team in the state of Pennsylvania except the Phillies. Lajoie dodged that by joining the AL Cleveland club and not playing in any games that took place in Pennsylvania. In 1903, the court reversed the decision. Although Lajoie was allowed to play anywhere, he stayed with Cleveland for 13 seasons. He won the AL batting title in both 1902 and 1903, batting .378 and .344, respectively. Because of his immense popularity, the team's name was changed to the Naps in 1903. Lajoie batted .376 in 1904, for his fourth title. That year he led the league in many offensive categories, including hits, with 208, and RBI, with 102.

Lajoie was so good and so popular when he played for the Cleveland Bronchos that they actually changed their name to the Cleveland Naps.

Nap Lajoie

Lajoie also developed a penchant for arguing with umpires on behalf of his teammates. In fact, he was suspended in 1904 for spitting tobacco juice into an umpire's eye.

Lajoie became player-manager of the Naps in 1905. That season, he developed blood poisoning after getting spiked. The infection was caused by the blue dye in his socks, and it was so serious that amputation of his leg was considered. Because of this incident, MLB created a new rule that all players must wear sanitary white socks under their colored hose, which was cut to fit into their cleats. This was the birth of the iconic "stirrup." Lajoie was wheelchair bound for a good part of the season but was able to return in August. Nap the manager was certainly not as good as Nap the player. Lajoie did not have the patience to mentor and manage younger players, and he expected them to be more dedicated to the game. This period also saw the rise of the Detroit Tigers' young batting star, Ty Cobb. While Lajoie batted in the .300s as player-manager, the brash young Cobb nosed ahead to take the batting title in 1907, 1908, and 1909. Lajoie asked the Cleveland Naps owner, Charles Somers, to replace him as manager so he could focus on his offense, and this was granted during the 1909 season. In five seasons as player-manager, Lajoie had compiled a 377–309 record and led the Naps to a second-place finish in 1908.

Without managerial responsibilities, Lajoie batted .383 in a controversial and exciting American League batting race in 1910. Lajoie and Cobb were dead even going into the last day of the season. The winner of the batting title would receive a brand-new

automobile from the Chalmers Motor Company. Going into a doubleheader against the St. Louis Browns on the last day of the season, Lajoie needed to get a hit in every at-bat to win the title. Interestingly, the manager of the Browns, Jack O'Connor, hated Ty Cobb so much that he instructed his third baseman to play well beyond the bag. Lajoie proceeded to drop down seven bunts in his first seven at-bats, with his last hit being a rope that he hit for a triple. Although American League president Ban Johnson declared Cobb the winner by less than a percentage point, both players were presented with new cars.

Lajoie had three more very productive years batting .365 in 1911, .368 in 1912, and .335 in 1913, but Ty Cobb was firmly established as the league's batting star. In 1914, Lajoie batted a paltry .258 with 108 hits at age 39. He then returned to his old team, Connie Mack's Athletics, to play out the string. After 21 seasons, Lajoie retired in 1916 with a career .338 average, 3,243

hits, and 1,599 RBI. Hired as player-manager of the 1917 Toronto Maple Leafs in the International League, Lajoie batted a lofty .380 to lead his team to the pennant. In 1918, he batted .282 as player-manager of the American Association's Indianapolis Indians before calling it quits for good.

In retirement, Lajoie dabbled in politics. He ran for sheriff of Cuyahoga County but lost his bid. For a brief period, he was commissioner of the Ohio-Pennsylvania League, and he had several business interests. Lajoie was elected to the Baseball Hall of Fame in 1937 with the highest percentage of votes and he participated in the first induction ceremony in 1939. Napoleon "Nap" Lajoie passed away from pneumonia on February 7, 1959, at the age of 84.

A stellar second sacker, five-time AL batting champ, three-time AL RBI leader, and Triple Crown winner, Lajoie certainly left his mark on our National Pastime.

WHEN IT COMES TO PRESENCE,
the huge and vibrant 1911 T3
Turkey Red Cabinets are in a class by
themselves. They are more than just
baseball cards, and it's easy to see why
when you are holding one of them in
your hands. In fact, you can enjoy them
from across the room in a way that is
hard to imagine with most standard-
sized trading cards. The large format
allows the viewer to appreciate every
detail, from the image of the game's
fiercest competitor to the rainbow-like
background that seems to symbolize a
slice of baseball heaven.

The set, which was issued by the
American Tobacco Company, is as
stunning as any collectible card issue in
hobby history. It contains 100 baseball
subjects but is numbered to 126
because cards 51–76 featured boxers.
That 26-card "break" is categorized
separately as the T9 set. The cabinet-
style cards, which measure 5¾″ x 8″
each, offer striking color lithography
on thick stock, surrounded by a
gray-colored frame. The cards could
be obtained through a redemption
program, where collectors could send in
coupons in exchange for these colossal
cards.

Three cigarette brands were involved
in the program: Turkey Red, Old
Mill, and Fez. While the fronts are
consistent in appearance, the content
on the reverse of each card can vary.
The backs will either display one of four
different checklists or feature an ad
for Turkey Red Cigarettes, but the ad
backs are limited to the higher series.
The advertising backs are considered
tougher and more desirable than their
checklist counterparts. It is important

This PSA NM-MT 8 is one of two examples graded at that tier, with none higher in
the PSA Population Report.

to note that Cobb, who is found in the earlier series, can only be found with a checklist on the reverse.

For collectors today, the supersized format is both a blessing and, unfortunately, a curse. These titanic cards could be difficult to store and protect. Furthermore, the cards were often affixed to walls due to their eye-catching nature, so it is important to beware of pin or tack holes. These cards can still retain great visual appeal, but they will suffer the consequences during the technical grading process. In certain cases, those holes were filled or covered at some point for aesthetic purposes, which would result in an "altered" designation today. Remember that evidence of a puncture will usually prevent a card from achieving a grade any higher than PSA Poor 1 or Fair 1.5.

The full-body pose of Cobb used in the T3 set is virtually identical to his "Bat On Shoulder" image in the T206 issue, which is a close-up shot. There are subtle differences in color as a result of the artwork, but the position of Cobb is the same. In a set riddled with most of the era's top stars, from Walter Johnson to Cy Young, Cobb is the clear anchor. Cobb finds himself on so many iconic cards, but no other issue can claim the sheer magnetism of this hobby giant.

For collectors today, the supersized format is both a blessing and, unfortunately, a curse.

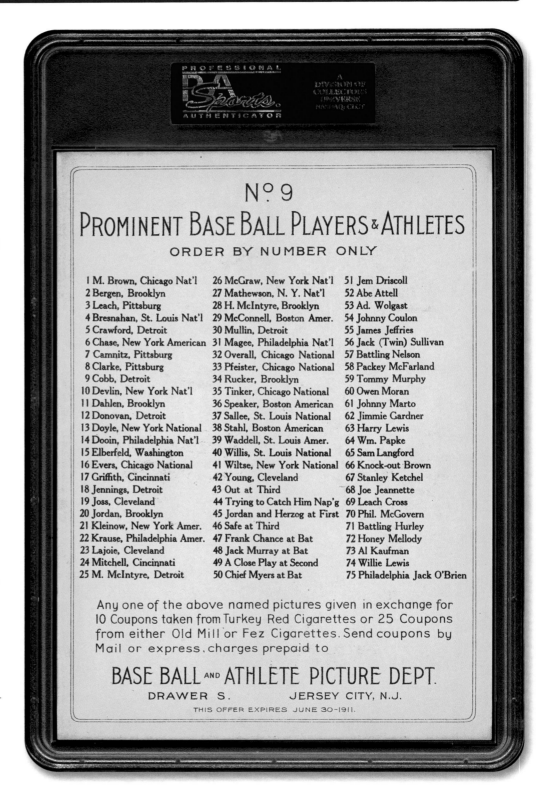

The Georgia Peach

When true baseball purists begin discussing the career and legacy of Ty Cobb, different emotions regarding his place in baseball history bubble up. Without doubt, the enigmatic Cobb is considered one of the top three or four greatest players of all time. His life and career, however, were very complex, and it is difficult to sort out what is fact and what is fiction. It is almost as though there are two Ty Cobb factions that exist. There are those who consider him a fierce competitor on the field who was only playing to win, and those who consider him an individual who was mad at the world, who had that same goal to win, but who did not care about the collateral damage. There are several Ty Cobb cards featured in this book with the T3 Turkey Red Cabinet card being the first. Here we are going to discuss Ty Cobb, the man, and later on we will get into his storied baseball career.

Tyrus Raymond Cobb was born in Narrows, Georgia, on December 18, 1886. Unlike many ballplayers from the Deadball Era, Cobb was brought up in an affluent home. His father, William, was a teacher and legislator who was even toying with the idea of running for governor of the state of Georgia. His mother, Amanda, came from a wealthy Georgia family. Young Ty idolized his father. In the young man's eyes, William was a brilliant educator who taught his son how to think independently and to always strive to succeed, no matter what the cost was. A major turning point in his life took place on August 8, 1905, when young Cobb was 18 years old. Apparently, Cobb's father suspected his wife of having an affair with another man. After telling his wife that he would be gone overnight at a farm

that they owned, he came back at midnight to confront both the wife and her supposed lover. When Amanda noticed a man peering into the bedroom window from outside, she pulled out a gun and shot the man with two bullets, killing him instantly. That man was William. Amanda claimed that she thought he was a burglar, but some evidence suggested otherwise, and she was arrested. Cobb's mother was indicted on manslaughter charges but was later acquitted. Rumors circulated that she was, in fact, involved with another man, but it was never proven. Young Cobb, who at the time was playing for the Augusta Tourists of the South Atlantic League, received a telegram calling him home. Needless to say, he was traumatized by the shocking, tragic event and all of the rumors that now swirled around his family. Most likely this time in his personal life contributed to the turbulence that would burden him the rest of his life.

Just a few weeks later, on August 30, 1905, Cobb made his major-league debut with the Detroit Tigers. Cobb had

Ty Cobb

However, there is no doubt that Cobb was very competitive, could be cantankerous, had a short fuse, and was generally not well-liked by his peers. When he was locked in a race for the 1910 American League batting title with Nap Lajoie of the Cleveland Naps, some of Cobb's teammates actually sent Lajoie congratulatory telegrams after he was declared the winner. Obviously, many of the issues that Cobb had were brought on by himself, but many incidents are now considered

difficulty adjusting to life in the north, and he was still reeling from the death of his father and the accusations against his mother. His teammates hardly spoke to him and hazed him by vandalizing his property. As a result, Cobb became a loner with a trigger temper, and he soon developed a reputation for carrying a chip on his shoulder. He feuded with teammates, opposing players, umpires, and fans, while becoming much more aggressive on the playing field. Some players and sportswriters claimed that Cobb sharpened his spikes to purposely hurt other players by sliding in to base with spikes high, and that a number of players covering second base or third base felt his wrath. On several occasions, Cobb did spike opponents, but he always maintained that it was never done intentionally. Cobb was also accused of being a racist after he got into a fight with a Black hotel employee but there is no evidence showing that Cobb was a racist. As a matter of fact, Cobb always said that he was in favor of integrating baseball. The racism stigma most likely comes from *Cobb: A Biography* written by Al Stump, which was used as the basis for the 1994 movie *Cobb* starring Tommy Lee Jones. Stump was the ghost writer of Ty Cobb's memoirs *My Life in Baseball*, which was published in 1961, soon after Cobb's death, but his portrayal of Cobb in the 1994 book was much more negative and some say Stump had a vendetta against Cobb. Many of his statements about Cobb have since been discredited.

baseball folklore. On a personal note, in 1908 Cobb married Charlotte "Charlie" Lombard, the youngest daughter of the wealthy businessman, Roswell O. Lombard, of Augusta, Georgia. The young couple lived at Lombard's country home "The Oaks" in Augusta in the offseasons. They had five children and were married nearly 40 years, but Cobb had a strained relationship with his wife, and he and Charlie finally divorced in 1947. Cobb married again in 1949 to Frances Fairbairn Cass, but they divorced in 1956.

Nevertheless, Ty Cobb was a brilliant businessman. He made wise financial investments in new companies like Coca Cola and General Motors. He was also very philanthropical, donating large sums to various charities and helping indigent retired ballplayers behind the scenes. In today's dollars, Cobb's net worth would be more than $100 million. As portrayed by Stump, Cobb became reclusive and turned to alcohol as his health declined. However, *Heart of a Tiger*, a book written by grandson Herschel Cobb, portrays Cobb as a loving grandfather. Enigmatic and complex? Absolutely. Should we believe everything written about him? Probably not. This is the framework of Ty Cobb the man. On page 52 we will examine the career of Ty Cobb, one of the greatest ballplayers of all time.

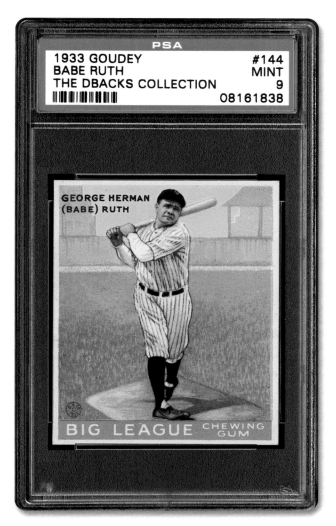

This PSA Mint 9 is one of four examples graded at that tier, with none higher in the PSA Population Report.

THE 1933 GOUDEY BASEBALL CARD SET HAS often been referred to as one of "The Big Three" in the sport, along with the 1909–1911 T206 and 1952 Topps sets. The Goudey issue rests comfortably in the middle of those two classics, nearly 20 years apart from each. When it comes to card count, the Goudey set is technically the smallest of the three but the pound-for-pound star power of the 240 cards within (if you count Napoleon Lajoie at #106) is unparalleled. There are two cards each of Hall of Famers like Jimmie Foxx, Lou Gehrig, Rogers Hornsby, and Mel Ott, but the true foundation of the staple set is a quartet of Babe Ruth cards.

Ruth can be found on card numbers 53, 144, 149 and 181. While the #53 (Yellow) and #149 (Red) Ruth cards are virtually identical in design outside of background color differences, the #144 (Full Body/Batting Pose) and #181 (Green – Dugout Steps) offer a different view of the slugger altogether. The Goudey Gum Company of Boston decided to package their cards with a piece of their Big League Chewing Gum, which ushered in a new era as a Golden Age of card manufacturing began. The hobby had already experienced "T-cards" (Tobacco), "E-cards" (Candy), and Cracker Jacks, but this was first time that cards and gum were nestled together in one wrapper. The rest is history.

The artwork used in the 1933 Goudey design was based on original photographs by Charles M. Conlon, arguably the most renowned sports photographer in baseball for the first half of the twentieth century. Three of the four Ruth cards (# 53, #144 and #149) were created from the same,

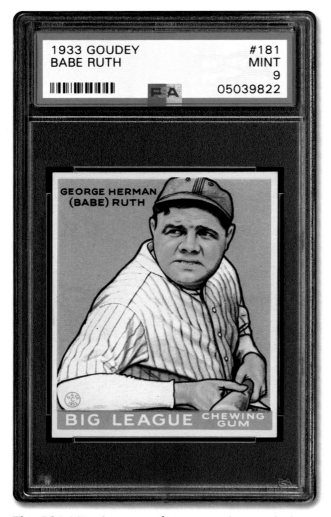

This PSA Mint 9 is one of six examples graded at that tier, with only one higher in the PSA Population Report.

classic batting image. Two (#53 and #149) are close-up shots, while one (#144) shows Ruth from head-to-toe, swinging on a small dirt patch against bright green grass in the background, amongst other things. This card, unlike the other three, was double printed. One version has slightly better registration than the other. The prevailing thought is that the #144 Ruth was inserted a second time on one of the sheets to replace the missing #106 Lajoie.

Despite being more plentiful in overall number, the #144 card is believed to be slightly tougher to find in high grade than the #181 Ruth. If we were to rank all four Ruth cards by condition difficulty, from toughest to easiest, it would look like the following: #53, #149, #144 and #181. Ruth was included in the 1935 Goudey set after his absence from the regular 1934 Goudey release (Ruth did appear on an

oversized 1934 Goudey Premium), but the 1933 Goudey quartet represented his last stand as the biggest active name in the game.

The Bambino

Continued from page 18.

The 1933 Goudeys feature Babe Ruth toward the end of his exceptional 15-year run with the Yankees, but let's take a look at his early years in New York. After six years with the Boston Red Sox, where he compiled an 89–46 record with a 2.19 ERA, Babe Ruth joined the New York Yankees in 1920. With his giant personality, the birth of the Roaring Twenties, and the general excitement that existed in New York City, this was a marriage made in heaven for Ruth, the Yankees, and baseball fans across America.

By the time "The Babe" got to the Yankees, his conversion from pitcher to full time outfielder was complete. After a slow start, Ruth began to hit home runs at a record pace. Fans flocked to The Polo Grounds to see "The Bambino," "The Sultan of Swat," and his amazing power. By the end of July, Ruth had hit 37 home runs. Although the Yankees finished in third place in 1920, Babe Ruth's debut in pinstripes was the talk of the baseball world. Ruth shattered the home-run record, going deep 54 times, while driving in 135 runs and batting .376. Although baseballs were manufactured differently, which ended the Deadball Era, and some pitches, like the spitball, were declared illegal, Ruth still hit more home runs that season than some entire teams. The nation had a genuine baseball superstar and even opposing players would step up the dugout stairs when Ruth came up to the plate.

Off the field, Ruth embraced the New York City nightlife, dining and drinking late into the night, smoking cigars, and having fun with fans all over the city. On the road, it was the same thing. The Babe never found a gin mill he did not like, and he usually had an entourage with him. To support their new star, the Yankees assembled more pieces to the team puzzle by building up their pitching and developing talented young players. In 1921, the team won the American League pennant, but lost the Series to the New York Giants in eight games. Ruth had a phenomenal year batting .378 and hitting an amazing 59 bombs to break his own home run record. He also led the league with 177 runs and 168 RBI, while banging out 204 hits. The World Series was a different story. Because of an elbow injury, Ruth batted a mere mortal .313 in only 16 at-bats. Going into the 1922 season with a new $52,000 contract, Ruth batted only .315 with 35 home runs. Besides having an off-year, Ruth managed to get into several scrums with opposing fans in the stands and even with a few umpires. The Yankees again won the American League pennant only to lose the Series to the New York Giants once again. Ruth had a miserable Series with only two hits and a paltry .118 batting average.

After sharing the Polo Grounds with the Giants for a decade, the Yankees moved into their own ballpark in 1923. Owner Jacob Ruppert's new ballpark was designed to help Ruth,

a lefty pull hitter. The dimension down the right-field line at the new Yankee Stadium was a short 295 feet, tailor made for Ruth. The new ballpark would soon be known as "The House That Ruth Built." The Babe rewarded his fans in 1923 with a .393 batting average while leading the league with 41 home runs and 130 RBI. The Yankees went to the World Series, this time beating the Giants in six games with Ruth leading the way batting .368 with three home runs. It would be the first of many championships at the new Yankee stadium. During the offseason, Ruth went on a barnstorming tour thrilling fans across the country. The Babe was especially wonderful with the kids, playing sandlot ball with them, patiently signing autographs, and often

Babe Ruth

The Babe was especially wonderful with the kids, playing sandlot ball with them, patiently signing autographs, and often visiting sick children in the hospital during his exhibition tours.

visiting sick children in the hospital during his exhibition tours. Even though some of his offseason antics were a bit over the top, Ruth came back in 1924 with another banner season leading the league with 46 home runs, 143 runs, and his .378 average. It would be the first and only batting title won by Ruth. The Yankees came up short in 1924, finishing second to the Washington Senators, who went on to defeat the Giants in seven games for the World Series title.

Ruth went off the rails during the offseason between 1924 and 1925. Instead of staying in shape for baseball, his weight ballooned up to 256 pounds. Between the hot dogs, beer, cigar smoking and simply not taking care of himself, Ruth was terribly out of shape. In spring training, he fell ill with an intestinal issue. Some reporters claimed it was due to the food and alcohol he was consuming. In any event, the incident became known as "The Bellyache Heard 'Round the World." Although it has never been confirmed, the doctors said that Ruth had developed a minor intestinal abscess and they performed a procedure that kept him out of the lineup until June. Ruth was hospitalized for six weeks. There has

always been speculation about what really happened. The fact that he was allowed to leave the hospital periodically to work out alone and with the team led some to believe that Ruth was actually addressing his excessive drinking. Others maintained that he did, in fact, have a stomach issue. Never in the hunt for the 1925 pennant, the Yankees finished in seventh place. Ruth's numbers were down significantly, to .290 with 25 home runs, good numbers for any other ballplayer, but less than average for Babe Ruth.

After that season, the 31-year-old slugger finally decided to curb his extracurricular activities and focus on getting back into shape so he could extend his baseball career. With a regimen of a strict diet and exercise, Ruth lost 44 pounds. For the next several seasons he hit a stretch that no other hitter ever reached. The new and improved Babe Ruth tore up the American League in 1926, batting .372 and slamming a league-leading 47 home runs and 153 RBI. With the addition of 23-year-old first baseman Lou Gehrig in his second full year, and a strong supporting cast, the Yankees went on to win the AL pennant only to lose the Series to the St. Louis Cardinals in seven games. In Game Four of that World Series, Ruth hit three home runs.

As a footnote to the 1926 World Series, the legend of Babe Ruth continued to manifest itself. Supposedly, Ruth made a promise to 11-year-old Johnny Sylvester, who was in the hospital, that he would hit a home run for him in the next game. Ruth had never met the boy, but he made the promise through a friend. Of course, Ruth hit a home run. Never one to turn down a great publicity opportunity, Ruth later visited the boy in the hospital and the press picked up the story which eventually became baseball lore.

The story continues on page 101.

EVEN TO THIS DAY, THE 1952

Topps Mickey Mantle is mistakenly referred to as a rookie card when in fact the only recognized rookie card of "The Commerce Comet" resides in the 1951 Bowman set. After he briefly joined the club in 1950, without a plate appearance, the New York Yankees began the center field transition from Joe DiMaggio to Mantle in 1951, as it was the final season for "Joltin' Joe." These were big shoes to fill for the youngster from Oklahoma, but Mantle rose to the occasion in a way that few could imagine at the time, eventually becoming the biggest star in the game for nearly two full decades.

This PSA Gem Mint 10 is the sole example to reach PSA's highest grading tier.

The Mantle card, which is part of the tougher high-number series (253-324), is one of three key rookies that anchor the 324-card release. The set, which begins with a #1 card of fellow Yankees Hall of Famer Whitey Ford, also features the rookie issue of Willie Mays. For years, fans would argue as to who the greatest center fielder of the era was, Mantle or Mays? At the time, some would even toss Duke Snider's name into the debate for fun, and all three patrolled the middle of the outfield for New York-based teams. Mays proved to have superior longevity over the course of his career as Mantle's body would break down over time, but the Yankees legend took a backseat to no one in his prime.

Collectors have long placed the 1951 Bowman issue in the upper echelon of sports card sets, not just because of the star-studded rookie trio noted above, but also due to the terrific design. The hand-painted color images, based on original photos, give the issue more of a classic artwork feel compared to the color-tinted look of the 1952 Topps set. Both are attractive in their own right. The Bowman Mantle rookie, like other cards in the set, can suffer from print defects, wax stains along the reverse, poor registration, and subpar centering. The white borders that frame each card are relatively thin, so the slightest shift, either vertically or horizontally, can impact the eye appeal.

The Mick

Continued from page 14.

The 1952 Topps Mantle and the 1951 Bowman Mantle, two of the most sought-after cards in the hobby, represent the first two years of Mickey Mantle's storied career. In the mid-1950s and 1960s, Mantle became a beloved superstar. Between 1955 and 1957, Mantle hit his stride, becoming the most dominant hitter in the American League. The Yankees won the 1955 pennant, but lost to "Dem Bums," the Brooklyn Dodgers, in a seven-game Series. Although Mantle had a very good season, batting .306 and blasting a league-leading 37 homers, a pulled hamstring limited him in the Series, and he batted only .200 in three games.

The Mick shifted his career into high gear during the 1956 and 1957 seasons, winning back-to-back MVP Awards. In 1956, he led the league with 52 home runs, .353 BA, and 130 RBI to win the Triple Crown. The AL MVP, Mantle was also named the AP Male Athlete of the Year. This time the Yankees beat the Dodgers in a seven-game Series with Mantle hitting .250, three homers, and four RBI in the Fall Classic. Mantle followed that in 1957 with a .365 average and went yard 34 times. He led the league with 121 hits and 146 walks and was again named AL MVP. The Yankees won the 1957 pennant but lost the seven-game Series to the Milwaukee Braves led by Eddie Mathews and Hank Aaron. Mantle batted just .263 with five hits and one home run in the Series due to a Game Three collision with the Braves' Red Schoendienst that injured his right shoulder and impacted his ability to hit left-handed for the rest of his career.

A complete ballplayer and the baseball idol of millions of fans, Mickey Mantle is a baseball legend.

The American League juggernaut Yankees returned to the World Series in 1958, this time turning the tide on the Milwaukee Braves in seven games. After a slow start, Mantle recovered to make his sixth All-Star appearance, bat .304, and lead the league with 42 home runs, 127 runs scored, and 129 walks. He had a decent Series, hitting two home runs and six hits to go along with a .250 average. The 1959 season was a good example of "how Mickey Mantle would fare, so would the Yankees." A .285 batting average with 31 home runs and 75 RBI would be considered a very good season by many players. To Mickey Mantle it was adequate, at best. That season the Yankees finished in third place, only four games above .500. Interestingly, MLB decided to test the waters with two All-Star games and Mantle played in both, not bad for an adequate season.

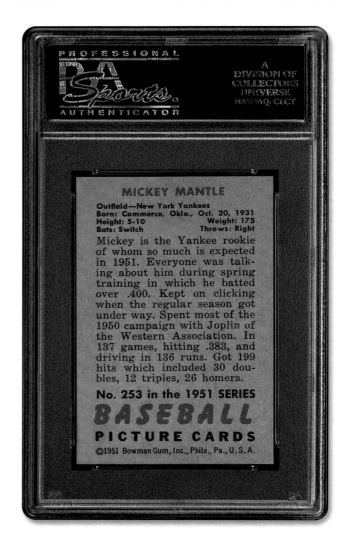

In 1960, the Yankees acquired power-hitting outfielder Roger Maris from the Kansas City Athletics. This proved to be the beginning of a magical stretch for the pinstripes. The tandem of Mantle and Maris made life miserable for opposing pitchers. Mantle knocked in 94 RBI and topped the league with 119 runs and 40 round trippers that season while Maris added 39 homers and 112 RBI...a formidable one-two punch. The Yankees returned to the World Series and Mantle batted .400 with three home runs and 11 RBI, but they lost the exciting seven-game contest to the Pittsburgh Pirates on Bill Mazeroski's famous Series-winning walk-off home run.

The 1961 season proved to be one of the most thrilling in baseball history. Mantle and Maris, known as the "M&M Boys," battled each other to break the single-season record of 60 home runs held by the legendary Babe Ruth. Maris

prevailed, hitting 61 home runs, and was named AL MVP. Considering Mantle missed ten of the last 12 games of the season due to injury, his 54 home runs, 163 hits, and .317 average are impressive. The Yankees won a league-leading 109 games and defeated the Cincinnati Reds in five games for the 1961 Series championship. Although he missed a total of 39 games due to injuries in 1962, Mantle batted .321 with 30 homers and was named AL MVP. He also became a $100,000 ballplayer, joining a very elite club.

The 1963 season proved to be troublesome for Mantle. He played only 65 games due to an injury in a June game against the Baltimore Orioles. Mantle broke his foot while chasing a ball hit by Oriole's third baseman, Brooks Robinson, and he could not return until August. Although chosen for the All-Star team, Mantle was unable to play. The Yankees were swept by Sandy Koufax and the Los Angeles

Dodgers in the 1963 World Series, with Mantle batting only .133. The Mick came roaring back in 1964, batting .303 with 35 homers. The Yankees lost the 1964 Series to the St. Louis Cardinals, but Mantle blasted Series career home runs 16, 17, and 18 to surpass Babe Ruth's record of 15 Series homers.

Going into the 1965 season, age and injuries began to catch up with Mantle. The 33-year-old star batted only .255, and the Yankees finished in sixth place. Other factors also played into the deterioration of his skills, namely, nightlife and alcohol. After his father died at an early age, Mantle believed his days were numbered and he decided to live large. He drank into the night and sometimes into the morning, and this would eventually be his downfall. Mantle bounced back somewhat in 1966, batting .288 with 23 home runs. He moved to first base in 1967 and 1968, batting just .245 and .237, respectively. One bright spot took place in May 1967 when Mantle attained the prestigious 500 Home Run Club milestone. Mantle played in the last game of his brilliant career on September 28, 1968 and retired in March 1969. In 18 storied seasons, he had compiled a .298 BA (.330 right-hand, .281 left-hand), 536 home runs, 1,509 RBI, and 1,676 runs. In June 1969, his number "7" jersey was retired at Yankee Stadium on Mickey Mantle Day with 70,000 fans in attendance. He was elected to the Hall of Fame in 1974, his first year of eligibility.

Due to unsuccessful business ventures, Mantle initially experienced financial difficulties in retirement but he later profited from the boom of the sports

memorabilia industry and regularly made signing appearances at card shows. After years of alcohol abuse, Mantle entered the Betty Ford Center in 1993, but it was too late. He had developed liver disease. To his credit, he began speaking about the dangers of alcohol across the country. During a liver transplant, doctors found an aggressive cancer that had spread and sadly, on August 13, 1995, Mickey Mantle passed away at age 63.

The face of the Yankees franchise for his entire career, "The Commerce Comet" was a 20-time All-Star, seven-time World Series Champ, and three-time American League MVP. He won the Triple Crown in 1956, smacked 536 home runs, won a Gold Glove and a batting title, but he was so much more than stats and awards. A complete ballplayer and the baseball idol of millions of fans, Mickey Mantle is a baseball legend.

"SHOELESS" JOE JACKSON HAS ONE OF THE MOST compelling stories in all of sports. From humble beginnings to becoming arguably the best hitter in the game to being connected to one of the most infamous moments in baseball history, Jackson's tale is intriguing and complicated. To this day, arguments rage on as to how involved Jackson was in the 1919 Black Sox Scandal. That shred of uncertainty has, in some ways, kept the tale alive, decade after decade. The legend of Jackson has not been harmed by it, but instead the interest in his collectibles has increased because of it. Of all the examples available to us, Jackson is the perfect "what could have been" figure to evaluate.

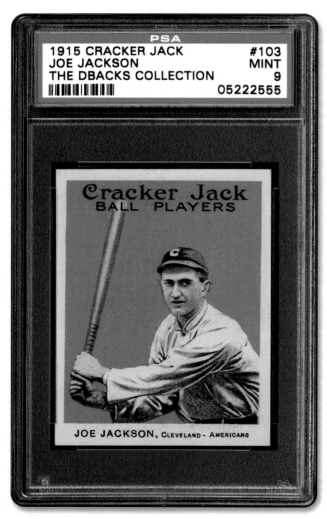

This PSA Mint 9 is one of two examples graded at that tier, with none higher in the PSA Population Report.

There aren't very many different Jackson cards to choose from, and there is no doubt that some others are far more valuable grade-for-grade, but the Cracker Jack Jackson cards are his most popular. The eye-grabbing color and pleasing image of Jackson make this his most visually attractive issue. In 1914, Cracker Jack decided to include cards with their sticky, sweet treat. The set, which totaled 144 cards, was stacked with the stars of the day, from Ty Cobb to Walter Johnson to Honus Wagner. In 1915, the company decided to repeat the basic design but expanded the offering to 176 cards. The 1914 and 1915 Jackson cards appear identical on the front, but the reverse on all the cards in the 1915 release was printed upside down.

While there is also a subtle difference in paper thickness and often the strength of the red color in the background, the most significant difference between the two lies in their difficulty. The only way to obtain the 1914 Jackson was by purchasing boxes of the candy. In 1915, the cards continued to be included in the Cracker Jack boxes, but a redemption program was available to the public where they could obtain an entire uncirculated set and an album to store the cards in. Interestingly, the 1915 Cracker Jack issue is more popular today since collectors have more high-grade cards available to them. For many collectors, the 1914 set is almost too tough to attempt.

In the collectibles world, Jackson is one of the rare cases where being blessed by the Hall of Fame isn't required for collectors to pursue him. To the contrary, they are fascinated by Jackson. Fans continue to explore every plausible explanation for his downfall and every possible outcome if his career would have been uninterrupted. Today, Jackson is more myth than man, and anything connected to him automatically rises to a level that mere mortals could never reach.

Shoeless Joe

Putting the infamous Black Sox Scandal aside for a moment, the discussion of "Shoeless" Joe Jackson as one of the greatest hitters to play the game merits consideration. Trailing only Ty Cobb, Oscar Charleston, and Rogers Hornsby with his .356 lifetime batting average, and with his tremendous defensive skills, Jackson was one of the original superstars of the game.

Born in rural Pickens County, South Carolina, in 1887, and raised in neighboring Greenville, Joseph Walker Jackson was the oldest of eight children. He never went to school because, from a very young age, he worked in the local textile mill to help support the family. Jackson learned to play baseball on the Brandon Mill team before he joined the Carolina Association's Greenville Spinners in 1908, where he got his nickname. In a June game, around the sixth inning, Jackson told his manager, Tommy Stouch, that he had blisters from his new cleats and asked if he could beg out of the game. Stouch nixed that idea, so Jackson took off the cleats and played in his stocking feet. Some say he played barefoot. Greenville fans good naturedly called out "Joe, you shoeless sonofagun." A reporter from *The Greenville News* heard the calls and dubbed him "Shoeless Joe" in his report of the game. The nickname stuck. Jackson's favorite bat also had a nickname. Made locally by a fan, the dense hickory bat measured 36 inches, weighed a hefty 48 ounces, and was darkened with tobacco juice. Jackson named it "Black Betsy" and used it throughout his career. A natural athlete with a sweet swing, the 6-foot-1, 200-pound Jackson boasted a .346 average right out of the gate, attracting Connie Mack's attention.

The 20-year-old slugger signed with Connie Mack's Philadelphia Athletics in July 1908. Because he had never learned to read or write, Jackson signed his contract with an X, but he later learned to trace his name on contracts. For the next two seasons, Jackson bounced between the minors and the parent club, but the shy country boy never adjusted to the big city. Some of his teammates made fun of his illiteracy and country ways, and finally Mack realized that Philadelphia was not a good fit for Jackson. He was traded to the Cleveland Naps in 1910 and had a much easier adjustment to the Cleveland team because many of the other players were from the south. This was the real beginning of his relatively short but illustrious career.

Jackson came out like gangbusters in 1911, batting an incredible .408 and banging out 233 hits. He followed up with a .395 average and led the league with 226 hits in 1912. His run with the Naps was very productive and he was at or near the top of the league in most offensive categories. During the offseason Jackson worked the Vaudeville circuit, attracting crowds wherever he appeared. In 1914, the Naps experienced a downturn. No longer contenders, they struggled at the gate. The newly formed Federal League

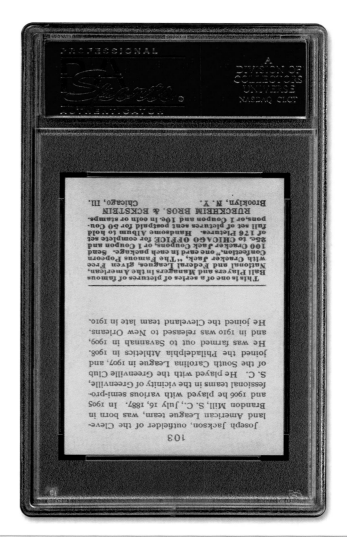

How good was Shoeless Joe Jackson? As the great Ty Cobb stated, "He was the finest natural hitter in the game of baseball."

offered Jackson $10,000 a year in 1915 to jump from the American League, but the Cleveland ownership traded Jackson to the Chicago White Sox before he could jump to the new league. Little did Jackson realize this was the beginning of the end for him. The trade, by the way, was the most expensive in baseball at the time. Jackson had a very successful first full season with the 1916 White Sox, batting .341, banging out over 202 hits, and leading the league with 21 triples. In 1917, with a talented lineup featuring the likes of Ray Schalk, Eddie Collins, Buck Weaver, and Chick

media circus, the eight players were acquitted by a jury, but despite that, Commissioner Kenesaw Mountain Landis expelled all eight players from baseball forever. Jackson claimed he never agreed to participate in the fix, that his name was used without his consent. He was given money, but Jackson maintained he attempted to return it before the Series and that he even tried to meet with Comiskey, but the owner would not see him.

With his professional career over, Jackson played for several semi-pro teams under different names, and fans were mostly respectful when they realized he was "Shoeless" Joe Jackson. In retirement, he operated a successful restaurant and liquor store in his hometown and enjoyed teaching local neighborhood kids how to play baseball. In September 1951, Cleveland fans voted Jackson to the Indians Hall of Fame. He died soon after of a heart attack in Greenville, South Carolina, on December 5, 1951, at age 64.

The legacy of Joe Jackson continues to be controversial. Along with the other banned 1919 Black Sox, he is not eligible for entrance into Cooperstown. Some people feel that he was innocent because he was not involved in the plans to throw the World Series. He played to win, but he accepted the money anyway. Was it right or wrong? It is said he used the money to pay his sister's hospital bills. How good was Joe Jackson? As the great Ty Cobb stated, "He was the finest natural hitter in the game of baseball." The story of "Shoeless" Joe Jackson is one of the saddest stories in baseball history.

Gandil, the White Sox won the pennant and defeated the New York Giants in six games to take the World Series championship.

Many players joined the military during the World War I, which drastically depleted the 1918 team. Jackson lost most of the season to war work in a Delaware shipyard. In 1919, the White Sox came back with a vengeance to clinch the pennant and face the Cincinnati Reds in the World Series. That season, Jackson batted .351 and played great defense but the White Sox had many internal issues. There were factions on the team that did not like each other, and most players on the team disliked owner Charles Comiskey because they believed he tried to save money at their expense, and he viewed them strictly as a commodity.

There are conflicting accounts about what really happened relative to the 1919 World Series. Disgruntled with

the miserly Comiskey, first baseman Chick Gandil got involved with mobsters to make more money. He approached several players, including Jackson, offering them various amounts of money to fix the Series. There were several middlemen acting as conduits between Gandil and the mobsters, who were betting very heavily on the Reds to win. Cincinnati did, in fact, win the Series, and rumors soon began to circulate that eight White Sox players were involved in the fix. To his credit, Jackson had a great Series batting .375 with 12 hits, but some say his defensive play was suspect.

The White Sox fared well in 1920 and at 32 years old, Jackson was in his prime, batting .382 with 218 hits. Sadly, on September 28, 1920, his career abruptly ended. Jackson and the other alleged co-conspirators were indicted for throwing the 1919 World Series. After a lengthy court case and

OVER THE PAST SEVERAL YEARS, SOME VINTAGE

cards have gained tremendous momentum in the market as collectors have either gained more appreciation for certain issues or changed their view entirely about them. One such card happens to feature Lou Gehrig, this time from the 1925 Exhibits set, which is considered by many to contain the rookie of the "The Iron Horse." Yet, while that specific Gehrig card has escalated in value more than any other in that time frame, the issue that is most closely associated with the Yankees icon, and his most visually attractive, is the pair of beauties found in 1934 Goudey set.

In 1934, Gehrig would have one of his finest seasons. He finished the season with a .363 batting average, 49 home runs and 166 RBI, which resulted in a Triple Crown for the lethal left-handed hitter. Amazingly, Gehrig only finished fifth in the MVP voting that year, a year that was somehow typical for the soft-spoken gentleman. For nearly a decade, Gehrig lived in the shadows of his charismatic teammate, Babe Ruth, but the 1934 season represented a passing of the torch. It was Ruth's final year in New York and the "Sultan of Swat's" skills had clearly started to decline. Even though Gehrig had put up remarkable numbers for years, the Yankees became *HIS* team in 1934. Gehrig was now the centerpiece.

In some ways, the 1934 Goudey set mirrors what was happening on the field. Gehrig, not Ruth, was also the centerpiece of the 96-card set. In fact, Ruth was absent from the issue altogether, and that does limit the set's overall

This PSA Mint 9 is one of three examples graded at that tier, with none higher in the PSA Population Report.

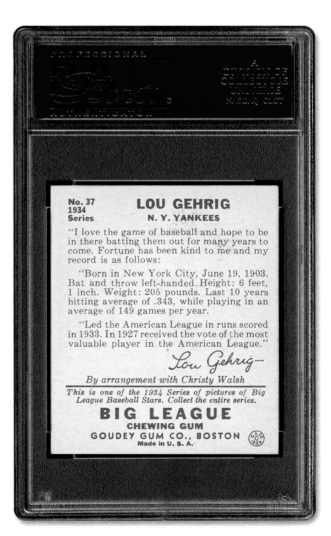

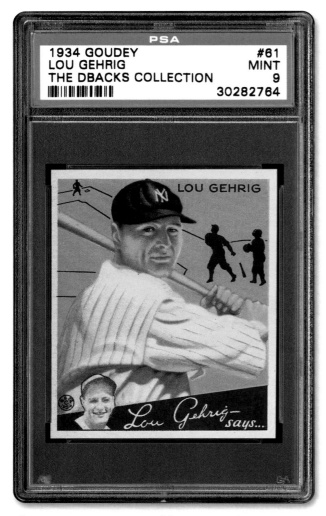

This PSA Mint 9 is one of four examples graded at that tier, with none higher in the PSA Population Report.

appeal to a degree. Some collectors, however, will argue that the 1934 Goudey design is even more attractive than its 1933 predecessor, which is stunning in its own right. The #37 portrait is widely viewed as the most eye-appealing card to ever feature Gehrig. The smiling headshot against the brilliant yellow background makes the card "pop" in an extraordinary way. The #61 card, which is also gorgeous, shows Gehrig in an intense batting pose with a heavy mix of blue and green colors throughout. This 1934 Goudey duo captures Gehrig's essence better than any other issue in hobby history.

Most of the cards in the set exhibit a "Lou Gehrig says..." banner at the base of the front. The reverse of the #37 card specifically features a quote from Gehrig, which reads, "I love the game of baseball and hope to be in there batting them

out for many years to come. Fortune has been kind to me..." A short time later, in 1939, Gehrig would be diagnosed with the debilitating disease, ALS, that now bears his name. We learn a lot about ourselves in times of adversity. What we already knew about Gehrig is that he was class personified, from beginning to tragic end.

The Iron Horse

The career of Lou Gehrig was one of monumental achievement and profound sadness. Remembered as "The Iron Horse," Gehrig and teammate Babe Ruth combined to become the most devastating one-two punch in baseball history.

Born in Manhattan to German immigrant parents, Henry Louis Gehrig developed an early love of baseball after his family relocated to the Washington Heights section of New York City, near the Polo Grounds and Hilltop Park where the Giants and Highlanders/Yankees played. At 17 years old, Gehrig gained attention in 1920 when his Commerce High baseball team played at Cubs Park in Chicago and he hit a grand slam out of the ballpark. He attended Columbia University on a football scholarship but also played baseball. Because money was tight in the Gehrig household, he decided to play semi-pro baseball in the Eastern League under an assumed name. Gehrig got caught and lost his freshman year college eligibility. When he regained eligibility in 1923, the slugging sophomore annihilated college pitching, catching the attention of Yankees scout Paul Krichell, who signed Gehrig in April 1923 for $400 per month with a $1,500 bonus. Gehrig left college to pursue a professional baseball career.

Assigned to the Class A Hartford Senators, the young slugger decimated minor-league pitching for parts of two seasons. He produced offensively in short stays with the big club in both 1923 and 1924. Wally Pipp, the Yankees regular first baseman, was injured in 1925, which gave Gehrig a chance to take over at first base. In his first full season, he batted a healthy .295 with 20 home runs and 68 RBI to earn the starting first baseman position. The 23-year-old Gehrig broke out in 1926, batting .313 with 16 home runs and 109 RBI while leading the league with 20 triples. The fact that he was playing alongside the best player on the planet motivated Gehrig. That season, Ruth had a typical "Ruthian"

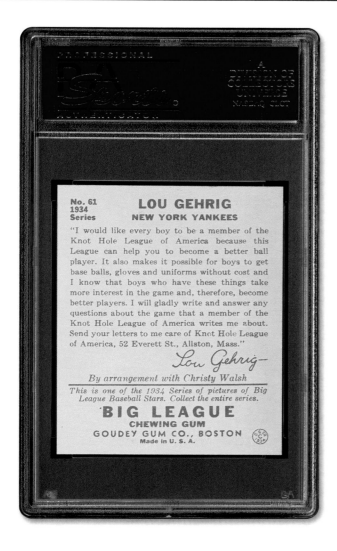

the Pirates in the World Series with Ruth leading the way, but Gehrig had a successful Series, batting .308. Although Ruth had a better season statistically than Gehrig, the young slugger was named the 1927 American League Most Valuable Player. According to the rules at the time, Ruth was not eligible because he was a previous MVP Award winner. Following the 1927 season, Ruth and Gehrig partnered in a barnstorming tour featuring Gehrig's Larrapin' Lous and Ruth's Bustin' Babes. The tour was a financial success for both players, with Ruth, of course, making more money. That year the Yankees awarded their new young star a $25,000 contract.

With 101 wins, the Yankees repeated in 1928, beating the Philadelphia Athletics for the pennant and sweeping the St. Louis Cardinals in the World Series. Again, Gehrig and Ruth carried the Yankees on their backs. Gehrig batted an incredible .545 with four home runs to go along with nine RBI. Ruth batted an amazing .625 and hit three home runs in Game Four. The Yankees wore uniform numbers for the first time in 1929. Ruth's number "3" and Gehrig's number "4" indicated where they were hitting in the lineup. Gehrig had another strong season, batting .300, hitting 35 homers, and knocking in 125 runs, but the Philadelphia Athletics ran away with the American League pennant, winning 104 games and finishing 16 games ahead of the Yankees.

The 1929 season did not end well for the Yankees and the next several months were even worse. In September, manager Miller Huggins died unexpectedly from a blood infection. His death especially affected Gehrig, who considered Huggins a father figure. A few weeks later, the stock market crashed, turning the entire country upside down. With the disastrous 1929 behind them, the Yankees and new manager, Bob Shawkey, looked forward to the new decade. Gehrig had a monster year in 1930, batting .379 with 41 home runs, 220 hits, and a league-leading 173 RBI. By the end of the season, Gehrig's consecutive games streak remained intact and baseball reporters dubbed him "The Iron Horse." Because they only won 86 games in 1930, finishing third behind the Athletics and the Washington Senators, Yankees ownership brought in a new manager, Joe McCarthy, to right the ship.

year batting .372 with 47 home runs. The Yankees won the 1926 pennant but lost the Series to the St. Louis Cardinals in seven games. Gehrig got a nice taste of postseason play, batting .348 in 23 at-bats.

Dubbed "Murderers' Row" by the press, the 1927 Yankees are considered the greatest baseball team ever assembled. With the devastating duo of Ruth batting third and Gehrig batting cleanup, and a cast of great players, the Yankees won 110 games that season. Baseball fans across the country were fascinated by the summer-long home run race between Ruth and Gehrig. The 24-year-old Gehrig kept pace with Ruth all season until Ruth went on a September tear to finish with a record 60 home runs compared to Gehrig's 47 homers. Gehrig also batted an amazing .373 with 218 hits while topping the league with 173 RBI and 52 doubles. Remarkably, he had played in every game since he came in as a pinch hitter on June 1, 1925. The Yankees swept

With McCarthy at the helm, the Yankees finished in second place behind the Athletics in 1931, and Gehrig had another tremendous year batting .341 while topping the league with

Lou Gehrig

Everett Scott. That year, Gehrig was chosen as starting first baseman for the first-ever All-Star Game. Now the primary offensive force for the Yankees, he led the American League with his .363 average, 49 homers, and 166 RBI to earn the Triple Crown in 1934. After that season, the 39-year-old Ruth left the Yankees to finish his career with the Boston Braves, and Lou Gehrig was named team captain. A young rookie named Joe DiMaggio joined the Yankees ranks in 1936. Gehrig welcomed the young phenom just as Ruth had welcomed him. That season Gehrig, like Ruth, showed the rookie how it was done, batting .354 with 152 RBI and leading the league with 49 home runs and 167 runs. He was also named the AL MVP. The Yanks went on to win the 1936 Series, beating the New York Giants in six games.

In 1937, Gehrig had another terrific year batting .351 with 37 home runs and 158 RBI and he played in his 1,965th consecutive game. The Yankees beat the Giants again for the 1937 World Series title. Gehrig hit .295 with 29 home runs in 1938 but his skills seemed to diminish. He tried using a lighter bat, with mixed results. The 35-year-old Gehrig did play through several injuries, but something was not right. The Yanks went on to win the American League pennant and sweep the Chicago Cubs in the World Series. After a difficult spring training in 1939, it became obvious that Gehrig was not well. He was losing weight, and even collapsed twice. Hitting less than .200 by the eighth game of the season, Gehrig took himself out of the lineup. The streak of The Iron Horse had ended on April 30, 1939, at 2,130 straight games.

185 RBI, 163 runs, and 211 hits. His 46 home runs tied with Ruth for first place in the league. With the country in the Great Depression, ballpark attendance was down significantly, and Gehrig took a pay cut to $23,000. He turned in another fine performance in 1932, with 34 home runs and a .349 average. The best day of his career came on June 3, 1932, when he hit four home runs against the A's at Shibe

Park. The Yankees won 107 games for the AL pennant and swept the Chicago Cubs in the 1932 World Series with Gehrig batting an astounding .529, with three home runs and nine hits.

Gehrig's consecutive game streak was catching the attention of baseball fans everywhere. In August 1933, he broke the record of 1,307 consecutive games set by former Yankees teammate

Lou Gehrig was inducted into the Hall of Fame by special election in 1939. For a brief time, he worked as parole commissioner for Mayor Fiorello La Guardia of New York City, but the disease progressed rapidly. On June 2, 1941, the great Lou Gehrig passed away at age 37. Thousands of fans attended his funeral. Flags were lowered to half-staff in New York City and at ballparks around the country. Gehrig's inspirational life story was told in the 1942 movie *The Pride of the Yankees*, starring Gary Cooper. He was voted the greatest

Although Gehrig stayed with the ballclub, his condition worsened, and he soon left the team to be examined at the Mayo Clinic. The doctors diagnosed him with Amyotrophic Lateral Sclerosis (ALS), an incurable disease affecting nerves and muscles that is now known as Lou Gehrig's disease. At 36 years old, Gehrig was given three years to live. He retired on June 21, 1939, and on July 4, the Yankees held Lou Gehrig Appreciation Day. More than 42,000 fans were in attendance to see Gehrig's uniform number "4" retired. Many of the 1927 Murderers Row Yankees showed up, as did his teammates from over the years. The short speech made by Lou Gehrig still resonates today.

first baseman of all time in 1969 and had the highest number of votes for the MLB All-Century team in 1999. Gehrig was honored with a postage stamp in 1989. His number "4" was the first number ever retired in MLB history. In 2021, Major League Baseball established June 2 as an annual league-wide Lou Gehrig Day to honor him and raise funds for ALS research. A statue of Gehrig now stands with those of Jackie Robinson and Roberto Clemente in the "Character and Courage" area of the Hall of Fame. With his seven All-Star appearances, two MVP Awards, a Triple Crown, his .340 career average, 2,721 hits, 493 home runs, and his 2,130 consecutive games streak, there is no doubt The Iron Horse was the greatest first baseman of all time.

"Fans, for the past two weeks you have been reading about a bad break. Today, I consider myself the luckiest man on the face of the earth.

"I have been in ballparks for 17 years and have never received anything but kindness and encouragement from you fans. Look at these grand men. Which of you wouldn't consider it the highlight of his career just to associate with them for even one day?

"Sure, I'm lucky.

"Who wouldn't consider it an honor to have known Jacob Ruppert? Also, the builder of baseball's greatest empire, Ed Barrow? To have spent six years with that wonderful little fellow, Miller Huggins? Then to have spent the next nine years with that outstanding leader, that smart student of psychology, the best manager in baseball today, Joe McCarthy?

"Sure, I'm lucky.

"When the New York Giants, a team you would give your right arm to beat, and vice versa, sends you a gift—that's something. When everybody down to the groundskeepers and those boys in white coats remember you with trophies—that's something.

"When you have a wonderful mother-in-law who takes sides with you in squabbles with her own daughter—that's something.

"When you have a father and a mother who work all their lives so you can have an education and build your body—it's a blessing.

"When you have a wife who has been a tower of strength and shown more courage than you dreamed existed—that's the finest I know.

"So, I close in saying that I might have been given a bad break, but I've got an awful lot to live for."

—Lou Gehrig, June 21, 1939

Mickey Mantle
game-used bat
circa 1966; 1998
Michael Jordan game-used
jersey; 1966 Roberto Clemente
game-used jersey; Satchel Paige
signed baseball and glove worn in 1948
World Series; Ty Cobb tobacco tin, circa
1909; Babe Ruth signed baseball; game-used
leather football helmet, circa 1920s. *The Mike Heffner
Collection.* The cards are images of the actual cards in the
Diamondbacks Collection.

3

The Rest of the Best

★ ★ ★ ★ ★ ★ ★ ★ ★ ★ ★ ★ ★ ★

The cards featured in this chapter complete the list of the top twenty sports cards in the sports collectibles world.

From the exceptional 1954 Topps Hank Aaron and 1986 Fleer Michael Jordan, both rated PSA Gem Mint 10, to the highest-ranking example of the difficult 1935 National Chicle Bronco Nagurski, to other iconic cards like the 1955 Topps Roberto Clemente, the 1941 Play Ball Joe DiMaggio, and the 1948 Bowman George Mikan, these remarkable pieces of cardboard complete the "Top 20" list of arguably the greatest sports cards in the hobby.

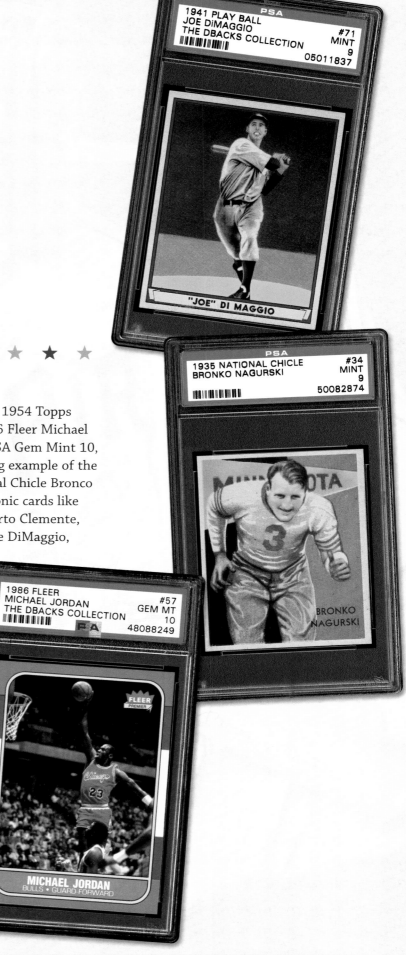

IN A SET DEFINED BY ITS HISTORICAL importance, star power, and difficulty, the 1948/1949 Leaf Satchel Paige card still stands as its most critical piece. Yes, the issue is home to a number of significant cards, including the iconic Jackie Robinson rookie, but the Paige card is the one component that causes collectors the most trouble from a scarcity and financial standpoint. For set builders of any grade quality, securing a Paige card is the single acquisition that puts them in a reasonable position to complete the entire project. With time, effort, and money, it becomes an attainable goal...but Paige is priority one. Major League Baseball fans were only able to get a small sample of Paige's mound magic when he was well beyond his peak, but it was just enough to imagine what he must have been like in his prime.

One of the key reasons for its rarity is the fact that the Paige card is one of 49 short prints in the 98-card set, which is oddly skip numbered. To put this in the proper context, there are approximately 10 times more Leaf Robinson cards graded in the PSA Population Report than there are of Paige. In addition to the card being printed in lower numbers versus the "regular" cards, no Paige had been graded higher than PSA NM-MT 8 at the time of this writing, making it one of the few stars in the set without an example graded NM-MT + 8.5, Mint 9, or Gem Mint 10 to date. Poor centering, print quality, registration, and varying degrees of border toning are all condition obstacles associated with the Paige card.

Finally getting an opportunity in the big leagues was bittersweet for Paige. Like most players in the Negro Leagues, Paige yearned for the chance to showcase his exceptional skills on the mound. In the case of Paige, however, his MLB debut came at 42, an age when most players are long retired. Paige had pitched against major-league players in exhibitions nearly two decades earlier, including the likes of Babe Ruth, so the lanky legend knew he had the ability to compete. Even at that advanced age, Paige won six of his seven starts in 1948 and over 72,000 fans witnessed his first home start in Cleveland that year. The pent-up desire to watch him was massive. Like Robinson, Paige did make an appearance in the Bowman set around the same general time, but the Leaf issue is his most sought-after card, by far.

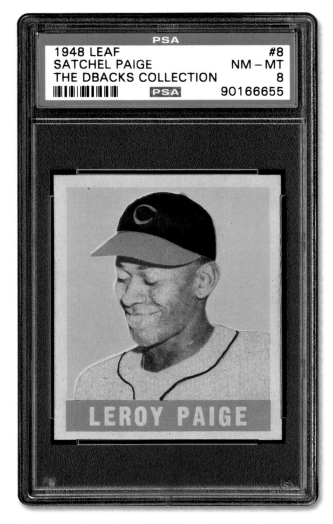

This PSA NM-MT 8 is one of five examples graded at that tier, with none higher in the PSA Population Report.

Satchel

Had Leroy "Satchel" Paige pitched his entire career in Major League Baseball, one can only imagine how many games he would have won and how dominant he would have been. Some say that between his seasons in the Negro Leagues and his barnstorming days, Paige won close to 1,500 games. That is likely an exaggeration, as Paige would have had to average roughly 35 wins per season, but according to those who saw him play, he was as dominant as any pitcher in the majors. Part showman and part trailblazer, Paige probably threw more pitches over a 40-year span than anyone in baseball history, and he helped change the face of baseball.

A product of the Deep South, Leroy Robert Paige was born on July 7, 1906, in Mobile, Alabama. As a young boy growing up in poverty, he worked at the local train station shining shoes and carrying passenger's suitcases to the hotel. The few cents he earned helped to keep him fed and shoes on his feet. The enterprising youngster wanted to carry more than one or two bags at a time, so he started using a pole he could hang several bags on and carry over his shoulder. Supposedly one of the boys he was working with yelled, "You look like a walking satchel tree." The nickname "Satchel" was born and stuck with him for the rest of his life. Of course, when a 12-year-old boy is not supervised, a lot can happen. The young Paige was truant from school on many occasions and was known to rifle through a suitcase or two while on the job. As a result, he ended up in reform school and was sentenced to five years at the institution. It was in reform school that Paige learned to pitch. The gangly 6-foot-3 right-hander was taught the proper mechanics of how to deliver a baseball by Coach Ed Byrd. With his long strong legs and high kick, Paige was able to fire the baseball past even the strongest kids. His motion was quite different than the average pitcher. Besides the leg kick, he had very large hands which made it easy for him to hide the ball. That coupled with the fact that he would almost snap the ball when it left his hand made it nearly impossible to hit.

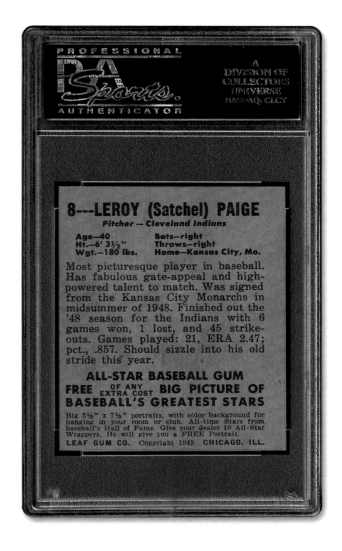

Part showman and part trailblazer, Paige probably threw more pitches over a 40-year span than anyone in baseball history, and he helped change the face of baseball.

Paige pitched for local semi-pro teams, including the Mobile Tigers, before launching his professional career in 1926 with the Chattanooga Black Lookouts. He brought his blazing fastball to the Birmingham Black Barons, where he played from 1927 to 1930. There he registered an 11–4 record with 121 strikeouts in 1928 and an 11–9 record with 189 Ks in 1929. After brief stints with the Baltimore Black Sox, Homestead Grays, and the Cleveland Cubs, Paige joined the Pittsburgh Crawfords, sticking with them for the most part from 1931 to 1937. He is credited with a 13–3 record and 152 strikeouts in 1934. Paige did leave the team a few times,

pitching briefly with the Bismarck Club in North Dakota and the Kansas City Monarchs during his salary disputes with the Crawfords. Because of his exceptional ability, showmanship, and engaging personality, Paige quickly became one of the biggest stars in his league, drawing large crowds whenever he played.

He parlayed this popularity into successful barnstorming tours and exhibition games in the offseason. Although MLB was segregated, these games offered the opportunity for integrated play, and audiences across the country were introduced to Negro League stars like Paige, Josh Gibson, Buck Leonard, Cool Papa Bell, and Oscar Charleston. In 1932, Satchel Paige and future Hall of Famer Dizzy Dean formed two barnstorming teams for exhibition play. In 1934, Paige's team beat Dean's in four out of six exhibition games. Wildly popular, and financially successful, the Dean-Paige barnstorming continued into 1945. In addition to his

Although Paige was known to move from team to team for the best paycheck, his primary team was the Kansas City Monarchs, where he played from 1935 to 1936, 1939 through 1948, 1950, and 1955. Paige being Paige, he also had stints with the 1938 Newark Eagles, the 1943 New York Black Yankees, the 1943 Memphis Red Sox, and the 1946 Philadelphia Stars during that period. His highpoint, though, was pitching the Monarchs to Negro League pennants in 1940, 1941, 1942, and 1946. The Monarchs won the Negro League World Series in 1942 and legend has it that in Game Two Paige deliberately walked batters so he could face the legendary Josh Gibson with the bases loaded. He proceeded to strike out Gibson on three pitches.

In 1946, Paige barnstormed throughout the country with future Hall of Famer Bob Feller, playing in 25 different cities. Feller's All-Stars versus Paige's All-Stars became a major drawing card. Although Feller's MLB team won the majority of the games, Paige's team certainly held their own, with Paige pitching very well against the best players in Major League Baseball. An excellent self-promoter, Paige would have his outfielders sit in the grass and watch him strike out batter after batter. For his pre-game warmup in exhibition games, Paige would throw pitches over a gum wrapper that he used for home plate, wowing fans with his exceptional command. He claimed that he would strike out the first nine batters he faced, and usually did.

In 1948, at age 42, Satchel Paige was signed by the Cleveland Indians and became one of the first Black players in the major leagues.

barnstorming teams, Paige also played in Latin America and the Caribbean. Fans in Cuba, the Dominican Republic, South America, Mexico, and Puerto Rico got to see the Paige phenomenon. Paige and several of his Pittsburgh Crawfords left the team during spring training in 1937 to play for the Dragones de Ciudad Trujillo in the Dominican Republic. This was a team owned by the notorious dictator Rafael Trujillo, who paid generously to attract the talent needed to win the championship. The team did, in fact, win the title in the last inning of the final game, but upon their return to the States, they found they were banned from the Negro National League for the rest of that season. Paige and his teammates ended up barnstorming across the country in their Trujillo All-Stars uniforms. Paige played in the Mexican League in 1938, and when he pitched the Brujos de Guayama team in the Puerto Rican League to the title in 1939, he dominated the competition, setting league records with his 19 wins and 208 strikeouts, records that still stand to this day.

The story continues on page 122.

12 1941 Play Ball Joe DiMaggio #71

IN A SET FILLED WITH THE BIGGEST NAMES of the day, the 1941 Play Ball Joe DiMaggio remains its most coveted card. That year, DiMaggio found himself in a summer-long fight for hitting supremacy with his friendly rival in Boston, Ted Williams. It wasn't the kind of competition where two players were vying for the exact same batting average or home run title. It was a battle of unworldly performances. Williams hit an uncanny .406 for the season, while DiMaggio compiled a 56-game hitting streak. The question for fans at the time was, "Which one of these feats was more extraordinary?"

The 72-card Play Ball set was the third installment during a three-year (1939–1941) run for the brand. From a set builder's view, while it is clearly smaller in terms of card count versus its two predecessors, it is the most aesthetically pleasing and desirable of the three Play Ball releases. The injection of color into the 1941 design separates it from the previous 1939 (black and white) and 1940 (sepia tone) sets. The DiMaggio in particular, which is basically a colorized version of his 1940 Play Ball card, has a beautiful look. The legendary centerfielder is shown finishing his classic swing against a trio of distinct colors, from bright yellow at the base to lime green just above it to deep purple that dominates the middle and upper half. It is all surrounded by a thin layer of rich blue that helps frame the image inside the light-colored borders.

The card, which contends with some print and border toning issues, is seen less often in high grade compared to the Williams in the same set. The DiMaggio is part of the high-number (37–72) series, but a vast difference in difficulty between the two series overall does not seem to exist based on current data. The card of "Joltin' Joe," perhaps as a result of it being the second to last in the set, is tougher to locate in top grades on its own merit. DiMaggio is not only surrounded by superstars like Jimmie Foxx, Carl Hubbell, and Pee Wee Reese, but he is joined by his two brothers, Dom and Vince, as well. It is, however, Joe's set and it was his year. It was DiMaggio, not Williams, who was named AL MVP in 1941...a model of consistency for his entire career.

This PSA Mint 9 is one of five examples graded at that tier, with only one higher in the PSA Population Report.

Joltin' Joe

Two years after Babe Ruth departed the Yankees for the Boston Braves, a 21-year-old rookie arrived in New York to take his place in the lineup alongside 33-year-old Lou Gehrig. Joe DiMaggio would continue the tradition of the great Yankees players who dominated the American League. The pinnacle of his extraordinary career came in 1941 when DiMaggio hit safely in 56 consecutive games, a record that has never been broken. "The Streak" was closely followed on the radio by mesmerized baseball fans throughout the country. Suddenly, the 26-year-old "Joltin' Joe" DiMaggio was a household name and a baseball hero.

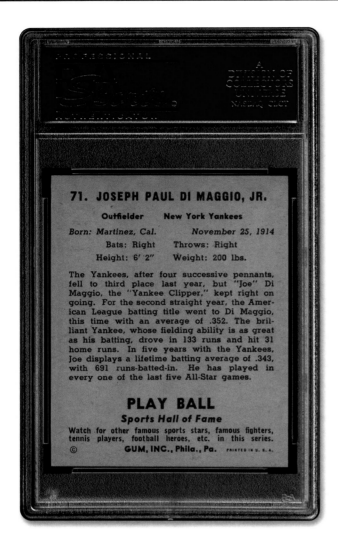

on the PCL scene when he batted .340 and broke the league record by hitting safely in 61 consecutive games in 1933. The Yankees took notice and bought DiMaggio's contract in December 1934 for $25,000 plus five players to be named later. Because DiMaggio had injured his knee in August of 1934, the Yankees were concerned he would not be able to play at a high level. The contract stipulated that DiMaggio would stay in the PCL for a season to prove what he could do. After he tore up the Pacific Coast League during the 1935 season and was named the Most Valuable Player of the league, the Yankees brought him up to the big club.

Not just an offensive threat, DiMaggio was also one of the best fielders and baserunners in the league. A natural athlete, the tall, dark, and handsome young outfielder played with such speed, grace, and confidence that he made it seem effortless.

When DiMaggio joined the Yankees for spring training in 1936, the expectations of the organization, fans, and sportswriters were very high. They expected a new superstar and Joe DiMaggio did not disappoint. On May 3, 1936, DiMaggio assumed Babe Ruth's place in the lineup, batting third, in front of the great Lou Gehrig. DiMaggio had a fabulous rookie year batting .323 and his 29 home runs set a Yankees rookie record that he held for 81 years until Aaron Judge broke it in 2017. That rookie season he also banged out 206 hits to go along with 125 RBI. He led the league with 15 triples, and was voted to the American League All-Star team, his first of 13 All-Star appearances. Not just an offensive threat, DiMaggio was also one of the best fielders and baserunners in the league. A natural athlete, the tall, dark, and handsome young outfielder played with such speed, grace, and confidence that he made it seem effortless. DiMaggio became an instant celebrity, appearing in national magazines and newspapers, but he also became a hero to Italian Americans across the country. "Joltin' Joe" DiMaggio had arrived. The Yankees went on to win the 1936 World Series, beating the New York Giants four games to two. The young DiMaggio had an excellent Series, batting .346

Giuseppe Paolo (Joseph Paul) DiMaggio was born in Martinez, California, on November 25, 1914, to Sicilian immigrant parents, Giuseppe and Rosalia. Soon after, the DiMaggio family moved to San Francisco where Giuseppe worked as a fisherman, just like he had in Sicily. Unlike his brothers, young Joe had no interest in working on the boat with his father or becoming a commercial fisherman. Along with two of his brothers, Vince and Dominic, Joe developed a love of baseball at an early age and they began playing for local amateur teams in the San Francisco area. All three brothers ended up playing in the major leagues. In 1932, when he was 17 years old, Joe DiMaggio got a chance to play for the San Francisco Seals of the Pacific Coast League. Vince DiMaggio, who was already a member of the team, made the recommendation to management that they give Joe a try, because he thought his brother had special talent as a ballplayer. With a salary of $225 a month, the teenager joined the Seals. In less than a year, Joe DiMaggio exploded with nine hits, and he returned to San Francisco to a hero's welcome. This would be the first of nine World Series championships for Joe DiMaggio.

For the next few seasons, DiMaggio and the Yankees continued to dominate the major leagues, winning three more consecutive championships. "Joltin' Joe" led the American League with 46 home runs, 151 runs, and 418 total bases in 1937 while batting .346, and he was voted to the All-Star Team for a second consecutive time. The Yankees dominated the Giants in the Series four games to one, although DiMaggio batted a vanilla .273 in the Series.

In 1938, the Yankees won yet another World Series championship, this time sweeping the Chicago Cubs. During the season, DiMaggio once again had strong offensive output, batting .324 with 32 home runs and 194 hits, but he had another vanilla Series batting .267 with only four hits. The 24-year-old DiMaggio achieved his first MVP recognition in 1939. He batted an amazing .381 for the American League batting title and slammed 30 home runs while playing flawless outfield. The Yankees won the 1939 World Series, defeating the Cincinnati Reds in a four-game sweep. That year, a new nickname was given to DiMaggio by the Yankees' game announcer. Because of his speed and graceful play in the outfield, "Joltin' Joe," would now also be known as "The Yankee Clipper." In the offseason, the young superstar married 21-year-old Dorothy Arnold, an actress he met while filming the movie *Manhattan Merry-Go-Round*. This would be the first of two marriages for DiMaggio. His second marriage would make world headlines.

DiMaggio had another banner year in 1940, capturing a second American League batting title with his .352 average while swatting 31 homers, but the pinstripes finished third in the American League. The 1940 season however, was just a prelude to what DiMaggio would accomplish.

The story continues on page 107.

WHEN YOU STOP AND THINK ABOUT all the awe-inspiring cards that Ty Cobb is connected to, it makes you wonder if any other name in the hobby comes close. From an early appearance in the majestic 1902–1911 Sporting Life Cabinets W600 set to the unique 1933 Goudey Sport Kings issue, Cobb was a fixture in many of the best releases during the pre-WWII era. One of the Cobb cards that rose to the top of that vast list is his 1911 T205 Gold Border. It's an issue that elicits adulation and frustration at the same time, so much so that some collectors choose to avoid the challenge altogether, no matter how deep their pockets might be. The set had a hard act to follow after the success of T206, but the American Tobacco Company came through with this stunning creation.

The set, which contains anywhere from around 208 cards to roughly 221 cards depending on whether we account for a number of errors and variations, was the first to include statistics on the back of each card. It is also one of the most condition-sensitive issues ever released. It is certainly much smaller than the contemporary 524-card T206 issue, but it is still one of the larger sets of the time and it provides a superior challenge for any collector seeking to assemble one in mid-to-high-grade condition. The same ornate design that enhances its beauty operates as the set's Achilles heel. The lavish borders that surround each card are exceedingly fragile. Wear is revealed with the slightest touch or chip. It has nowhere to hide. From an aesthetic standpoint, the contrast between the white paper underneath and the dark borders can accentuate the negative impact on eye appeal.

As one would imagine, Cobb is the leading name in the set, along with a horde of top stars such as Walter Johnson, Christy Mathewson, Tris Speaker, and Cy Young. The Cobb card is, by far, the most valuable component. It is also clearly tougher to find in any grade than the most difficult of the four basic Cobb cards in the T206 set. Well over 950 copies of the "Green Portrait" Cobb, the scarcest of the T206 Cobb quartet, had been graded by PSA at the time of this writing, compared to about 650 T205 Cobbs. Less than 35 of those examples graded PSA EX-MT 6 or better, which showcases just how elusive this Cobb card is in top condition. Beauty might be in the eye of the beholder, but the striking nature of the T205 design makes this Cobb a timeless piece of cardboard art.

This PSA NM-MT 8 is one of three examples graded at that tier, with none higher in the PSA Population Report.

The Georgia Peach

Continued from page 28.

When a ballplayer's career spans 24 seasons, it is almost a foregone conclusion that the last several years of that career would probably be mediocre at best. In Ty Cobb's case, those 24 seasons represent just how dominant a ballplayer he really was. Think about a 41-year-old player batting .323 and banging out 114 hits playing part-time in 393 plate appearances. As a matter of fact, Ty Cobb never hit below .300, except for his very first season when he batted .238 as an 18-year-old rookie. For 23 consecutive seasons, Cobb batted well over .300. Like Cal Ripken's 2,632 consecutive

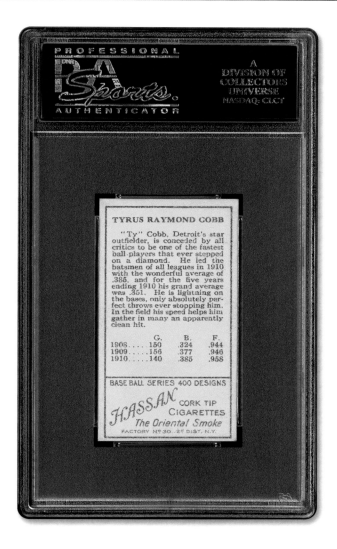

jealous of the young star, and the worse they treated him, the more defiant he became. Cobb appeared in 41 games and batted .238 during his rookie season but his manager saw something in the young player that he thought was very special. Despite his difficulties with teammates, Cobb won a starting outfield job in 1906, and batted .316 with 113 hits in 394 plate appearances. He missed part of the season due to stress that was brought about by his strained relationship with his teammates. However, 1907 proved to be the breakout season for the 20-year-old Cobb. After a move to right field under new manager Hughie Jennings, Cobb led the league with his .350 batting average, 212 hits, 119 RBI, and 53 stolen bases. By this time, the controversial young phenom was becoming the talk of the baseball world. Cobb's stellar yet aggressive play engendered strong feeling in fans and players. They either loved him or hated him. That season the Tigers won the American League pennant but lost the Series to the Chicago Cubs. Cobb did not contribute much to the Series, batting a weak .200 with four hits in 20 at-bats. He had another excellent season in 1908, batting a league-leading .324 and 188 hits, while also topping the league in doubles, triples, and RBI. The Tigers won the 1908 pennant but lost the Series to the Cubs a second consecutive time, four games to one. This time, however, Cobb had a great Series, batting .368 with seven hits and four RBI.

Cobb's stellar yet aggressive play engendered strong feeling in fans and players. They either loved him or hated him.

Cobb's reputation for being hotheaded followed him wherever he played. During the 1908 season, he was arrested for a "road rage" altercation with a motorist who offended him. Cobb's relationship with teammate and future Hall of Famer Sam "Wahoo" Crawford was also a problem. Initially, Crawford was a mentor to the young outfielder but as Cobb got better, Crawford perceived him to be a threat. Animosity developed between the two players, and they did not speak for years even though they played side by side in the Tigers outfield. Cobb had an outstanding season in 1909, leading the league again in just about every offensive category. He won the Triple Crown by leading the league with his .377 average, 107 RBI, and nine home runs. His

game streak, Nolan Ryan's strikeout record of 5,714, Ricky Henderson's stolen base record of 1,406, Joe DiMaggio's 56 game hitting streak, Pete Rose's 4,256 hits or Cy Young's 511 wins, Ty Cobb's lifetime batting average of .366 will probably never be surpassed. On page 27, we touched upon a family tragedy that shaped Cobb's personality and a few of the controversies that dogged him throughout his career. Although those controversies impacted the way he was perceived by teammates and fans, he still managed to be one of the era's most dominant forces between the lines.

After a brief stint in the minors, with the Augusta Tourists of the South Atlantic League being his last stop, Cobb came up to the big leagues in 1905. The Tourists had sold the rights to Cobb to the American League Detroit Tigers for $700. The 1905 and 1906 seasons proved difficult for the young outfielder from an acceptance standpoint. His teammates treated him badly because many of them were

Athletics, Cobb allegedly slid into third base with spikes high, cutting the arm of future Hall of Famer Frank "Home Run" Baker. Cobb claimed that it was a fair slide and the league agreed, but Philly fans disagreed and threatened him physically. That same season, he also got involved in an altercation with a Black hotel night watchman in Cleveland, which led to Cobb's arrest for attempted murder. The civil suit was settled out of court when Cobb pleaded guilty to a lesser charge.

One of the most exciting and controversial batting title contests in baseball history took place in 1910. Cobb and Larry "Nap" Lajoie of the Cleveland Naps were involved in a heated race for the title. The prize for the winner was a brand new Chalmer's automobile. Cobb sat out the last two games of the season to preserve the lead that he had at the time, but Jack O'Connor, the manager of the St. Louis Browns had other plans. The Naps were playing the Browns on the last day of the season in a doubleheader. O'Connor hated Cobb so much that he had his third baseman play way beyond the bag, almost into shallow left field. Lajoie bunted seven consecutive times, going 7-for-7 and hit a triple in his final at-bat to win the batting title. However, American League president, Ban Johnson, declared Cobb the winner by less than a percentage point on his batting average. The automobile company decided to give both players a new car. Years later, it was discovered that there was an error with Cobb's stats and that Lajoie did, indeed, have the higher batting average. The controversary about the 1910 batting championship continues to this day.

216 hits and 76 steals also topped the league that season. The Tigers won the pennant to make it back to the World Series for the third consecutive season. This time they lost to the powerful Pittsburgh Pirates and their superstar Honus Wagner in an exciting seven-game contest. For the second time in three seasons, Cobb did not have a good Series, batting a paltry .231. That same season, the surly Cobb had a few noteworthy episodes that further tarnished his reputation. In an August game against the Philadelphia

The story continues on page 91.

THROUGHOUT THE YEARS, THE MAJORITY of collector attention has gone towards the mainstream trading card issues. These are the brands that most hobbyists are familiar with. In the 1950s, the two big brands that dominated the scene in baseball were Topps and Bowman. Topps ultimately took over the market in 1956 after purchasing Bowman and eliminating their lone national competitor. During that time, however, some of the most desirable regional sets were created and the demand for them defies the general collecting rule.

One such card is the 1954 Wilson Franks Ted Williams. In fact, one could argue that this card is the most important regional issue ever produced. The Williams card, which is the key to the 20-card set, offers a combination of extreme difficulty with tremendous eye appeal due to the attractive design. The majority of the known copies were included with packages of hot dogs, which explains why so many of them are found in rough condition today. That said, a few hundred uncirculated Wilson Franks cards entered the market in the 1980s. As a result, some high-grade copies exist for an issue that had to contend with so many natural packaging pitfalls.

The white borders on the cards are extremely narrow, which leaves little room for error when it comes to centering. In the case of Williams, the entire background of the card is white, thus making the card appear "borderless." Less than perfect centering isn't as much of an eyesore with the Williams card as it is with some of the others in the set, like those of Bob Feller and Roy Campanella, where there is great contrast between the bold-colored background and light borders. This gives professional grading services a little more flexibility when it comes to evaluating the centering impact on the Williams card.

In 1954, Williams played in more than 100 games for the first time since 1951. Williams saw limited action in 1952 and 1953 as his career was interrupted by military service in Korea. Bowman did not include Williams in their 1952 or 1953 sets, nor did Topps. The following year, the image of Williams could be found in both. In fact, Topps included him twice as the first and last card in their 1954 set, but make no mistake about it, the Wilson Franks card is the year's crown jewel and the most valuable Williams card period, grade-for-grade, in the hobby today.

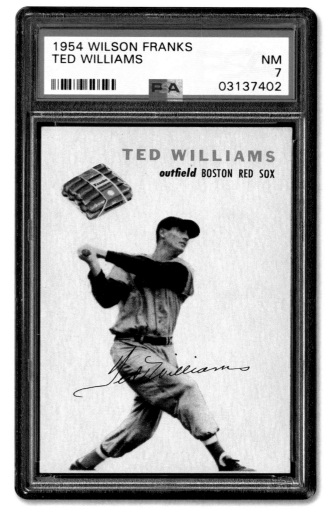

This PSA NM 7 is one of nine examples graded at that tier, with seven unqualified copies graded higher in the PSA Population Report.

The Kid

Who was the greatest hitter that ever lived? The discussion has been going on for years. The list usually gets whittled down to two lefties—Babe Ruth and Ted Williams. There are others who could be considered the best "All-Around" player based on their five-tool abilities to hit for average, power, fielding, running the bases, and throwing, but for the sheer ability to hit a baseball, "The Sultan of Swat" and "The Splendid Splinter" vie for the top of the list. The argument for Williams can certainly be made when you consider he lost five years in his prime to active service in World War II and the Korean War.

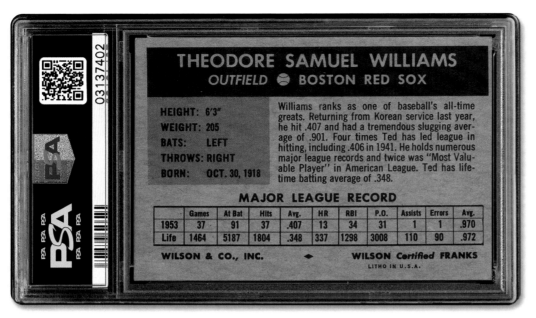

THEODORE SAMUEL WILLIAMS
OUTFIELD ● BOSTON RED SOX

HEIGHT: 6'3"
WEIGHT: 205
BATS: LEFT
THROWS: RIGHT
BORN: OCT. 30, 1918

Williams ranks as one of baseball's all-time greats. Returning from Korean service last year, he hit .407 and had a tremendous slugging average of .901. Four times Ted has led league in hitting, including .406 in 1941. He holds numerous major league records and twice was "Most Valuable Player" in American League. Ted has lifetime batting average of .348.

MAJOR LEAGUE RECORD

	Games	At Bat	Hits	Avg.	HR	RBI	P.O.	Assists	Errors	Avg.
1953	37	91	37	.407	13	34	31	1	1	.970
Life	1464	5187	1804	.348	337	1298	3008	110	90	.972

WILSON & CO., INC. ◆ WILSON Certified FRANKS
LITHO IN U.S.A.

Determined to be one of the greatest hitters in baseball, Williams constantly worked to perfect his swing.

The 1954 Wilson Franks card features Williams as a mature ballplayer, more than halfway through his storied 19-year career spent entirely with the Boston Red Sox. A decorated US Marine combat pilot, the 34-year-old Williams had recently returned from Korea to pick up where he left off, batting .407 in 1953 and .345 in 1954, but let's not get ahead of ourselves.

Theodore Samuel Williams was born on August 30, 1918. in San Diego, California, to Samuel and May Williams. Samuel was a photographer and May, of Spanish-Mexican descent, was an Evangelist working for the Salvation Army. Young Ted started playing baseball at local playgrounds and excelled, often playing with older kids. Realizing that he had a special gift to succeed at the sport, the brash young ballplayer starred as both a pitcher and hitter at Herbert Hoover High School in San Diego. In 1936, the 17-year-old prospect signed with the San Diego Padres of the Pacific Coast League, although he already had offers from both the New York Yankees and St. Louis Cardinals. Williams did not sign with one of the major-league clubs because he was still in high school, and his mother thought he was just too young to leave home. His first year with the Padres was promising. He batted a decent .271 in 42 games. After graduating from high school in 1937, Williams played a full season for the Padres, batting .291 and hitting 23 home runs, helping them to the Pacific Coast League championship. Red Sox General Manager, Eddie Collins saw

Williams play while he was in the area scouting a few other players, and the Sox immediately bought his contract. "The Kid," as he became known, was assigned to the Red Sox AA affiliate Minneapolis Millers in 1938. With the tutelage of the Millers' coach, future Hall of Famer Rogers Hornsby, paired with his own natural athletic ability, Williams became the star of the team. He won the Triple Crown, batting .366 with 43 home runs, but his stint in the minors was short-lived, as he was promoted to the big-league club the very next year.

The rookie made his major-league debut playing against Lou Gehrig, Joe DiMaggio, and the World Series champion New York Yankees on Opening Day in Yankee Stadium. Williams had one hit in four at-bats, and that was just a taste of what was to come. The media hype in Boston and across the country was torrid in 1939 when "The Kid" from San Diego joined the Red Sox, and the brash Williams rose to the occasion. Coming out of the gate, he batted .327 with 31 home runs and set a major-league rookie record knocking in 145 runs. The Boston newspapers gushed over the 20-year-old phenom. In 1940, after moving to left field, he had an excellent season, batting .344, slamming 23 home runs, knocking in a league-leading 134 runs, and he was voted to his first of 19 All-Star Games. However, the season was not without controversy. Unfortunately, the young, unfiltered Williams complained that his salary was too low, and that was reported in the newspapers. He was also quoted as saying that he hated the city of Boston and the Boston sports reporters. From that point on, Williams battled with the press, and this would continue throughout his career. Occasionally the young Williams lost his focus in the outfield because he was taking practice swings. Boston fans booed him when he missed plays and after that, Williams vowed never to tip his cap to the fans. One Boston columnist in particular, Dave Egan, carried a major grudge against Williams, criticizing his play, the fact that he never tipped his cap to the fans, and his refusal to talk to the local scribes.

Determined to be one of the greatest hitters in baseball, Williams constantly worked to perfect his swing. A perfectionist and student of the game, he talked about the mechanics of

> *His main strategy at the plate was to wait for the right pitch and swing hard.*

baseball with other hitters and pitchers he met and tried incorporating any tips he picked up. His main strategy at the plate was to wait for the right pitch and swing hard. "Teddy Ballgame" became such a threat that opposing teams created the now famous "Williams Shift" as a defensive strategy. Because of his patience at the plate, Williams often drew walks, and over the course of his career he led the American League in walks eight times.

The hard work, discipline, and practice paid off for Williams. In 1941, he delivered an offensive performance that is considered one of the best, if not the overall best, of all time.

Continued on page 112.

STATISTICALLY, ROBERTO CLEMENTE STACKS UP
with the best players of his generation. The Pittsburgh Pirates right fielder could do it all, from his hitting prowess to his cannon-like arm. Clemente would earn four NL batting titles and 12 Gold Gloves in his career, along with two championships in 1960 and 1971. From a skillset standpoint, Clemente checked all the boxes. Clemente's appeal, however, goes far beyond base hits and outfield assists. He was a cultural icon and a hero to people from all walks of life. Clemente's stellar on-field performance was overshadowed by the kind of man he was. Simply put, statues of athletes are erected because of individuals like Clemente.

The 1955 Topps set is home to several key cards; from the likes of Jackie Robinson, who helped lead the Brooklyn Dodgers to a championship that year; to a second-year issue of Hank Aaron; to a trio of great rookie cards in Harmon Killebrew, Sandy Koufax, and of course, Clemente. The Clemente card, in particular, which is part of the high-number series (161–210), has always been considered one of the tougher cards to obtain in high grade from the 206-piece set. You can certainly see the difference in difficulty between the three key rookie cards by perusing their existing populations by grade. Finding well-centered copies is one of the bigger challenges for collectors, but the Clemente card also appears to exist in significantly fewer numbers overall compared to the Koufax rookie. At the time of this writing, over 50 percent more Koufax cards were submitted to PSA for grading versus those featuring the Pittsburgh immortal.

The story of Clemente is so captivating yet so tragic it's hard to believe. As the first Latin American player inducted into the Hall of Fame in 1973, Clemente inspired countless international players to pursue their dreams. Over the last few decades, the player representation in MLB from Latin American countries has increased dramatically. Clemente was a pioneer in that regard, but he cared most about helping others

in need. When Clemente perished during a mission to earthquake victims in Nicaragua, the game lost a superstar and the world lost a humanitarian. The stature of Clemente, as a player and a person, combined with the undeniable popularity and aesthetic beauty of the 1955 Topps issue, creates an extraordinary level of demand for this special card.

The Great One

One of those rare five-tool players, Roberto Clemente certainly hit for average and hit with power, although his power numbers would most likely have been considerably higher had he not played in the expansive Forbes Field. Defensively, he was amazing, winning twelve Gold Gloves. His throwing arm was the best in baseball and his speed, while not blazing, was far more than adequate. For some reason, during the early part of his career, Clemente did not get the accolades that he probably deserved. In any event, by the time his career had tragically ended, Clemente was considered one of the greatest players in National League history.

A multi-sports talent, Clemente decided to focus on baseball and signed a contract with the Cangrejeros De Santurce team of the Puerto Rican League in 1952 at the age of 18.

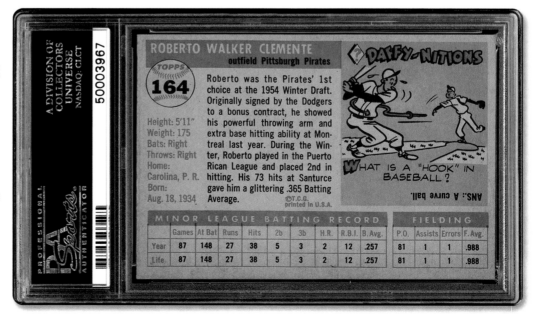

From a skillset standpoint, Clemente checked all the boxes. Clemente's appeal, however, goes far beyond base hits and outfield assists.

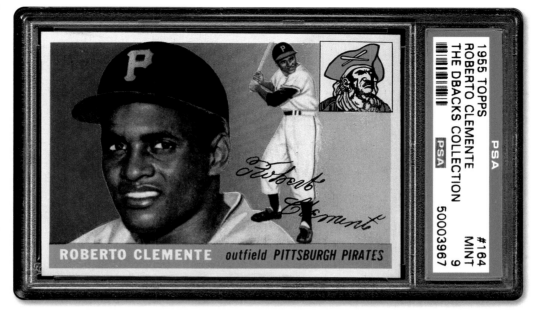

This PSA Mint 9 is one of 11 examples graded at that tier, with only one higher in the PSA Population Report.

Although he sat on the bench his first year, Clemente became a starting outfielder in his sophomore season, batting a respectable .288. In February 1954, Clemente signed a contract with the Brooklyn Dodgers, who sent him to their minor-league affiliate, the Montreal Royals. The Dodgers tried to "hide" Clemente, playing him sparingly, because they did not want to lose him in the Rule 5 draft. That plan didn't work. In November of 1954, Branch Rickey's Pittsburgh Pirates drafted Clemente and that was the beginning of an 18-year marriage between the Pirates and their charismatic superstar. Before reporting to Pittsburgh, Clemente played the winter season with Santurce, helping them to the Caribbean Series title. On April 17, 1955, 20-year-old Clemente made his major-league debut for the Pirates. That year he batted .255 with 121 hits. Not bad, but not historic. However, his defensive skills and base-running ability set him apart from the other young players in the league. It all began to take shape in 1956, when Clemente batted .311, with 169 hits and seven home runs. During the offseasons, Clemente stayed sharp by playing in the Puerto Rican League. This endeared him to his fans in Puerto Rico because he never forgot his roots. Heading into the 1957 season, Clemente experienced some lingering back issues due to a car accident in 1954. As a result, he slumped to a .253 average and played in only 111 games. The Pirates finished in seventh place, just ahead of the lowly Cubs. In 1958, Clemente bounced back with a .289 average and helped the Pirates climb to second place because of his defense and improved batting. He worked through some nagging injuries in 1959 to bat .296, but the new decade would be very good for Clemente.

In 1960, Clemente made his first All-Star team, batted .314 with 179 hits and 94 RBI, and slammed 16 homers. More importantly, the Pirates won the National League pennant for the first time since 1927 and defeated the New York Yankees in the World Series with the historic Bill Mazeroski walk-off home run in Game Seven. Clemente's defensive prowess was becoming the talk of the league. He played the outfield with reckless abandon, often sacrificing his body. In 1961, Roberto Clemente the superstar won the National League batting title with his .351 average and won his first of twelve Gold Gloves. Through all of this, Clemente continued to play winter ball in Puerto Rico because he felt that it was an obligation to his fellow countrymen.

Overall, Roberto Clemente emerged during the early 1960s to be one of the two or three greatest players in the National League. Despite the injuries, the young star just kept getting better and better. From 1963 through the end of the decade, Clemente was as good as anyone. From 1964 through 1967, he put together phenomenal numbers. He batted .339 in 1964 for his second batting title and led the league with 211 hits. On a personal note, he married Vera Christina Zabala in the offseason, and started managing in the Puerto Rican League. He won the batting crown a third time in 1965 with his .329 average. Though he only batted .317 in 1966, he registered his 2,000th career hit and was named the NL Most Valuable Player. In 1967, he led the league with

Roberto Clemente

209 hits and capped off that great run with a .357 batting average to win his fourth batting title.

When you look at his overall body of work during the 1960s, Clemente's stats were remarkable. The 1966 National League MVP won four NL batting titles, was an All-Star every year except 1968, and won a Gold Glove every year. In the early 1970s, Clemente and the Pirates had another nice run. The team moved from Forbes Field to Three Rivers Stadium in late June of 1970. That season, Clemente batted .352, followed by a .341 batting average in 1971. The Pirates won the National League East division in 1970 but were eliminated by the Cincinnati Reds. In 1971, the Pirates again won the NL East and defeated the overwhelmingly favored Baltimore Orioles in seven games in the World Series. Clemente had a fabulous Series, batting .414 and winning the Series MVP Award. In 1972, Clemente's average dipped to .312, but he won his 12th straight Gold Glove, and was again an All-Star. On September 30, 1972, Clemente hit another milestone with his 3,000th hit. Sadly, it would be his last.

Clemente was known for his charitable work during the offseason to help the less fortunate. On December 23, 1972, Managua, Nicaragua, suffered a devasting earthquake. Clemente raised funds to send medicine, food, and relief packages to the survivors. He and four others decided to ride in the cargo plane with the supplies to supervise their distribution. Shortly after takeoff, on December 31, 1972, the plane experienced engine problems and turned around to return to San Juan airport. Tragically the plane crashed

into the Atlantic Ocean, just one mile from the coast. Clemente's body was never recovered.

He was voted into the Hall of Fame the very next year with a special election, becoming the first player from Latin America to be inducted. Major League Baseball established the Roberto Clemente Award, given annually to a player for accomplishments on and off the field. In 1973, President Richard Nixon honored him with the Congressional Gold Medal. His widow Vera fulfilled his dream with the

Roberto Clemente Sports Complex for young people in Puerto Rico, and today the Roberto Clemente Foundation honors his legacy of helping those less fortunate. One of the greatest to ever play the game, with 3,000 career hits, 15 All-Star appearances, 240 home runs, 12 Gold Gloves, a NL MVP Award, a World Series MVP trophy, four batting titles, and a host of other offensive and defensive titles, Roberto Clemente, "Arriba," "The Great One," leaves a legacy of baseball excellence and humanitarianism.

THERE ARE CERTAIN CARDS, ALBEIT A LIMITED
number of them, that possess a symbolic value...one that
extends far beyond the featured player or the set in which it
resides. The 1954 Topps Hank Aaron is one of those cards.
The card itself is the centerpiece of one of the most desirable
issues in hobby history, and the man pictured is one of the
finest players to ever step between the white lines. That
said, the image of the card offers something more. When the
hobby became a nationwide phenomenon in the 1980s, this
was one of the cards that acted as a virtual logo for an entire
industry. That sentiment remains true today.

First, let's talk about the set and the card. The 1954
Topps set, a 250-card issue that begins and ends with
Ted Williams, is one of the most eye-catching releases of
the decade. Booming with color, this set has long been a
collector favorite. In addition to its outstanding aesthetics,
the set offers three major rookie cards in Ernie Banks, Al
Kaline, and of course, Aaron's only mainstream rookie.
"Hammerin' Hank" was included in some early regional
issues such as Spic and Span and Johnston Cookies, but
the Topps card is the unquestioned Aaron card to own.
Condition obstacles include poor centering, print defects
in the orange background, and chipping along the green
reverse.

Second, let's talk about the man. Much like pioneer Jackie
Robinson, Aaron's legacy is built on more than the success
he had on the field, it was just as much about the way he
did it. No one word is broad enough to describe what Aaron
meant to the game of baseball or embody his essence, but
"class" is certainly one of them. Year after year, Aaron was a
model of consistency at the plate and a role model for young
people to emulate. As he approached the career home run
record, one of the most hallowed records in sports, Aaron
never wavered or let his success alter his character. He was
courageous without being cocky, a lesson some modern
athletes could learn. Aaron let his bat do the talking for him,
and his 1954 Topps rookie card, like the man himself, has an
ability to communicate so much without saying a word.

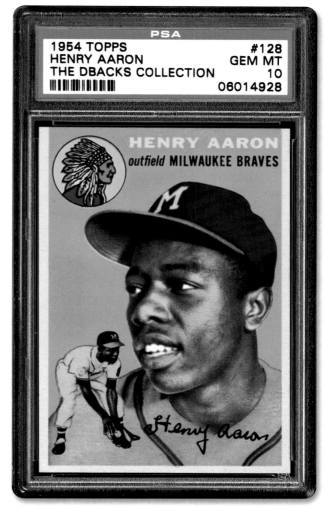

This PSA Gem Mint 10 is one of two examples to
reach PSA's highest grading tier.

Hammerin' Hank

Considered by many to be the greatest home-run hitter of
all time, Henry "Hank" Aaron's 23-year run in the majors
may never be duplicated. The quiet, unassuming Aaron
was skilled defensively, a whiz on the basepaths, and broke
"unbreakable" offensive records. On the way, "Hammerin'
Hank" overcame prejudice to become a beloved baseball
hero.

Born and raised in Alabama, Hank Aaron practiced baseball
as a youngster by hitting rocks and bottle caps with a sawn-
off broom stick. An outstanding high school athlete, Aaron
tried out for the Brooklyn Dodgers when he was 15 years

old, but because he held the bat with an unorthodox cross-handed grip they were not interested. Later in his high-school career, Aaron played with the semi-pro Mobile Black Bears for $3 per game. In 1951, Negro American League scout, Bunny Downs, signed the young prospect to the Indianapolis Clowns for $200 a month. Although only with the Clowns for three months, Aaron batted .366 in 26 games helping them to the 1952 Negro League Series championship.

Because of his Negro Leagues success, Aaron received contract offers from both the New York Giants and Boston Braves in 1952. Braves Scout, Dewey Griggs offered Aaron more money and he signed immediately. During his first minor-league stop in Wisconsin with the Eau Claire Bears, coaches worked with Aaron to eliminate the cross-handed grip, and the results paid off immediately. Aaron batted .336, was voted to the league All-Star team, and named Rookie of the Year, but the 18-year-old slugger had to deal with being away from home and being on the receiving end of racism. Fans taunted him, and he had to stay in separate hotels on the road. In 1953, Aaron moved up to the Class A Jacksonville Braves. Despite the racial taunts, Aaron won over fans in the Deep South with his sparkling performance. He was voted MVP with his .362 average, 22 home runs, 208 hits, and 125 RBI, while leading the Braves to the league championship. In the minors, Aaron played shortstop and second base, but in 1953 he was converted to the outfield while playing ball in Puerto Rico.

By the mid-1960s, Hank Aaron had become a home run machine, perennial All-Star, and an excellent fielder with three Gold Gloves.

Heading into the 1954 season, Aaron was invited to the major-league camp. Because of his excellent performance he earned a spot on the Milwaukee Braves roster. Although he was limited to 122 games due to a fractured ankle, Aaron had a successful rookie season, batting .280 with 13 home runs and 131 hits. In 1955, he played in his first of 25 consecutive All-Star games. The 21-year-old outfielder batted .314, slammed 27 home runs, and drove in 106 runs, to help the Braves to a second-place finish behind the Brooklyn Dodgers. "Hammerin' Hank" took it to another level in 1956. He won the National League batting title with his .328 average, blasted 26 home runs, topped the NL with 200 hits and 34 doubles, and was named *The Sporting News* NL Player of the Year. Again, the Braves finished in second place behind the Brooklyn Dodgers. After manager Charlie Grimm was replaced by Fred Haney, everything came together for the Braves in 1957. Aaron walloped 44 home runs to top the league while batting .322. He led the league with 118 runs and 132 RBI and was voted NL MVP. The Braves won the pennant to face and defeat the New York Yankees in seven games. Aaron had a great Series, batting .393 with eleven hits and three home runs, leading the way to the Braves' first and only world championship in Milwaukee.

In 1958, Aaron picked up where he left off, batting .326 with 30 home runs and winning his first Gold Glove. The Braves again won the NL pennant but lost the Series in seven games to the Yankees. The next few seasons were phenomenal for Aaron. In 1959, he slammed 39 home runs, topped the league with 223 hits, and won his second NL batting title with his .355 average. Again, the Braves were in pennant contention but wound up in second place. The highlight of that season for Aaron was hitting three home runs in a June game against the San Francisco Giants. Heading into the 1960s, Aaron continued his homerun onslaught while also hitting for average and playing solid defense. In 1960, Aaron hit his 200th home run. In 1963, he joined the 30–30 club, stealing 31 bases and hitting a league-leading 44 home runs to go along with a .319 batting average. His 121 runs and 130 RBI also topped the NL. By the mid-1960s, Hank Aaron had become a home run machine, perennial All-Star, and an excellent fielder with three Gold Gloves. Unfortunately, fan support in Milwaukee had dwindled. Following the 1965 season, the team pulled up stakes and moved to Atlanta.

Aaron continued to hit home runs. In 1966, the 32-year-old slugger hit his 400th home run and led the league with 44 bombs and 127 RBI. In 1968, the Braves were in the middle of the pack in the National League, but Aaron maintained his record pace, smashing his 500th homer in July. In 1969, he passed Mickey Mantle by hitting his 537th home run. Now there were only two players left to surpass, Willie Mays and Babe Ruth. The Braves won the 1969 NL West but lost the league championship to the "Miracle" Mets. That season, Aaron batted .300 with 44 home runs, 164 hits, and 97 RBI. Over the next several years, the Braves were mediocre at best, but by this time all eyes were on Aaron and his quest for the home run crown. In May 1970, the 36-year-old Aaron became the first MLB player to notch 3,000 hits and 500 home runs. Entering the 1971 season, Aaron wasted no time, crushing his 600th home run on April 27, and in August he hit his 40th home run to

set the NL record for most 40-home-run seasons, with seven. He wound up slamming 47 homers, a career high.

The 1972 season was all about Hank Aaron and his quest to break the home-run record. On August 6, he blasted number 661, surpassing Willie Mays. Would Aaron surpass Ruth's "unbeatable" record of 714 homeruns? As 1973 approached, Aaron received thousands of letters every week from fans all over the country. Most of America was cheering for him, but there were some who wanted him to fail. He received hate mail with racist taunts, some even threatened his life. He managed to stay above the fray and the 1973 season proved to be historic for Aaron, who smashed 40 home runs at the age of 39. More importantly, he slammed home run number 713 on September 29. He was just one home run shy of the great Ruth's record, but

Aaron's fans would have to wait. The next home run would not come until the 1974 season.

The media circus and the pressure affected Aaron, but the trickle-down effect on his teammates and especially on opposing pitchers was glaring. What pitcher wanted to be remembered as the guy who gave up the tying or record-breaking home run? The baseball world would not wait very long to find out. On April 4, 1974, in the first game of the season, Aaron crushed number 714 off Jack Billingham of the Cincinnati Reds to tie Ruth. Four days later, on April 8, the Braves were playing the Los Angeles Dodgers in Atlanta before an electric crowd of 53,775, the largest to ever attend a Braves game. The entire country was tuned into the game on national television. With Al Downing of the Dodgers on the mound in the fourth inning, Aaron made history, blasting number 715, breaking the "unbreakable" record of the legendary Ruth. The iconic image of Aaron circling the bases and two college students jumping out of the stands and running down the third base line will always be remembered. As announcer Vin Scully accurately portrayed it: "What a marvelous moment for baseball; what a marvelous moment for Atlanta and the state of Georgia. What a marvelous moment for the country and the world. A Black man is getting a standing ovation in the Deep South for breaking a record of an all-time baseball idol. And it is a great moment for all of us, and particularly for Henry Aaron."

Aaron made history, blasting number 715, breaking the "unbreakable" record of the legendary Ruth.

By the time the 1974 season ended, Aaron had hit his 733rd home run. With the record now in the bank, the only question was what Aaron's final career home run number would be. Aaron requested a trade to the American League so he could extend his career as a designated hitter. He ended up back in Milwaukee, as the Brewers new designated hitter. By that time, the 41-year-old Aaron was not hitting for average anymore, and his power numbers dropped to 12 home runs in 1975 and 10 in 1976. However, Aaron had another milestone to reach. In 1975, he broke the all-time RBI record of 2,213 held by Ruth. Aaron hit the 755th and final home run of his career in July 1976 and retired at the end of the season at age 42.

He returned to Atlanta to work in the Braves front office and owned several auto dealerships and restaurants in the Georgia area. The 25-time All-Star was elected to the Hall of Fame in 1982 with 97.8% of the vote. From ballparks in his name to being awarded the Medal of Freedom by President George W. Bush, the list of his honors and accolades goes on and on. In 2007, Barry Bonds broke Aaron's home run record, but the home run chase was rife with controversy because of performance enhancement drug allegations leveled against Bonds. Aaron took the high road though, and graciously congratulated Bonds on his achievement. "Hammerin' Hank" is usually listed in the top four or five greatest players in the history of the game. On January 22, 2021, Hank Aaron passed away of natural causes at the age of 86, leaving a legacy of character, determination, and excellence.

TRAVELING THROUGH SPORTS HISTORY WILL often reveal how much the game, and the players, have changed over the years. There are times when you might wonder how an athlete of the past would stack up against the athletes of today. Currently, there is no doubt that the average player is bigger, stronger, and faster than most who played decades ago. In the case of Bronko Nagurski, however, it would be interesting to see how the modern players would deal with him rather than the other way around. Some guys look like they could bend iron with their hands or run through a brick wall, and Nagurski is one of them. As Steve Owen of the New York Giants once said of him, "The only way to stop Nagurski is to shoot him before he leaves the dressing room." He looks like a football player. His name sounds like a football player. His 1935 National Chicle card is the beneficiary of all of it.

National Chicle, which is also responsible for the 1934–1936 Diamond Stars series in baseball, decided to jump into the football card market, one that went relatively unserved until the late-1940s when Bowman and Leaf entered the fold. Topps would soon join those two manufacturers in the 1950s, but the 1930s were another story. For their lone gridiron effort, the Cambridge, Massachusetts, company utilized a design that was virtually identical to their baseball cards, which had an Art Deco appearance. The 36-card set contains some iconic names from the college and professional ranks, such as Knute Rockne (#9), and it features a tough high-number series (25–36), which are believed to have been produced in far fewer numbers as national interest in the release declined after the first run (1–24).

The Nagurski card lies in that tougher, high-number series. In addition, the card is often found with poor centering, making high-grade or eye-appealing copies challenging to locate. Collectors might also notice some variance in border shade due to toning of the paper, which is common to National Chicle football and baseball cards. Each sport tends to identify its Holy Grail. While there are some high profile, modern manufactured rarities that have sold well into seven figures in recent times, the Nagurski card is still viewed as the most coveted vintage prize in football card collecting. The man was one of the first to enter the hallowed halls of Canton as a charter member in 1963, and the card is the undisputed key to the first mainstream football set to capture the attention of collectors. For those who focus on cardboard giants, it's Bronko or bust in the land of the pigskin.

Bronko

One of the most devastating two-way players in the history of National League Football, Bronislau "Bronko" Nagurski was a dominant force as a professional football player and a professional wrestler. A product of Rainy River, Ontario, Canada, Nagurski and his family moved across the border to International Falls, Minnesota, when he was five years old.

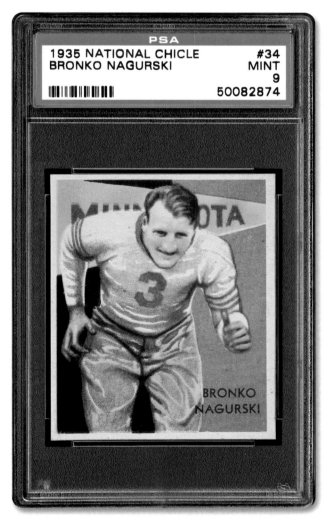

This card is the sole example to reach the PSA Mint 9 grading tier with none higher in the PSA Population Report.

He grew up working on the family farm and helping in his father's general store. The hard farm work soon transformed the young Nagurski into a solid 6-foot-2, 235-pound strongman.

The head football coach at the University of Minnesota, Clarence "Doc" Spears, discovered Nagurski on a scouting trip and was so impressed with his size, strength, and speed that he immediately signed him to play for the Golden Gophers. Nagurski developed into an outstanding running back and a solid defensive tackle, becoming the best two-way collegiate player in the country. He starred at Minnesota from 1927 through 1929 and actually played four different positions at one time or another: fullback, tackle, end, and guard. Playing in the Big Ten Conference, Minnesota posted an 18–4 record over the course of Nagurski's career and won the Conference Title in 1927. Nagurski was a 1929 consensus All-American at tackle and All-American at fullback that same year.

Nagurski caught the eye of George Halas, the owner and head coach of the National Football League's Chicago Bears, who signed him to a contract in 1930 for approximately $5,000. For a period of seven seasons, Nagurski punished opponents with his brutal offensive and defensive play. A devastating multi-talented player offensively, Nagurski was a straight-ahead running back who ran over and through the defense on a regular basis. Nagurski could also throw the football with the best of them. He perfected the jump pass where he would fake a run straight into the line of scrimmage, then jump up and throw a quick pass to a receiver. This was a key component in the 1932 Bears' title win.

In 1933, Nagurski passed for two touchdowns, including the game-winning score in the NFL's first official championship game, a 23–21 victory over the New York Giants. That year, to supplement his income in the offseason, Nagurski turned his sights on professional wrestling, and he quickly became a box office star. Because of a salary dispute with the Bears in 1937, coupled with the fact that Halas wanted him to give up wrestling, Nagurski retired from football. He continued with his wrestling career and went on to win the "real" professional heavyweight championship, the National Wrestling Association (NWA) title, in 1939 by defeating the great Lou Thesz. Nagurski bested Ray Steele in 1941 for his second NWA title.

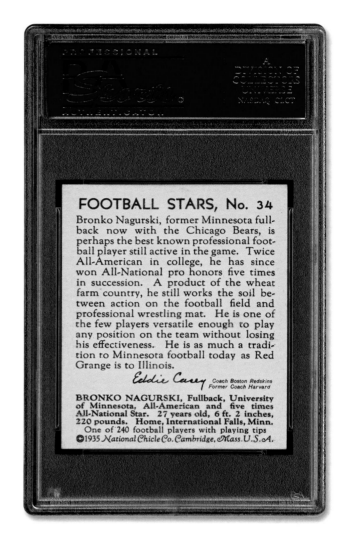

With the outbreak of World War II, Halas was shorthanded and convinced the 35-year-old Nagurski to come back to the Bears in 1943. Nagurski agreed to play tackle but went back to the fullback position late in the season before retiring from football for the second time. That year he led the Bears to the 1943 title vs. the Washington Redskins, scoring a touchdown in his final NFL game. Over his career, Nagurski led the Bears to several division titles and three NFL championships, rushing for over 2,700 yards and completing 32 passes, which does not tell the story of how great he really was.

After his playing career ended, he was the backfield coach for the UCLA Bruins for the 1944 season. Nagurski continued his wrestling career until 1960 and finally called it quits. He operated a thriving service station in his hometown until 1978 when he retired because of the nagging injuries that

he had suffered as an athlete. Nagurski lived a relatively quiet life near the Canadian border and enjoyed following his son's football career. Bronko Nagurski Jr. was an All-Star offensive tackle for the Hamilton Tiger-Cats in the Canadian Football League from 1959 through the mid-1960s.

The honors and accolades Nagurski received in recognition of his professional football career are impressive. In 1963, he was elected as a charter member of the National Professional Football Hall of Fame in Canton, Ohio. The two-time NFL champ was a first-team All-Pro on four different occasions, and the 1932 NFL rushing touchdowns leader. Nagurski was voted to the NFL 75th Anniversary All-Time Team, the NFL 1930s All-Decade Team, and his number "3" jersey was retired by the Bears. He also had the honor of participating in the coin toss at Superbowl XVIII in 1984.

His collegiate honors include induction to the inaugural class of the College Football Hall of Fame in 1951, and his number "72" jersey was retired by the Gophers in 1979. The Bronko Nagurski Trophy, which is awarded annually to the Top Defensive Player in college football, was established in 1993. He was named to the *Sports Illustrated* NCAA Football All-Century Team at tackle, and he is ranked 14th on

ESPN's list of the 150 Greatest Players in College Football's 150-Year History. In addition, Nagurski was inducted to the National Wrestling Hall of Fame in 2009. The Bronko Nagurski Museum in his hometown of International Falls, celebrates the life, career, and legacy of this incredibly versatile, powerful athlete. On January 7, 1990, Bronko Nagurski passed away from cardiac arrest at age 81.

WHEN IT COMES TO THE FOUR MAJOR SPORTS

in the hobby and the collectors who pursue trading cards, there is no greater frustration than the one found in vintage basketball. There is simply not much to choose from. Sets were sparse from the 1940s through the 1960s, when so many iconic players were active. On the other hand, the lack of options makes the sets that were released all the more important. Collectors often refer to a "Big Three" in vintage basketball, which includes the 1957 Topps and 1961 Fleer sets. You could argue a fourth set, 1969 Topps, should be included in that group as well, but it all started with 1948 Bowman and the key to that issue is the George Mikan rookie.

Mikan was the sport's first major star, hence his nickname "Mr. Basketball." He was also the game's first dominant big man. While possessing an intimidating size for the time at 6-foot-10, 245 pounds, Mikan's look and genial personality away from the court was more "Clark Kent" than Superman. On the court, however, Mikan was an unstoppable force. Unlike the red-caped superhero, Mikan just kept the glasses on while doing his thing. The card showcases the center driving towards the basket and it suggests that defenders better get out of the way. Before they became a staple in Los Angeles, Mikan led the Minneapolis Lakers to five championships in six years, which brought the word "Dynasty" into pro basketball for the first time.

The 1948 Bowman set was comprised of 72 cards, and it does feature some other noteworthy rookie cards, like those of Hall of Famers Red Holzman, Buddy Jeannette, Jim Pollard, and Arnie Risen to name a few, but no card comes close to the iconic nature of the Mikan. The card, which appears in the tougher high-number (37–72) series, has to contend with centering issues and varying degrees of toning along the edges. Keep in mind that some of these cards exhibit a slightly rougher cut than others, but it is generally not considered a detractor from a grading perspective. There is no doubt that the sport and basketball card collecting itself have both changed dramatically over the years, but there is always a beginning and a history. From a hobby perspective, the Mikan rookie is a pillar and a symbol of what was to come from a sport that eventually became a global sensation.

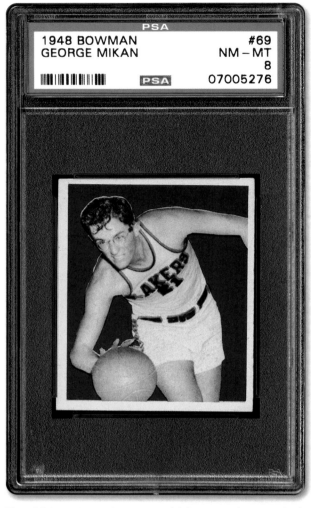

This PSA NM-MT 8 is one of 23 examples graded at that tier, with only five unqualified copies graded higher in the PSA Population Report.

Mr. Basketball

One of the original trailblazers of the NBA, George "Mr. Basketball" Mikan certainly left his mark on the sport. Considered the first real superstar in professional basketball, the dominant center preceded the likes of Bill Russell, Bob Cousy, and Wilt Chamberlain. As a matter of fact, because of the 6-foot-10, 245-pound Mikan's dominance, the league changed some rules to level the playing field for opposing players.

Born in Joliet, Illinois, in 1924, Mikan had grown to a height of 6-foot-10 and weighed well over 200 pounds by the time he was a senior in high school, but he was

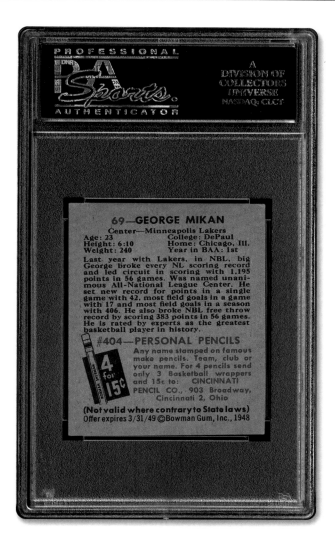

With the DePaul Blue Demons from 1942 through 1946, Mikan was a three-time All-American and was named the 1944 and 1945 Helms NCAA College Player of the Year, averaging 23 points per game. In 1945, DePaul won the National Invitational Tournament (NIT) which was as prestigious as the NCAA tourney is today. Mikan averaged a tidy 40 points per game and was voted the tourney MVP. The most sought-after player in the country after his collegiate career ended, Mikan signed with the Chicago American Gears of the National Basketball League (NBL). As a rookie during the 1946–1947 season, Mikan averaged just under 17 points per game, led the Gears to the 1947 league championship, and was voted the Most Valuable Player. The following season, the Gears' owner started a rival league, the Professional Basketball League of America. He failed miserably, and the Gears closed shop a few weeks into the season. Mikan ended up in a lottery and wound up back in the NBL with a brand-new franchise, the Minneapolis Lakers.

His initial season with the Lakers (1947–1948) proved to be the year that Mikan established himself as the best player on the planet, averaging 28 points per game, again winning the MVP Award, and leading the Lakers to the 1948 NBL championship. The Lakers moved to the Basketball Association of America (BAA) the next year and Mikan continued to dominate, leading the Lakers to the 1949 BAA championship. That August, the BAA merged with the NBL to form the National Basketball Association (NBA), which initially featured 17 teams.

awkward, uncoordinated, and wore thick eyeglasses. Mikan's fortunes changed at DePaul University when he met the 28-year-old basketball coach, Ray Meyer. Under Meyer's tutelage, Mikan developed his skills and coordination by jumping rope, dancing, and learning the fundamentals of the game. He also developed a devastating left-handed hook shot opposing players could not defend. Eventually, he also developed a right-handed hook shot which made him almost unstoppable. Mikan beefed up to 245 pounds with his training program which made it nearly impossible to move him from underneath the basket. Defensively, Mikan developed the art of goaltending which was legal at the time. He would swat a ball away as it was dropping into the basket, making it extremely difficult for the opposing team to score. Because of Mikan, goaltending was later declared illegal.

Again, Mikan was the most dominant player by far, leading the league with his 27-points-per-game average and taking the Lakers to the first-ever NBA championship vs. the Syracuse Nationals in 1950. He continued to dominate the league the next season, even though teams developed new strategies to defend against him. With no shot clock in place at the time, opposing teams began to "stall" the ball by not shooting. The strategy was to keep the game close until the last minute or two. As a matter of fact, in a November 1950 game against the Fort Wayne Pistons, the final score was 19–18. Fans did not like it nor did NBA officials, but it was not until four years later that the shot clock was implemented.

Known as "the Mikan Rule," the NBA expanded the inside perimeter around the basket from six feet to twelve feet at

George Mikan

the beginning of the 1951–1952 season, because of Mikan's dominance. However, Mikan still put up impressive numbers, averaging in the mid-20s and grabbing about 14 rebounds per game. On January 20, 1952, he scored an amazing 61 points in a game vs. the Rochester Royals, his career best. Mikan continued to be one of the dominant forces in the game, leading the Lakers to three consecutive NBA championships—1952, 1953, and 1954. He retired at the end of the 1954 season as the NBA All-Time scoring leader. Between Chicago and Minneapolis, Mikan played on seven championship teams over his stellar career.

After a stint as GM of the Lakers, Mikan came back for one last hurrah for the 1955–1956 season. In 37 games, Mikan averaged almost 11 points per game, but his skills had diminished, and he retired for good at the end of the season. He finished with a 23.1 lifetime average along with an average of 13.4 rebounds per game after they started keeping that statistic. Mikan maintained a national presence after his playing days were over. He ran for Congress in 1956 for the state of Minnesota's third district but lost the closely contested race. He was head coach of the Lakers for part of the 1957–1958 season, but they finished dead last with a 19–53 record. Mikan had studied law in the offseasons, and after his unsuccessful coaching experience he decided to go into practice. The Lakers had struggled at the gate without Mikan's star power and moved to Los Angeles before the 1960–1961 season.

In 1967, Mikan became the first commissioner of the American Basketball Association (ABA), a new rival league that was formed to compete against the NBA. He was instrumental in instituting the three-point line to make the game more exciting for the fans. Mikan resigned in 1969 and returned to his law practice. The ABA disbanded in 1976, but several of the teams, a new host of stars, and the three-point shot were all incorporated into the NBA. Mikan later led a group focused on bringing pro basketball back to Minnesota. Because of their efforts, a new NBA franchise, the Minnesota Timberwolves, arrived in 1989.

Mikan developed diabetes and because of escalating medical costs, he lobbied the NBA to increase pension funding for

older players. Mikan's condition worsened, and he died from complications on June 1, 2005 at age 80.

George Mikan's career will go down as one of the greatest of all time. He was inducted as a charter member the Naismith Memorial Basketball Hall of Fame in 1959, named the greatest player in the first half of the twentieth century by the Associated Press in 1951, and voted one of the Top 50 Players in NBA History in 1996. A seven-time champion, Mikan was a four-time All-Star, six-time All-NBA First Team, three-time NBA scoring champ, MVP, and the list of his achievements goes on and on. In 2001, "Mr. Basketball" was honored with a nine-foot bronze statue depicting his famous hook shot which stands at the entrance of the Target Center, the Minnesota Timberwolves arena.

OVER THE PAST FEW YEARS, there are a few names from the vintage sports card world that have ascended to new heights as greater collector appreciation has emerged for their accomplishments. Two that come to mind are Jackie Robinson, for somewhat obvious reasons, and this man...Willie Mays. Still regarded by many as the greatest five-tool player in the history of the sport, Mays has started to be viewed in the light he deserved for so many years. No position player, past or present, could hit, hit with power, run, field, and throw at his level over the course of a 20-plus-year career.

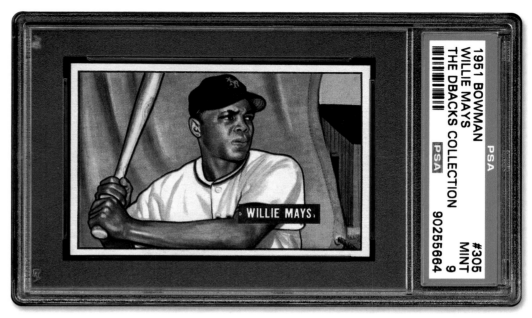

This PSA Mint 9 is one of eight examples graded at that tier, with none higher in the PSA Population Report.

This classic card, which is Mays' only recognized rookie, has long been desirable, but in recent times it has gradually started closing the gap on the 1951 Bowman set's fellow anchor—the Mickey Mantle rookie—when it comes to market value. In addition to both the Mays and Mantle rookie issues, which both reside in the tougher high-number series (253-324), an inaugural card of Whitey Ford completes the trio of keys to this very popular set. The colorful artwork has long made this 324-card Bowman release a collector favorite. In terms of difficulty, the card itself is often found with below-average centering. Since the card images were framed with relatively thin white borders, subpar centering can hinder the eye appeal in a meaningful way.

Although Mays is depicted with an intense stare as he wields his favorite weapon, the joy this icon brought to the game was evident in a smile that could light up an entire stadium. Even his name, much like Mantle's, seems like a product of Hollywood casting. From virtually every angle, Mays appears to be the prototype for the perfect baseball player. His rookie card has similar qualities. It bridges the gap between the visual appeal of issues like the Goudeys from the pre-war era and the photography-based card designs that would soon dominate the product scene later in the 1950s. From the perspective of historical importance, the Mays rookie is a must for the collector of baseball gods.

Say Hey Kid

Baseball historians often talk about "The Best." Who was the best all-around hitter of all time? Who was the best power hitter of all time? Who was the best outfielder? Shortstop? You get it. When the discussion of the *BEST* all-around player of all time comes up, the name Willie Mays is at the forefront.

> *No position player, past or present, could hit, hit with power, run, field, and throw at his [Mays] level over the course of a 20-plus-year career.*

Mays was a five-tool player who could hit for average, hit for power, field, run, and throw. A 24-time All-Star, Mays won 12 Gold Gloves, hit 660 home runs, had a .301 lifetime batting average, led the National League in in stolen bases four times, and had a rocket for an arm.

Willie Howard Mays was born on May 6, 1931, in Westfield, Alabama, to William "Cat" and Anna Mays. He lived with his father from a young age after his parents separated. Cat Mays played semi-pro baseball, but he made it a point not to force the game on his son. An exceptional athlete, the young Mays attended Fairfield Industrial High School, but could not play baseball there because they did not have a school team. Instead, Willie played semi-pro ball with the Gray Sox and the Fairfield Industrial League team alongside his father. In 1947, Mays joined the Birmingham Black Barons of the Negro American League. Because he was still in high school, Mays only played in the Barons' weekend home games. At the age of 16, he played in 28 games and batted .262 for the Barons, who were the defending league champs, and he had the opportunity to participate in the Negro League World Series.

Famous for hitting balls in the ballpark, Mays became famous for hitting balls in the middle of the street. It was not uncommon for him to play stickball with the neighborhood kids and then take them to the soda shop after the game.

Mays had a couple of productive seasons with the Black Barons, the highlight being in 1948, when he batted .311 in 75 games. The young outfielder attracted the attention of major-league scouts. The consensus was that although Mays had star potential, he needed to improve his overall hitting. At the urging of Brooklyn Dodgers catcher Roy Campanella, who played against Mays in a barnstorming game, the Dodgers took a look at him, but they were not interested because the young prospect had difficulty hitting the curveball.

The Boston Braves also scouted him, but it was the New York Giants who pulled the trigger, signing the future star. Giants scout, Eddie Montague said Mays was the best young player he had ever seen. In 1950, the Giants signed Mays to a $4,000 contract and assigned him to the Class B Trenton Giants. Mays had an immediate impact, batting .353 in 306 at-bats. He achieved this despite having to deal with the racist segregation of the era. He was forced to sleep in Black-only motels and use Black-only restrooms when the team traveled. Some of Mays' white teammates would sneak over

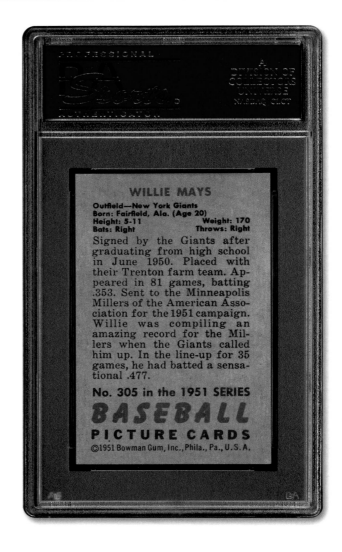

to his Black-only motel and sleep on the floor in solidarity with their young teammate.

Mays jumped up to the AAA Minneapolis Millers in the American Association in 1951. After the young star tore up the league, batting .477 in 35 games, the fifth-place Giants were eager to bring him up to New York. Mays was hesitant about joining the big-league team because he felt he would not be able to hit major-league pitching. Manager Leo Durocher would hear none of that, and Mays debuted in center field for the Giants on May 25, 1951. He started off badly, going 1-for-26 out of the gate, and was extremely discouraged. Durocher told Mays that he was the best center fielder he had ever seen and then he told him to pull his pants up higher to create a more favorable strike zone. With that encouragement and advice, Mays turned the corner and began to hit. The 20-year-old went on to bat a respectable

.274 with 20 home runs and 68 RBI. Although those numbers do not exactly jump off the page, Mays was voted Rookie of the Year. Not only that, but in storybook fashion, the Giants won a three-game playoff against the Brooklyn Dodgers on Bobby Thomson's famous "Shot Heard 'Round the World," a game-winning home run in the bottom of the ninth that clinched the National League pennant. The Giants went on to lose the Series to the New York Yankees in six games. The 20-year-old Mays had a taste of his first World Series but batted only .182 in the Fall Classic.

The "Say Hey Kid," as Mays became known, lived with a family in Harlem, close to the Polo Grounds, and soon became close with the family and the neighborhood kids. Famous for hitting balls in the ballpark, Mays became famous for hitting balls in the middle of the street. It was not uncommon for him to play stickball with the neighborhood kids and then take them to the soda shop after the game. Kids would sometimes knock at Mays' door and ask him to come out and play a game. He would usually accommodate them, play a little stick ball, and then go to the ballpark.

The story continues on page 126.

OVER TIME, A LIMITED NUMBER OF SPORTS cards morph into something more than their technical attributes would amount to by themselves. The 1986 Fleer Michael Jordan is a prime example. There are plenty of Jordan issues manufactured throughout his playing career that are superior when it comes to scarcity and market value from a pound-for-pound perspective, but no single card of the post-1980 era possesses more symbolic value than this mainstream rookie card. It is, arguably, the most recognizable card on the planet, regardless of era or sport. The image alone acts as an ambassador for the hobby, and that kind of visual power is limited to just a handful of iconic collectibles.

The colorful borders are susceptible to chipping and wear, while print defects and modest centering issues can impact the grade. It is also, perhaps, the most widely counterfeited trading card ever produced so buyers must beware. Appropriately, the card resides in what many consider to be the most popular sports card set ever made. Of course, part of the 132-card set's immense appeal is due to the Jordan rookie's presence, but this legendary card is surrounded by fellow superstars of the period...and that era is often referred to as the Golden Age of Basketball. The 1980s began with the Magic Johnson/Larry Bird rivalry and the 1990s ended just before a Shaq/Kobe three-peat started in Los Angeles. Right in the middle of it all was a dominant run by a man who rose above the rest to earn the moniker of the GOAT.

There are plenty of terms and phrases that get overused in sports when paying compliments to its figures. Claiming that an athlete "transcends" sports is one of them. In the case of Jordan, however, it's abundantly clear. Jordan became a global star and a brand in the way that few others have ever achieved. His name, like Babe Ruth's, is synonymous with excellence. Jordan's competitive fire, like Tom Brady's, separates him from so many other greats who have stepped onto the hardwood. Jordan, like the two other legends noted here, is more than the stats and trophies reveal. Likewise, his 1986 Fleer rookie is more than just a card. It is the paragon of modern card collecting.

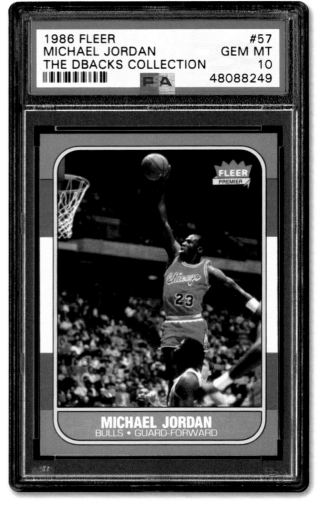

This PSA Gem Mint 10 is one of 319 examples to reach PSA's highest grading tier.

Air Jordan

When you look at the list of the greatest basketball players of all time, you will see names like Russell, Chamberlain, Jabbar, Lebron, Kobe, Shaq, Larry, Magic, and a host of others. However, there is only one player that sits at the very top of the mountain. Simply stated, Michael Jordon is the greatest player that ever stepped on a basketball court.

Born in Brooklyn, New York, in 1963, Michael Jeffrey Jordon did not make the varsity team at Emsley A. Laney High School until his junior year, but he wound up averaging 25 points per game and was awarded a scholarship to the University of North Carolina by legendary coach Dean

Smith. For three years, Jordon was a dominant force for the Tar Heels. He was the Atlantic Coast Conference (ACC) Rookie of the Year as a freshman and first team All-ACC in both his sophomore and junior years. With Smith's blessing, Jordan opted out of his senior year, declaring himself eligible for the NBA draft. He eventually returned to UNC to obtain his degree in the offseason.

In 1984, the Chicago Bulls drafted Jordon as the third pick in the first round. Little did they realize this pick would not only change the face of the franchise, but it would change the face of professional basketball forever. Michael Jordan became a superstar with mass appeal to both the older fans and, more importantly, a new young generation. He not only changed the game, but he created a remarkable brand that extended from fashion to food to entertainment. Right out of the gate, the 21-year-old Jordon averaged 28 points per game, bringing the Bulls to a higher level of competitiveness. Fans packed arenas across the country to get a glimpse of the young superstar. Jordan started the All-Star game as a rookie in 1985, but he scored only seven points. Evidently, some veteran players resented Jordon's popularity and decided to keep the ball away from him. Isiah Thomas of the Detroit Pistons supposedly led the charge to freeze Jordon out. The Bulls made the playoffs that year only to be defeated in the first round by the Milwaukee Bucks, but the future looked very promising for Jordan and the Bulls. Jordon was voted Rookie of the Year in 1984–1985, but he played in only 18 games the following season after breaking his foot in the third game. Without Jordon, the Bulls barely made the playoffs with a losing record. He made it back for the playoffs, and although the Bulls were swept by Larry Bird's Boston Celtics, Jordon's performance in Game Two was a glimpse of things to come. Jordan scored an amazing 63 points, breaking the record for a single playoff game set by the Lakers' Elgin Baylor in 1962.

The 1986–1987 season was arguably Michael Jordan's greatest. With his 37-points-per-game average, total 3,041 points, 236 steals, and 125 blocked shots, the nicknames began to surface. "His Airness," "Air Jordon," "MJ," "Black Cat," "Money," "Mr. June," "Superman," "Captain Marvel." Michael Jordan had become the face of the NBA. The following season, Jordan again dominated the league with a 35-point-per-game average to go along with a Most Valuable Player Award. He was also named Defensive Player of the Year. With a 50–32 record, the Bulls had certainly

turned the corner. They defeated the Cleveland Cavaliers in the first round of the playoffs, but they ran into Isiah Thomas's Detroit Pistons buzz saw and lost the semifinals in five games. The Jordan legacy grew in 1988–1989 when he led the Bulls to the Eastern Conference playoffs with his 32 points per game. One of the greatest Michael Jordon moments was when he hit a shot at the buzzer to beat the Cavs in the fifth and final game of the first round. "The Shot" is still a highlight film today. Again, the Bulls fell to the Pistons in the Finals. With the emergence of some excellent young players during the 1989–1990 season, the Chicago Bulls juggernaut really took shape. Scottie Pippen was becoming a bona fide force in the league, and assistant coach Phil Jackson took over as head coach. Jordon again dominated, averaging 33 points and six rebounds per game. Again, the Bulls lost to the seasoned Pistons in the Eastern Conference Finals.

Michael Jordan

The next three years catapulted Michael Jordan and the Bulls to the top of the NBA. The Bulls won 61 games in 1990–1991. Jordan won another MVP Award and averaged 31 points per game. The Bulls won their first championship, beating the New York Knicks, the Philadelphia 76ers and finally sweeping the Detroit Pistons in four games. In the NBA Finals, the Bulls defeated Magic Johnson and an excellent Los Angeles Lakers team in five games. Besides his 1991 MVP Award, Jordan was named the NBA Finals MVP for averaging 31 points, 11 assists, six rebounds, and two steals per game. The Bulls buzzed through the competition, compiling a 67–15 record during the 1991–1992 season. Jordon won another MVP trophy, and in the playoffs, the Bulls first dispatched the Miami Heat, then the New York Knicks in a tough seven-game series, and then the Cleveland Cavaliers in the conference finals. The NBA Finals found the Bulls battling the Portland Trail Blazers and the great Clyde "The Glide" Drexler. The Bulls defeated the Trail Blazers in six games with Jordon winning another NBA Finals MVP. The "threepeat" came to fruition after the 1992–1993 season when Jordan and company won their third NBA championship by defeating Charles Barkley and the Phoenix Suns. MJ averaged an amazing 41 points per game and again won the NBA Finals MVP Award, although Barkley was voted MVP for the season.

By this time, Michael Jordan was the most famous athlete on the planet, but the fame, outside business interests, and Olympic participation on the gold medalist "The Dream Team" began to catch up with him. The random murder of his father in July 1993 understandably took its toll. In October 1993, Jordan shocked the basketball world by announcing his retirement. Surprising everyone, he decided to try professional baseball. He signed with the Chicago White Sox and reported to their AA affiliate, the Birmingham Barons, in 1994. He also played in the Arizona Fall League for the Scottsdale Scorpions. Jordan's baseball career was short, but it was something his father had always wanted him to try. His career batting average was .202, two points above the Mendoza line, but his time in baseball revitalized him.

Jordon returned to the NBA in March 1995. After a few games to get the rust out, he carried the Bulls into the playoffs, and they made it to the Eastern Conference Semifinals. The Bulls went on to win the NBA championship for the next three seasons, defeating the Seattle SuperSonics in 1996, and the Utah Jazz in both 1997 and 1998. Jordan was NBA Finals MVP for all three contests. In January 1999, Jordon retired again, and in 2000, he became part-owner of the Washington Wizards. As president of basketball operations, Jordan received mixed reviews. He began to get the itch to get out on the court again and decided to play for his own team during the 2001–2002 season. Although he only played in 60 games because of injuries, the Wizards improved, but not enough to make the playoffs. That season, Jordan donated his salary to 9/11 related charities. In 2002–2003, his last season as a player, there were glimpses of his greatness. At 40 years old, Jordon averaged 20 points, six rebounds, and was named to the NBA All-Star team for the 14th time. After his retirement was announced, Jordan was honored at every NBA venue near the end of the season. His last points were two free throws, and he walked off the court for good to an amazing ovation.

In retirement, Jordan initially kept a relatively low profile making public appearances, enjoying his family, and playing in golf tournaments. In 2006, as a minority owner of the Charlotte Bobcats, he took over the position of managing member of basketball operations. In 2010, the NBA approved Jordan's bid to become the majority owner of the Bobcats (now the Charlotte Hornets). Jordan's business interests are legendary. He has been company spokesperson for Coca Cola, Hanes, Gatorade, McDonalds, Wheaties, and a host of other companies. In the 1980s, Nike developed the "Air Jordon" sneakers which became the rage for athletes and non-athletes worldwide. A complete Jordon brand was eventually developed and endorsed by professional athletes and celebrities. Jordon worked with Looney Tunes and Nike on commercials that featured him playing basketball with Bugs Bunny, and he later co-starred in the movie *Space Jam*. He is principal owner of 23XI, a NASCAR racing team, part-owner of the Florida Marlins baseball team, and special advisor to the board of DraftKings, a fantasy sports

and betting operation. And, oh yes, he is also involved in several car dealerships and restaurants and he owns a golf course in Florida. Needless to say, Michael Jordon is the first NBA player-billionaire. In 2020, the critically acclaimed documentary *The Last Dance,* detailed Jordan's years with the Bulls. From a philanthropic perspective, Jordon has pledged and raised millions of dollars for charities including Feeding America, Hurricane Relief, the Boys and Girls Club, Chicago area charities, and many others.

A six-time NBA Champion, six-time NBA Finals MVP, five-time NBA MVP, 14-time NBA All-Star, three-time All-Star MVP, nine-time All-NBA Defensive First Team, 10-time NBA Scoring Champ, 50th Anniversary NBA All-Time Team member, 1984 and 1992 Olympic Gold Medalist, 2009 inductee to the Naismith Memorial Basketball Hall of Fame, 2016 recipient of the Presidential Medal of Freedom, generous philanthropist, and successful businessman, Michael Jordan is truly the greatest of all time.

1957 Ty Cobb signed photo, Ty Cobb decal bat
circa 1908-1910, Cy Young cigar box circa 1910.
The Mike Heffner Collection.

4

Pre-War Legends (1900–1935)

★ ★ ★ ★ ★ ★ ★ ★ ★ ★ ★ ★ ★ ★ ★

These outstanding cards take us on a journey from the pre-war tobacco card days, through the Roaring Twenties, and into the Great Depression.

Some of the greatest professional athletes of all time graced the baseball diamond, gridiron, and Olympic stadiums during that period. Cy Young and Walter Johnson, two of the greatest pitchers of all time; the enigmatic but gifted Ty Cobb; and football, baseball, and Olympic track-and-field star Jim Thorpe are a few of the legends featured on these important pieces of cardboard art. The unique examples featured in this grouping are the 1909–1911 T206 Cy Young Portrait, 1909–1911 T206 "Magie Error," 1916 Famous & Barr Co. Jim Thorpe, and the underappreciated 1927 E126 and 1934 World Wide Gum Babe Ruth cards, all of which are the highest ranked specimens in the PSA population report.

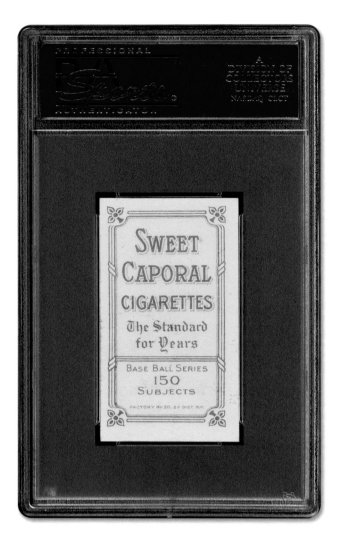

This card is the sole example to reach the PSA Mint 9 grading tier with none higher in the PSA Population Report.

LIKE ALL OTHER SPORTS, THERE IS NO DOUBT

that the game of baseball has changed since its inception. In-game strategies, scouting, training, and the way we evaluate performance has evolved. Sports has become a data-driven industry, and its athletes are seemingly able to do things physically that were once thought of as impossible. Along the way, however, their bodies seem to be breaking down at a much faster rate than in previous generations. There are varying opinions as to why this is happening. No matter what explanation has the most merit, the results are real. For these reasons and more, there are certain milestones and records that appear untouchable. One of them is Cy Young's career mark for wins at 511.

Within the T206 issue, a set that came out at the tail end of his illustrious career, Young can be found on three different cards and each one is distinct. The classic portrait, based on the work of renowned photographer Carl Horner, is joined by two additional poses. One appears to depict Young in mid-delivery (Glove Shows) and another seems to catch the unbreakable pitcher after completing a throw (Bare Hand Shows). When it comes to overall scarcity, all three poses appear to exist in similar numbers based on the population data available today, but the portrait is clearly the most sought-after Young of the trio. This is typical for all Hall of Famer cards in the release, and the rich green background on the portrait makes the eye appeal exceptional.

Interestingly, when it comes to naming the greatest pitcher of all time, most baseball historians would give the nod to others who have graced the mound. Young, however, is the name attached to the annual MLB award for pitching

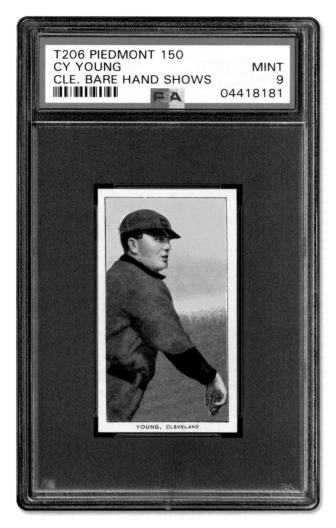

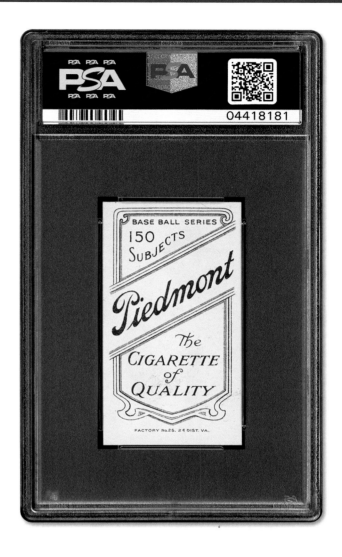

This PSA Mint 9 is one of three examples graded at that tier, with none higher in the PSA Population Report.

excellence and the impact on his collectibles should not be underestimated. Young's association with that award ensures that his name will remain at the forefront, generation after generation. The combination of Young's unfathomable career marks for durability and the fact that pitching's seasonal standard is named after him place his T206 cards in special company. Beyond its notable rarities, Young joins Ty Cobb, Walter Johnson, and Christy Mathewson as the backbone of this historic set.

There is no doubt that Young is featured on some earlier cards that are exceedingly tougher to find than his T206 trio, such as the black-and-white 1903 E107 Breisch-Williams card or the nearly impossible 1893 Just So rarity, a unique card as there is only one copy known at the time of

this writing. His T206 cards, however, are the most popular with collectors.

Cyclone

When a pitcher wins over 20 games on 16 different occasions, wins over 511 games for his career—more games than any other pitcher in baseball history—and gets the most prestigious MLB pitching award named after him, he is certainly going to get your attention.

A flame thrower during the first part of his illustrious career, Denton "Cy" Young adjusted as he got older to become a finesse pitcher with excellent command and a variety of pitches. Denton True Young was born in 1867, just two years after the conclusion of the Civil War. The 6-foot-2,

Cy Young

league championship the Spiders were swept by the Beaneaters. At the end of that season Young tied the knot with his hometown sweetheart, Robba Miller.

Between the 1892 and 1893 seasons, the pitching mound was moved back from 55 feet and 6 inches to today's regulation 60 feet and 6 inches. Although Young's earned-run average went up, he still won 33 games in 1893. The Spiders faltered in 1894, dropping to sixth place, but Young managed to put together a 26–21 season. He posted a magnificent, league-leading 35–10 record in 1895 to lead the Spiders to the Temple Cup championship vs. the Baltimore Orioles. Young won three of the five games in this championship contest that predated the World Series. Over the next three seasons, Young continued his dominance. In addition to his excellent fastball and curve, he developed what is known today as the changeup or "slowball," as he called it. In 1897, Young had a mediocre (for him) 21–19 season. His high point that year was pitching his first no-hitter in a game against the Cincinnati Reds on September 18.

The owner of the Spiders, Frank Robison decided to buy the bankrupt St. Louis Browns in 1898 and renamed them the Perfectos. As owner of both the Spiders and the Perfectos, Robison decided to transfer Young and a few other players to St. Louis. The hapless Spiders wound up losing 134 games because they were so depleted. Young had 26 wins in 1899 and 20 wins in 1900 after the team was renamed the Cardinals. A new league was formed in 1901 to compete with the National League. The fledgling American League

210-pound farm boy from Gilmore, Ohio, was a gifted athlete. From his late teens and into his early twenties, Young played for several semi-professional teams. In 1890, he played with the Canton team in the Tri-State League, and it was there that the hard-throwing righty got the nickname "Cy," short for cyclone. Although he was 15–15 for the last place Canton team, Young developed a reputation as the most overpowering pitcher around. In late June of that year, he was signed by the Cleveland Spiders of the National League for $300. He made his debut on August 6, 1890, against the great Cap Anson's Chicago Colts and tossed a three-hitter victory. Although the Spiders were a sub-.500 team, Young finished 9–7 in his inaugural season.

In 1891, the 24-year-old pitcher won 27 games and became the undisputed ace of the Spiders staff. Although his command of pitches was still developing, Young gained the reputation as a flame thrower. The 1892 season proved to be the breakout season for Young. He led the National League with his incredible 36–12 record, 1.93 ERA, and nine shutouts, while leading the Spiders to a second-place finish. An excellent Boston Beaneaters team took first place that year. The league had a split season with Boston winning the first half and Cleveland winning the second half, but in the

From April 25 through May 11, 1904, he pitched an amazing 25 consecutive hitless innings, still the MLB record today.

made great efforts to lure players from the NL ranks. Cy Young and his longtime batterymate Lou Criger jumped to the new league, which immediately gave the junior circuit credibility. Signed by the Boston Americans, the 34-year-old pitching ace continued to dominate. In 1901, Young led the league with 33 wins, a 1.62 ERA, and 158 strikeouts, earning the pitching Triple Crown title. He followed that with 32 wins in 1902 and 28 wins in 1903. At the end of that season, the first World Series took place, pitting the AL Boston Americans and Cy Young against the NL Pittsburgh Pirates and the great Honus Wagner. As starting pitcher for the Americans, Young became the first hurler to throw a pitch in a World Series game. Boston won that first world championship five games to three, with Young getting the wins in Game Five and Game Seven.

1904 was another stellar season for Young, who won 26 games and posted a sparkling 1.97 ERA. From April 25 through May 11, he pitched an amazing 25 consecutive hitless innings, still the MLB record today. In the middle of that streak, on May 5, 1904, he pitched a perfect game against the Philadelphia Athletics' Rube Waddell. Boston won the pennant that year, but there was no World Series because the NL pennant-winning New York Giants refused to play. For the next few seasons, the Americans were not very competitive, and they wound up in last place in 1906. Young's record dipped below .500 in both 1905 and 1906, but he bounced back with a 21–15 record in 1907. Young remained competitive by changing his style from a hard thrower to a command pitcher, painting the corners and using a lethal curveball. The Americans changed their name to the Boston Red Sox in 1908, and Young had a great season, winning 21 games with a miniscule 1.26 ERA. On June 30, 1908, the 41-year-old legend tossed his third no-hitter, this time against the New York Highlanders.

Young was traded to the Cleveland Naps in 1909, at the age of 42. That year, he won 19 games, but age was catching up with him. Although he developed arm problems, he won his 500th game in 1910. He retired in 1911 at the age of 44 with a 511–316 record, a 2.63 lifetime ERA, and 2,803 career strikeouts. Young returned to Peoli, Ohio, where he and Robba enjoyed retirement on their farm. Hurt financially by the Depression, Young sold the farm, moved in with friends, and worked as a retail clerk in Newcomerstown after his wife died in 1933. He was elected to the Hall of Fame in 1937, and Young attended the inaugural

class induction ceremonies in Cooperstown in 1939. On November 4, 1955, he passed away at the age of 88.

Over his noteworthy 22-year career, Cy Young led the league in wins five times, strikeouts twice, and ERA twice. He was a 16-time 20-plus game winner, with five of those wins in the exalted 30-plus game category. His 511 wins is a major-league record that will probably never be broken. Young also holds the records for innings pitched (7,356), games started (815), complete games (749), and consecutive hitless innings (25). The year after he died, MLB created the Cy Young Award, which is given annually to the best American League pitcher and the best National League pitcher. Cy Young certainly deserves his place in baseball history as one of the greatest pitchers to ever step on the mound.

IN A SET THAT IS DEFINED, IN PART, by its immense star power, Walter Johnson finds himself as one of several critical components. Outside of the great rarities that most collectors do not consider part of the basic set due to their astounding difficulty and monumental cost, Johnson joins Ty Cobb, Christy Mathewson, and Cy Young as the elite names in an unparalleled issue. Of the three preeminent hurlers of the era, it is Johnson that most baseball experts consider the best of the bunch. In fact, when it comes to naming the finest pitcher in baseball history, Johnson is one of the few that warrants serious consideration for the top spot. Johnson can be found in other classic sets like the 1909 T204 Ramly and 1914/1915 Cracker Jack issues, but the T206 cards are his most popular.

Johnson is represented twice in the T206 set. "The Big Train" is featured on one portrait with a yellow background and another pose where the pitcher is shown from the side view with his bare and glove hands pausing near his chest. The "Hands at Chest" Johnson is positioned against a blue background. As is the case with the dozens of other Hall of Famers in the set, the portrait of Johnson remains the more sought-after and valuable of the two poses as a product of renowned photographer Carl Horner. Interestingly, the Johnson portrait is one of the easiest T206 cards to find in top grade. It is believed that a discovery of uncirculated T206 cards in the late-1980s, dubbed "The Southern Find," accounts for most of these high-grade copies.

Despite Johnson's status in the all-time rankings, Mathewson and Young were featured on one more card each for a total of three in the T206 set. Johnson, who was just starting to find his groove during the 1909–1911 period, had not yet become a perennial star like the other pitching legends noted above. This might be the most logical explanation for Johnson appearing fewer times in the set. When his career was over, Johnson's numbers told the story. If his 417 victories and 2.17 ERA aren't enough, Johnson's 110 career shutouts, a record that still stands, should do the trick. The T206 set captures Johnson near the beginning of his run as the most dominant pitcher of his era, a career that earned him one of the first five spots in the Hall of Fame in 1936.

This PSA Mint 9 is one of six examples graded at that tier, with none higher in the PSA Population Report.

The Big Train

If you look at Walter Johnson's T206 card, you see a face filled with serenity. His friendly smile and welcoming eyes jump off the cardboard in an affable and welcoming manner. Unfortunately for the batters who faced him, Walter Johnson the pitcher was quite different. In a 21-season career from 1907 through 1927, all with the Washington Senators, the man they called "The Big Train" whistled fastballs past opposing hitters like a locomotive passing in the night. Along the way, he fashioned a career that made him an inaugural member of the Hall of Fame.

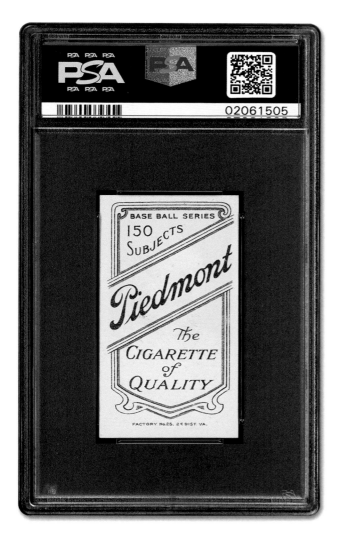

exhibiting pinpoint control that belied his youthful age. He also registered an ERA of 1.88. The Senators were smitten.

From 1910 to 1919, Johnson put together an incredible run of victories. In each of those seasons, he won 20 games or more. In that span, he led the National League in wins five times, ERA four times, strikeouts nine times, shutouts six times, and complete games six times. That decade of dominance alone would easily be enough to get a pitcher into the Hall of Fame. Johnson's 2.17 career ERA is one of those triple-take stats that boggles the mind. He added over 3,500 strikeouts to go along with 417 career wins. On six occasions, he led the American League in victories. Keep in mind that in the bulk of those seasons, his Senators were less than spectacular—a perennial second division club. Johnson can play and win the stat game with any pitcher in history, but one numerical column stands out above the rest. While a host of Strikeout Sultans have passed Johnson's 3,509 career Ks, he remains on the very short list of the game's greatest power pitchers. If the strikeout is indeed an art form, Walter Johnson was Michelangelo, Monet, and DaVinci dressed in a woolen baseball uniform and cleats. He topped the junior circuit in punchouts on 12 occasions, including every season from 1912 to 1919. In 1913, Johnson delivered one of the greatest seasons in the history of the game. He went 36–7 with a 1.14 ERA, 29 complete games, 11 shutouts, 346 innings pitched, and 243 strikeouts. That season, he earned the first of his two Most Valuable Player Awards.

Born in the fertile Midwest farmland that has yielded a bumper crop of big leaguers, Johnson was a native of Kansas. From humble beginnings, he would create a proud major-league resume. Perhaps Johnson's rural upbringing influenced his uncanny ability to retire batters. As a boy in Kansas, he helped his family work the farm and developed a passion and skill set for outdoor activities such as hunting and fishing. Ironically, while in Kansas, Johnson had few thoughts of a baseball career, but another boyhood development would change the course of his life. When the Johnson family moved to southern California, young Walter found he could play baseball year-round in the Golden State sunshine. He began playing semi-pro ball and took a natural liking to the mound. Word of the young hurler's talent began to spread, and in July of 1907, he was signed as a free agent by the Senators. He played for Washington that season at 19 years of age. In just over 110 innings pitched, Johnson struck out 71 batters and walked only 20,

The T206 set captures Johnson near the beginning of his run as the most dominant pitcher of his era, a career that earned him one of the first five spots in the Hall of Fame in 1936.

Eleven times in his career, Johnson posted an ERA of under 2.00, 11 times! He was, indeed, nearly unhittable. Johnson did not see the light of the World Series until 1924 at the age of 36. That season, the venerable Senator legend led the American League with 23 wins and 158 strikeouts. The ever-lowly Sens won the World Series in seven games against the Giants, and Johnson won his second league

Walter Johnson

MVP Award. In 1925, Washington returned to the Fall Classic and, once again, they rode the "Big Train" to get there. Johnson was 20–7, the last of his 20-win seasons. Alas, Washington

could not defend their unlikely 1924 crown. Manager Bucky Harris's crew fell to the Pittsburgh Pirates in seven games. The franchise known as the Washington Senators would make the World Series just one more time in their history, losing to the Giants in 1933. The highest yearly salary that Johnson ever earned was $20,000, in his final three seasons of 1925, 1926, and 1927. With his class, charisma, and consistency, one can only wonder what he would have earned in today's booming baseball salary structure.

After his playing career, Johnson managed in the minor leagues before managing the Senators from 1929 to 1932. With Washington, he tutored and mentored many of the players who would win the AL pennant in 1933. Johnson also served as manager of the Cleveland Indians from 1933 to 1935. Overall, in his seven-year managing career, Johnson's teams went 529–432 for a .550 winning percentage. In

addition to baseball, Johnson's post-playing career included civic leadership, broadcasting with the Washington Senators, playing in exhibition games, and politics. When baseball established the Hall of Fame in Cooperstown in 1936, Johnson was deservedly among the first five legends elected, joining the likes of Ty Cobb, Christy Mathewson, Babe Ruth, and Honus Wagner. Johnson dominated hitters and put up overall numbers that are mind boggling. Statistically speaking, it is confounding that Johnson remains among the all-time leaders in strikeouts over nine decades after his retirement. A baseball trailblazer, he defined the role of the power pitcher. His immortalization is based on demoralization—breaking the spirit of batters with a dazzling array of mound magic. This true legend passed away from a brain tumor on December 10, 1946, in Washington, DC, at age 59, but his legacy of excellence is eternal.

In a 21-season career from 1907 through 1927, all with the Washington Senators, the man they called "The Big Train" whistled fastballs past opposing hitters like a locomotive passing in the night.

OFTEN REFERRED TO AS ONE OF THE THREE BIG
rarities in one of "The Big Three" baseball sets, the 1909–1911 T206 Sherry Magie has long been dubbed one of the error card kings of the collectibles world. While not nearly as scarce as the T206 Joe Doyle NY NAT'L (Hands Over Head) card, which is now considered the fourth great rarity in the set and its most elusive piece for those seeking true completion, the Magie is more recognizable. It has the advantage of being in the trade headlines for a longer time as one of the most challenging components in, arguably, the hobby's most coveted set. In addition, the image used was derived from the work of Carl Horner, a well-known photographer of the day.

When the T206 cards were initially released, the portrait card featuring Magee had his name spelled incorrectly as "Magie" instead. The error was corrected quickly, but some Magie cards did escape and fall into the hands of collectors. It is important to note that the Magie error can only be found with a Piedmont 150 back. Furthermore, in comparison to the Doyle rarity, Honus Wagner, and Eddie Plank cards, the Magie error is the most common of the four. At the time of this writing, less than 140 examples had been graded by PSA according to their population report. For context, the Plank, which is the second most common of the quartet, had less than 80. When it comes to condition, the Magie is extraordinarily challenging. Only seven copies have graded PSA EX 5 or higher, which makes it a condition rarity on top of a general rarity.

In some cases, great rarities, errors, or variations are connected to players who were not standouts in their day. Magee might not be a Hall of Famer or household name in the way that Ty Cobb or Honus Wagner are, but he was a superb player. During his 16-year career, played during the Deadball Era, Magee was amongst league leaders in home runs on several occasions. He won a batting title in 1910 and led the NL in RBI four times. Magee also stole 441 bases and was regarded as a fine defensive outfielder. As a player, it's easy to get lost in the T206 set. "The Monster" is a virtual abyss of legendary names, but Magee held his own in the field. The lore around his error keeps his T206 card high on the list of collector demand.

This card is the sole example to reach the PSA NM-MT 8 grading tier with none higher in the PSA Population Report.

Sherry

Had the Sherry Magee error card never existed, it is not very likely that many hobbyists would even know who he was. Like so many other great Deadball Era players, Magee may have remained under just about everyone's radar except for the real baseball history buffs. Taking the famous card and putting it aside for a moment, let's take a look at Sherry Magee the ballplayer.

During his years with the Phillies, Magee was one of the best players in baseball. An excellent hitter, fielder, and speedster on the basepaths, he was one of the most dominant players

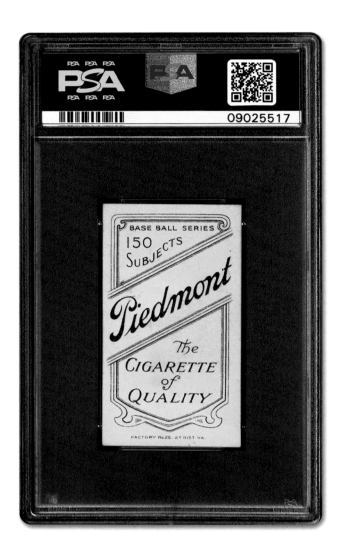

Unfortunately, along with his talent came a player with a fiery temper and combative style of play.

In 1907, Magee had an outstanding year. His .328 batting average was good for second in the National League, behind Honus Wagner. Magee led the league with 85 RBI and stole 46 bases. However, it seemed that the better he played, the more difficult he was to play with. It was a common

---

During his years with the Phillies, Magee was one of the best players in baseball. An excellent hitter, fielder, and speedster on the basepaths, he was one of the most dominant players in the National League.

---

occurrence for the hot-headed Magee to get into scraps with both players and umpires, and it was not unusual for him to be tossed from a ball game. Magee had a spectacular year in 1910, leading the league in almost every offensive category. He batted a lofty .331 for the National League batting title, led the league with 110 runs and 123 RBI, and had 49 steals. However in 1911, the short-tempered, irascible Magee got himself into trouble in a game against St. Louis on July 10. With two men on in the third inning, Magee was up at the plate. Umpire Bill Finneran called Magee out on a called third strike, which probably should have been called a ball. Magee threw his bat up in the air in disgust, so Finneran promptly threw him out of the game. He rushed the umpire and punched him in the face drawing blood and knocking him out. The rest of the umpiring crew as well as the managers rushed out to help Finneran while Magee's teammates escorted him off the field. After Finneran came to, he went after Magee but the two were separated by the players and managers. The Phillies went on to win the game, but National League President Thomas Lynch suspended Magee for the remainder of the season. After Magee issued a public apology, the suspension was reduced to 36 games. Regrettably, by the time he returned to play, the Phillies were out of the pennant race.

in the National League. Born in Clarendon, Pennsylvania, Sherwood Robert Magee was a star while playing on an area semi-pro team. Philadelphia Phillies scout Jim Randall got wind of the young kid with the great bat and quick temper and signed him immediately. Two days later, on June 29, 1904, the 19-year-old was the starting left fielder for the Phillies. In his initial season, the fledgling left fielder batted a very respectable .277 with 101 hits in 364 at-bats, to establish himself as one of the rising stars of the game. At 5-foot-11 and 179 pounds, the muscular Magee was talented and competitive. Over the next several seasons, he showed the ability to dominate a game either with his bat, glove, or speed. In 1905, he batted .299 and stole 48 bases. Magee continued his dominance on the basepaths in 1906, swiping 55 bases, a Phillies record he held until it was broken by Juan Samuel in 1984. From a defensive standpoint, Magee was considered to have the best outfield arm in baseball.

The next season started badly for Magee. He was hit by a pitch during a pre-season batting practice, and a broken arm and wrist caused him to miss the first part of the season. Soon after he returned to play, Magee was injured again when he collided with center fielder Dode Paskert, but he recovered to post a .306 batting average that year. Phillies fans never really warmed up to Magee. During his 11 seasons in Philadelphia, the team was mediocre at best, usually finishing in fourth, fifth, or sixth place, yet Magee was usually among league leaders in many batting categories. The fans thought Magee's personal stats meant more to him than anything.

Magee batted .306 again in 1913 and the Phillies finished in second place. Despite his troubled relationship with fans and management, Magee was named team captain in 1914. In addition to his normal left-field position, that year he played shortstop, first base, and second base while batting .314 and leading the league with 103 RBI, 171 hits, and 39 doubles, but the Phillies finished in sixth place.

Although he hoped to be chosen to replace Red Dooin as Phillies manager at the end of the season, Magee was passed over in favor of Pat Moran. Frustrated, Magee asked to be traded to a winning team, and he was traded to the world champion Boston Braves

in December of 1914. There was bad luck from the start in Boston. He broke his collarbone and injured his shoulder soon after arriving for spring training. That first year, Magee batted .280 but ironically, the Braves finished second to the 1915 pennant-winning Phillies. Things never really worked out for Magee with the Braves. He was waived in 1917 and was eventually picked up by the Cincinnati Reds. Magee had a few decent seasons with the Reds, batting .321 in 1917, and batting .298 and leading the league with 76 RBI in 1918. Illness kept him out of the lineup for most of 1919, but Magee did appear in the 1919 World Series as a pinch hitter before Cincinnati released him at the end of the season.

Magee played seven more seasons in the minor leagues with mixed success,

finishing up with the Baltimore Orioles as player-coach. After retiring in 1926 at the age of 41, Magee was not quite done with baseball. He reinvented himself as a big-league umpire and was actually quite good at his new profession. Things were looking good for the future but in early March 1929, Magee contracted pneumonia. His condition worsened quickly, and he passed away in Philadelphia on March 13, at the age of 44.

The first big Phillies star of the twentieth century, Sherry Magee posted a .291 lifetime batting average, 2,169 hits, and 441 stolen bases. He had 23 steals of home, including two in one game. One of the most colorful characters in baseball history, Magee was considered for the Hall of Fame in 2008 but was not elected.

This PSA NM-MT 8 is one of eight examples graded at that tier, with none higher in the PSA Population Report.

WHEN COLLECTORS DISCUSS THE T206 ISSUE, it's
hard not to start with a conversation about the legendary Honus Wagner rarity, but this set is built around Ty Cobb. Make no mistake about it; Cobb was the star of the day. Many baseball historians will argue that, along with Babe Ruth, the fierce competitor belongs in the argument for the best player in the first half of the twentieth century. In fact, when the first Hall of Fame class was announced in 1936, it was Cobb who led the inaugural five members with the highest number of votes. Considering the clout in that group, which included Ruth, it tells us just how much Cobb was revered.

As most experienced collectors know, the T206 set is filled with rarities, variations, and thousands of different cards

if you factor in all the different advertising back/factory/ series combinations it offers. Most hobbyists, however, choose to focus on the basic set checklist, which can still be intimidating at 524 total cards. In the case of Cobb, there are technically dozens of different combinations to collect, but the foundation is built on four different cards in that basic set. Those cards include the Green Portrait, Red Portrait, Bat Off Shoulder and the Bat On Shoulder. Amazingly, Hal Chase appears on the most cards in the base set (5), but it is Cobb who steals the show.

The Green and Red Portrait Cobbs are virtually identical aside from the difference in background color. There are some subtle, distinguishing features in the uniform and face of Cobb, but they were both created from the original image taken by renowned photographer Carl Horner. The Green Portrait is, without a doubt, the toughest of all four Cobb cards in the basic set, but the Red Portrait is arguably

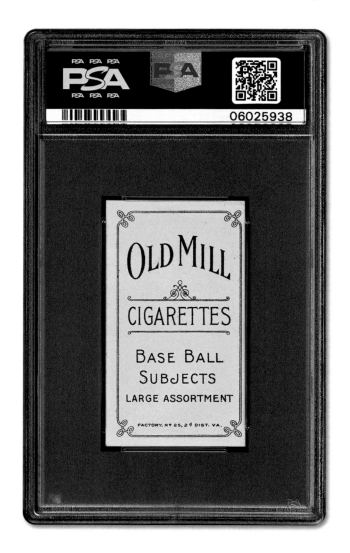

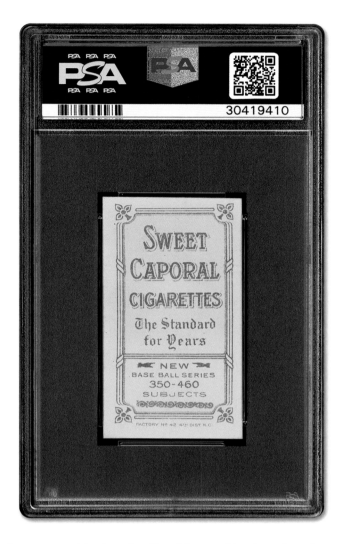

This PSA NM-MT 8 is one of 19 examples graded at that tier, with only two unqualified copies graded higher in the PSA Population Report.

the most popular. When it comes to the Red Portrait, it is important to note that the background can be found with wide variances in color. Some are found with a deep, rich, red color, while others appear more orange. Over the years, some have argued that the "orange" Cobb should be distinguished as a fifth card since the color is so distinct, but the majority of the hobby has kept them as one.

The two other Cobbs, the Bat On Shoulder and the Bat Off Shoulder cards, are not quite as popular but are highly desirable in their own right. The portraits of all the Hall of Famers included in the T206 issue have always garnered greater attention from collectors, so it's not surprising that the Green and Red Portrait Cobbs generate the most demand

of the quartet. The Bat On Shoulder card is viewed as the tougher of the two "Cobb with bat" poses. It would be his bat that made Cobb such a dominant player, combined with a nature that made him feared by opposing teams on the field.

The Georgia Peach

Continued from page 54.

By 1911, the feisty outfielder with the hair-trigger temper had battled his way to superstar status. That season was arguably Cobb's best. He batted an amazing .419 with 248 hits, led the league in most offensive categories, including stolen bases, and squeezed in a 40-game hit streak. Voted the 1911 American League Most Valuable Player, Cobb won another Chalmer's automobile. By this time, Ty Cobb was the most highly paid player in baseball and when fans came

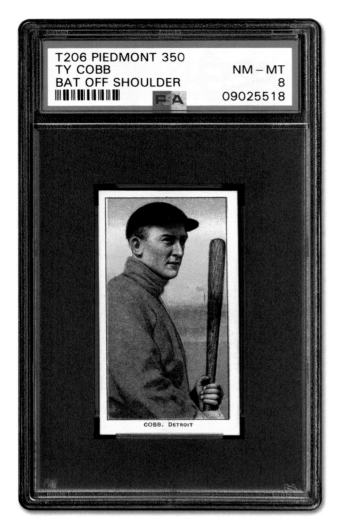

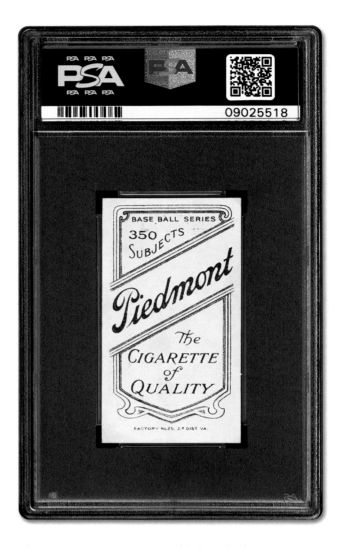

This PSA NM-MT 8 is one of 14 examples graded at that tier, with only five unqualified copies graded higher in the PSA Population Report.

out to see him, they either cheered him or heckled him. His hitting and base-stealing ability was something fans had never witnessed before. Over the next few seasons, Cobb continued his assault on American League pitching. Although the Tigers were a sub-.500 team and not very competitive, Ty Cobb was the star of the league. In 1912, he produced another amazing season, batting .409 and banging out 226 hits to lead the league. Again that season, his temper got the better of him. This time he jumped into the stands during a game and pummeled a fan who had been taunting him. Cobb was suspended by the league for 10 games. Even though he was not well-liked by his own teammates, they went on a one-game strike to protest Cobb's suspension, forcing the Tigers management to fill the roster with replacement players that day.

Over the next three seasons, Cobb led the league in batting average, posting .389 in 1913, .368 in 1914, and .369 in 1915. His 144 runs and 208 hits topped the league in 1915 and he broke the single-season record for steals with 96. That record stood until 1962, when it was broken by Los Angeles Dodgers speedster Maury Wills with 104 thefts.

Although Cobb was the league leader with 113 runs and 68 stolen bases in 1916, he lost the batting title to future Hall of Famer, Tris Speaker. In 1917, Cobb led the league in most offensive categories and regained his batting crown with his .383 average and 225 hits. Another incident took place in spring training that year during a game between the Tigers and the New York Giants. It all started when the New York Giants second baseman, Buck Herzog, taunted Cobb for arriving at the game late. Cobb slid into Herzog with spikes high and the two got into a brawl which actually carried over into Cobb's hotel room later that evening.

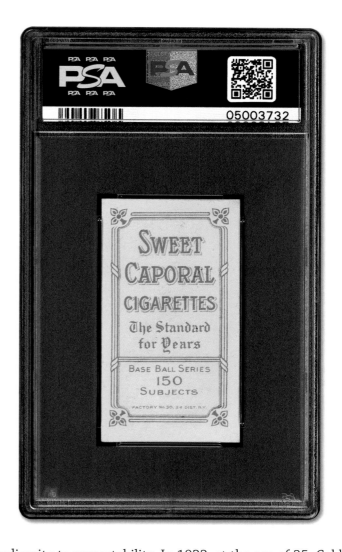

This PSA NM-MT 8 is one of 12 examples graded at that tier, with none higher in the PSA Population Report.

Cobb won the batting title again in 1918 with his .382 average, but because the country was entering World War I, he enlisted in the army in October. Captain Tyrus Cobb served in the Chemical Corps branch in Chaumont, France, under Major Branch Rickey. Captain Christy Mathewson and First Lieutenant George Sisler also served in the same unit. After several months, Cobb was honorably discharged along with the other major-league stars. Over the next several seasons, there was no slowing down for Cobb. He won the batting title in 1919 with his .384 average while pacing the league with 191 hits, and he registered hit number 3,000 in 1921 at age 34. Cobb accepted the job of player-manager of the Detroit Tigers in 1921 and for the next five years he led the team while continuing to dominate offensively. He actually did a nice job as manager, leading the Tigers from

mediocrity to respectability. In 1922, at the age of 35, Cobb batted an astounding .401, and in 1923 his Tigers finished in second place. Amazingly, Cobb kept his temper in check for the most part. After two game evictions as manager in 1921, he was only evicted three times in the next five seasons. In 1926, he resigned as manager and announced his retirement from baseball after rumors circulated that he and Cleveland Indians manager, Tris Speaker, were involved in fixing a game back in 1919. With no witnesses stepping up, Cobb was eventually exonerated. He wrapped up his managerial stint with a 479–444 record.

Prior to his tenure as player-manager, Cobb was considered the best player in the league, but suddenly all eyes were turning towards another emerging superstar. George Herman "Babe" Ruth would be the baseball star of the Roaring Twenties. The "Sultan of Swat" had arrived. Cobb resented the emergence of this new star and maintained

CRACKER JACK BASEBALL CARDS

are part of the fabric of the hobby, just like the confection is to the game itself. Within the back-to-back sets issued in 1914 and 1915 are some of the most desirable cards ever produced. From the Christy Mathewson rarity in the 1914 set to "Shoeless" Joe Jackson, perhaps his best-looking issue, iconic cards seem to run amuck in the product. There is no doubting, however, whom the biggest star of the day was—Ty Cobb. Unlike Jackson, Cobb appeared in a host of classic sets, which makes picking a favorite of the bunch nearly impossible. While there are certainly more valuable and scarce Cobb cards to consider, one could argue that no other image reflects his fiery personality better than the Cracker Jack.

Cobb brought an unmatched ferocity to the sport...at the plate, in the field, and on the basepaths.

that he was just as good as Ruth. In later years, though, he too agreed that Ruth was the best that ever stepped on a field. Cobb was coaxed out of retirement by his old friend Connie Mack, manager of the Philadelphia Athletics. His two seasons with the A's were very productive, with the highlight taking place on July 18, 1927, when Cobb logged career hit number 4,000. This was the same season that Ruth slammed 60 home runs. At the end of the 1928 season, despite batting .323 at the age of 41, Cobb retired for good.

He lived very comfortably in retirement, traveling extensively and spending time between his Atherton, California, estate and his Lake Tahoe getaway. Ty Cobb died from prostate cancer on July 17, 1961, at the age of 74. An extremely complex man who alienated many fans, teammates,

and opposing players, Ty Cobb's contribution to our National Pastime will never be disputed. The 12-time batting champion, 1909 AL Triple Crown winner, and 1911 AL MVP finished with 4,189 career hits, 897 stolen bases, and many other offensive milestones. As of this writing, Cobb's .366 lifetime batting average is still the highest in baseball history.

In 1936, Ty Cobb, "The Georgia Peach," was elected to the inaugural Hall of Fame class with the highest percentage of votes, more than fellow class members Babe Ruth, Honus Wagner, Christy Mathewson, and Walter Johnson. His 98.2% of the vote remained the highest voting percentage until Tom Seaver's induction in 1992.

Cobb is looking directly at the viewer with bat in hand, in the same way he stared down every pitcher who dared to throw one over the plate. His eyes communicate bad intentions without his mouth saying a word. Cobb brought an unmatched ferocity to the sport... at the plate, in the field, and on the basepaths. Cobb's ethos is captured against a rich, red background, which seems incredibly appropriate for the menacing combatant. In 1915, a year after their initial 144-card offering, Cracker Jack would deliver its second installment of baseball cards in a 176-card set. The 1914 cards are

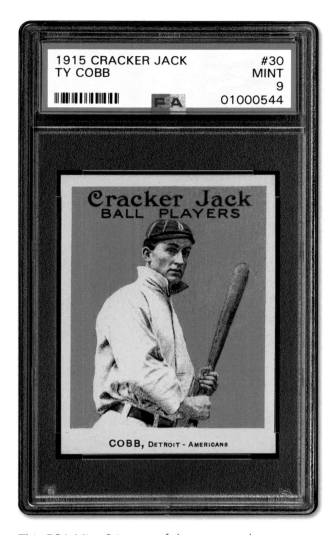

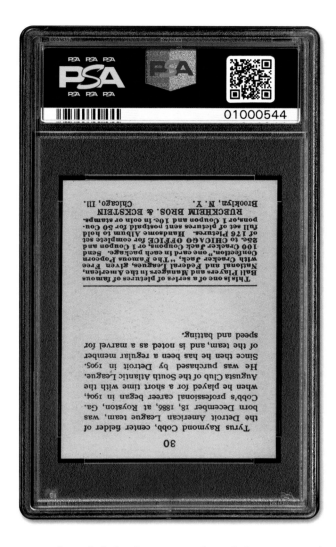

This PSA Mint 9 is one of three examples graded at that tier, with none higher in the PSA Population Report.

significantly tougher to find in top grades since the only way to obtain them was by extracting the cards from treacherous boxes filled with sticky treats.

In 1915, however, the company created a redemption program where collectors could acquire a full set, one that didn't have to navigate all the pitfalls associated with the packaging. For 100 coupons or one coupon plus 25 cents, the set could be yours. In fact, customized albums were offered as well in exchange for 50 coupons or one coupon plus 10 cents, so collectors could store their cards in style. For this reason, there are far more high-end 1915 Cobb cards in circulation today versus the 1914 issue. The two cards appear virtually identical but there are some subtle differences in paper thickness and color. The 1914 cards

were printed in slightly thinner stock and the 1915 cards often exhibit deeper color in the red background than their predecessors. In addition, the reverse on the 1915 cards was printed upside down so they could be read while mounted in the specially designed albums.

While there are certainly more valuable and scarce Cobb cards to consider, one could argue that no other image reflects his fiery personality better than the Cracker Jack.

IN THIS DAY AND AGE, IT IS HARD TO IMAGINE any athlete being able to excel at so many different sports the way Jim Thorpe did. We have witnessed some two-way stars in the past few decades, like Bo Jackson, Deion Sanders, and Brian Jordan, but Thorpe's physical exploits went far beyond baseball and football. In addition to barnstorming as a professional basketball player, Thorpe became the first Native American to win a gold medal in the Olympics. In fact, Thorpe earned two of them in 1912, one for his first-place finish in the decathlon and one for the pentathlon. Simply put, the sports world has never seen anything quite like him since, and the 1916 M101-5 issue was one of the few to capture Thorpe on cardboard.

Thorpe did appear on a handful of other baseball cards during his career, including those in the 1912 E270 Colgan Chips and 1922 Zee-Nut sets (which features Thorpe as a minor leaguer in the Pacific Coast League), but the black-and-white M101-5 card is his most popular and valuable. Felix Mendelsohn distributed this issue along with the virtually identical M101-4 set, and the cards exhibit either a blank back or one that showcases an advertisement on the reverse. The M101-5 advertisements range from baking company Standard Biscuit to clothing stores like Famous & Barr Co., which catered to young boys. Each back variety offers a different level of scarcity as they were printed in various numbers. A small find of cards featuring the Famous & Barr Co. backs were discovered in St. Louis in 2019, but the Thorpe card remains elusive. Less than 10 Famous & Barr Co. Thorpes had been graded by PSA at the time of this writing.

In the M101-5 set, Thorpe is pictured as a member of the New York Giants with bat in hand. Thorpe would play a total of six seasons in the big leagues as an outfielder, with most of the time spent with New York. He also had short stints with the Cincinnati Reds and Boston Braves. In New York, Thorpe had the chance to play for future Hall of Famer John McGraw. Felix Mendelsohn would release an additional set later in 1916, the M101-4 issue. Both sets contain 200 cards, but the checklists are slightly different. For example, Thorpe only appears in M101-5 on card #176. The card numbers can be found centered at the very base of the fronts. Even though the issues that depict Thorpe as a football player, such as the 1933 Goudey Sport Kings and 1955 Topps All-American sets, are more popular, the M101-5 Thorpe is his most desirable baseball card and it dates to his active days as a professional athlete.

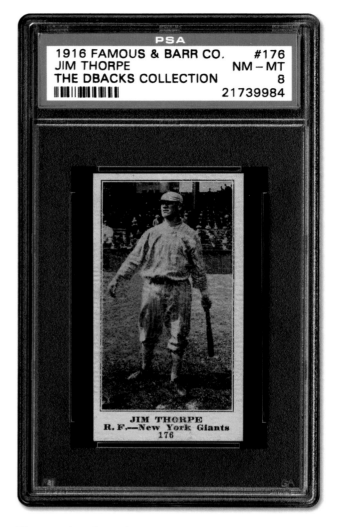

This card is the sole Famous & Barr Co. example to reach the PSA NM-MT 8 grading tier with none higher in the PSA Population Report.

The Legend

Considered one of the greatest all-around athletes if not *THE* greatest all-around athlete ever, Jim Thorpe excelled at whatever sport he participated in. An Olympic gold medal winner, professional football player, professional baseball player, and yes, professional basketball player, James Francis Thorpe did just about everything except sell hot dogs.

A product of the Carlisle Indian Industrial School in Pennsylvania, Thorpe was born on May 28, 1887, in Indian Territory near Prague, Oklahoma. A member of the Sac and Fox Nation, his Native American name was Wa-Tho-Huk which means "Bright Path." At Carlisle, Thorpe developed his track & field, football, and baseball skills under the tutelage of the legendary Pop Warner, but football was his passion. Considered one of the best running backs and kickers in the country, Thorpe led Carlisle to victories over Ivy League competitors Harvard, Yale, and Army. Named first team All-American in 1911 and 1912, Thorpe led Carlisle to a 12–1–1 season and the National Collegiate Championship in 1912 after his return from the Olympics.

At 24 years old, the 6-foot-1, 185-pound Thorpe had qualified for track and field events in the 1912 Olympics in Stockholm, Sweden. He traveled by ship with the US team, and it is said he used "visualization" to train during the voyage. Powerful, fast, and focused, Thorpe decimated the competition, winning gold medals in both the decathlon and pentathlon. He received a hero's welcome with a ticker tape parade in New York City upon his return to the States. More than six months later, it came to light that Thorpe had been paid a pittance to play semi-pro baseball during the summer months in 1909 and 1910. Although the rules stated that a protest against a gold medalist must occur within thirty days, the Olympic Committee promptly revoked his amateur status, took back his gold medals, and wiped his glorious achievements from the Olympic record books.

No longer constrained by amateur status, Thorpe turned his sights on professional athletics. In 1913, he signed with the New York Giants as a major-league ballplayer, and for the next six seasons he played outfield for the Giants, Cincinnati Reds, and finally the Boston Braves. Thorpe had mixed success as a part-time player, batting .252 for his career average. He did have one very good season as a part-timer, batting .327 with 159 at-bats in 1919, his last year with the Braves. He then played minor-league baseball through the 1922 season.

Thorpe started to play professional football in between his baseball seasons in 1915. That was the year he brought his star power to the Canton Bulldogs. An outstanding running back, kicker, and defensive back, Thorpe led the Bulldogs to the league championship in 1916, 1917, and 1919. Canton joined 13 other teams in 1920 to form the American Professional Football Association (APFA) and Thorpe was named the first president of the organization. That was before the AFPA became the NFL in 1922. Thorpe was player-coach of the 1920 Bulldogs, 1921 Cleveland Indians, and the 1922–1923 Oorang Indians, a pro football team solely made up of Native Americans. Named first-team All-Pro in 1923, Thorpe then played for the Rock Island Independents, New York Giants, Canton Bulldogs, Chicago Cardinals, and several barnstorming teams including the Tampa Cardinals before he retired after the 1928 season.

Thorpe's basketball career was not as eventful as his baseball and football careers, but it existed, nonetheless. The "Jim Thorpe and his World-Famous Indians" basketball team barnstormed for a few years in the late 1920s. Not much is known about this team except for the fact that they went from town to town entertaining crowds and featuring Thorpe as the star.

In addition to his tremendous versatility as a player in major sports, Thorpe was a successful coach. Because of his popularity throughout the country, Thorpe was in demand as a celebrity speaker about Indian affairs and other topics. He also travelled with his own song and dance troupe, "The Jim Thorpe Show," and later worked for the city of Chicago as the superintendent of parks and recreation. From 1931 to 1950, he was a character actor in several Hollywood

Jim Thorpe

the age of 64 in his Lomita, California, home. In 1982, the Olympic committee finally restored the gold medals that were taken from Thorpe. His name was reinstated in the Olympic record books, but only as a co-champion along with the medalists who were elevated after Thorpe was disqualified. He was inducted into the US Olympic Hall of Fame in 1983 and, to this day, advocates continue to lobby for Thorpe to be on record as sole champion of the 1912 Olympic decathlon and pentathlon.

When you look at his body of work, along with the honors he received, Jim Thorpe secured his legacy as one of the greatest athletes of all-time. His honors are too numerous to list, but here are just a few. In 1950, the Associated Press named him the "greatest American football player" and the "greatest overall male athlete" of the first half of the twentieth century. A member of the NFL's All-Decade team of the 1920s and the NFL's 50th anniversary All-Time team, "The Legend" was inducted to the Pro Football Hall of Fame as a charter member in 1963. He was inducted into the College Football Hall of Fame in 1951, and the USA Track & Field Hall of Fame in 1975. From 1955 to 2008, the Jim Thorpe Memorial Trophy was awarded annually to the NFL MVP. Since 1986, the Jim Thorpe Award has been given annually to the top defensive back in college football. The United States Postal Service honored Thorpe with commemorative stamps issued in 1984 and 1998. Jim "Bright Path" Thorpe will always be remembered as a truly special athlete.

movies, and he was technical advisor for the 1951 movie *Jim Thorpe-All American,* in which Burt Lancaster had the starring role. Although he always worked, Thorpe struggled financially to care for his eight children. As he got older, he even took menial jobs to provide for his family, working as a doorman, construction worker, ditch digger, security guard, and in the merchant marine.

On March 28, 1953, Jim Thorpe was stricken by a heart attack and died at

WHEN BABE RUTH WAS IN HIS PRIME, a prime that seemed to last longer than most, it was hard for contemporary stars to compete for attention. Even though fellow legend and teammate Lou Gehrig didn't crave it, no matter how well he performed on the field, "The Iron Horse" never seemed to escape Ruth's shadow until "The Sultan of Swat" spit his last breath at the game. The same phenomenon impacts the trading card world. Some cards demand the lion's share of collector interest, leaving other fantastic issues underappreciated or overlooked by comparison. With Ruth, his rookie-era cards and later-career Goudeys tend to command more collector curiosity than others, but some of the most interesting Ruth cards ever made have yet to enjoy the limelight.

The 1927 E126 American Caramel Ruth is one of them. The set, which contains 60 black-and-white cards, was the final release in a run that began in 1908 for American Caramel. In recent years, the Ruth cards that inhabit the sets from the 1920s have started to garner more respect from collectors, as prices have been steadily moving up across the board. The earlier E120, E121, and E122 sets were all distributed near the beginning of Ruth's rise to stardom in New York. The company ceased production in 1922 and returned five years later to issue the E126 set. It is believed that this set was printed in fewer numbers compared to American Caramel's earlier efforts. Even though the set itself is not as popular as some of the other sets issued by American Caramel, there are two aspects to the E126 Ruth that make it extremely attractive.

First and foremost, this card dates to Ruth's 60-home-run season, a number that was quite unfathomable at the time. Ruth's exploits are numerous and his stats are gaudy, but what he was known for beyond all else was his thunderous bat. Ruth changed the game from hit-and-run to hit-and-trot singlehandedly with it. Historians still debate which of his many prolific seasons was his best, and Ruth has several that warrant consideration, but 1927 is the one that helped define the legend the most. The game's best player reached 60 while playing for, arguably,

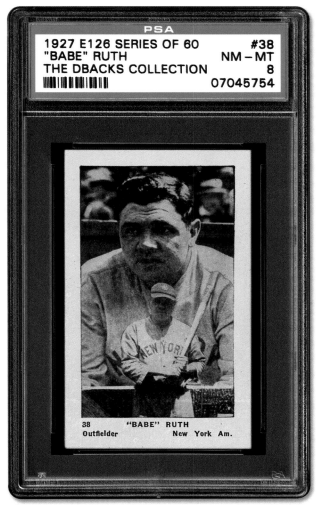

This card is the sole example to reach the PSA NM-MT 8 grading tier with none higher in the PSA Population Report.

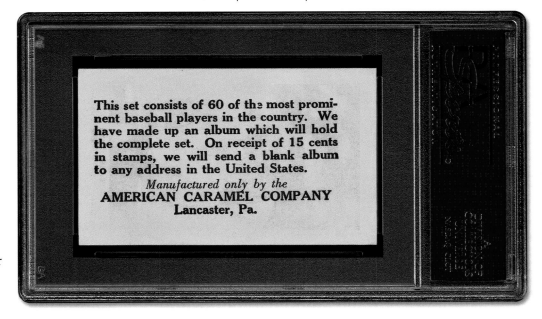

baseball's best team historically. That home-run mark lasted until 1961, when Roger Maris eclipsed it by one dinger.

Beyond its connection to this special season, the card itself was treated differently than all others in the set. The card features a montage, with a portrait of Ruth hovering above a smaller image of the slugger holding his favorite weapon. The powerful combination of images not only makes this a standout card in the set based on its unique design, but it is so fitting for the man who had an ability to command the stage more than any other player in baseball history.

OVER THE COURSE OF A CAREER, many athletes were featured on a variety of trading cards, from the familiar to the esoteric. When it comes to the incomparable Babe Ruth, his appearances were numerous, at least for the time. Ruth's career in cardboard begins with an ultra-rarity in the 1914 Baltimore News minor league set and continues on through a diverse menu of candy issues in the 1920s to a post-mortem cameo with Leaf not long after his passing. The card brand that Ruth is most closely associated with, however, is Goudey. The four Ruth cards that reside in the 1933 Goudey set are his most popular, but there is another Ruth issue that combines the same basic design with superior difficulty.

The World Wide Gum Company entered the fold in 1933, after partnering with Goudey, to issue the colorful baseball cards in Canada. In essence, World Wide Gum operated as a Canadian-based Goudey company per the arrangement. Their first "Canadian" effort, launched in 1933, closely resembled the American version. In 1934, World Wide Gum took a slightly different approach by utilizing both the 1933 and 1934 Goudey design in the same set. The lone Ruth card, which is #28 in the 1934 World Wide Gum issue, is largely based on the #53 card in the 1933 Goudey set. In fact, cards numbered 1–48 shared the 1933 look, while cards 49–96 were made with the 1934 Goudey design. Of course, Ruth was not included in the 1934 Goudey set at all, with Lou Gehrig taking over as the centerpiece.

While the general construction of the World Wide Gum cards mimicked their Goudey counterparts, there are a few differences that help collectors clearly distinguish the two issues. Since the cards were distributed in Canada, they were printed in English and French on the reverse. In 1934, the dual language approach was incorporated throughout after featuring bilingual text on only a portion of the cards the year before. Near the base of the card, "WORLD WIDE GUM CO., LTD. MONTREAL" is followed by "Printed in Canada" just beneath it, which further separates the Canadian version from Goudey. Interestingly, a statement appears on the back that reads, "This is one of a series of 240 Baseball Stars" even though the World Wide Gum set was only 96 cards. The 240-card mention is in reference to the 1933 Goudey set. Why the company left that in the text is a mystery.

To put its scarcity into proper perspective, PSA had graded less than 75 total examples of the 1934 World Wide Gum Ruth card at the time of this writing, while nearly 1,000 copies of the card it resembles most—the 1933 Goudey #53—were logged in the PSA Population Report. The American Goudeys are certainly more popular, especially when it comes to set building, but the World Wide Gum Ruth is an often-overlooked option for collectors seeking a loftier challenge or trying to fill the void left by the Goudey base product in 1934.

The Sultan of Swat

Continued from page 32.

The 1927 Yankees are widely considered the greatest baseball team ever assembled. With the likes of Ruth, Gehrig, and several more future Hall of Famers, the "Murderers' Row" Yankees won 110 games and swept the Pittsburgh Pirates in the World Series. That same season, Ruth was in a race for the home-run title with teammate Gehrig and after going on a hot streak in September, he left the young first baseman in the dust, hitting 60 homeruns to Gehrig's 47. It was an achievement that seemed untouchable until Roger Maris blasted 61 homers in 1961. The Yankees took up where they left off in 1928, finishing with 101 wins and sweeping the St. Louis Cardinals in the World Series. Ruth batted .323 during the regular season, swatting 54 home runs and batted an incredible .625 in the Series. For a second time, he hit three home runs in one game, Game Four, of the Series.

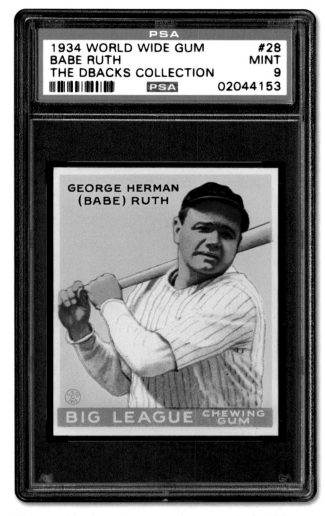

This card is the sole example to reach the PSA Mint 9 grading tier with none higher in the PSA Population Report.

In 1929, Ruth married longtime friend Claire Hodgson. He had married Helen Woodford in 1914, and they adopted a baby girl, Dorothy, in 1921, but because Helen was not interested in the limelight or Ruth's infidelities, they had lived apart for several years. Tragically, Helen died in a house fire in January of 1929, and Ruth married Claire in April of that same year. Although the 1929 season was a forgettable one for the Yankees, who finished 16 games behind the Philadelphia Athletics, Ruth had another successful season, batting .345 with 46 home runs and 154 RBI. He once again barnstormed after the season, and fans throughout the country came out to see the great Babe Ruth. Kids especially loved him, and the feeling was mutual. One day in Waco, Texas, Ruth invited kids to come out on the field during the exhibition game. Thousands of kids ran

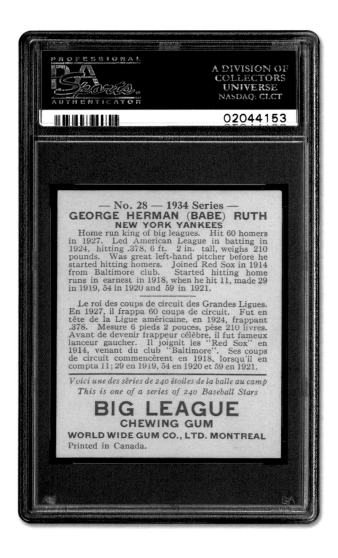

and throwing lemons at the 37-year-old slugger. In the first inning, Ruth hit a three-run shot off Chicago pitcher Charlie Root. In the fifth inning, with the count of two balls and two strikes, Ruth reportedly gestured to center-field before slamming a 500-foot home run to center-field. The incident became known as "Babe Ruth's Called Shot." There is no conclusive evidence in film footage that Ruth actually pointed to center-field, but as he rounded the bases, he taunted the Cubs bench indicating that he made the call. It all added to the legend of Babe Ruth.

Ruth was in a race for the home-run title with teammate Gehrig and after going on a hot streak in September, he left the young first baseman in the dust, hitting 60 homeruns to Gehrig's 47.

No longer in his prime, Ruth still had a decent season in 1933, batting .301 with 34 home runs and 104 RBI. He played in the first-ever All-Star game and appropriately hit the first home run in All-Star history. With his age, weight, and Father Time finally catching up with him, the 1934 season would be Ruth's last in pinstripes. Although he hit a respectable .288 with 22 home runs, he had a difficult time playing the outfield and even circling the bases was tough for him. For years, Ruth had lobbied to become player-manager of the Yankees, but with Joe McCarthy firmly entrenched, owner Jacob Ruppert denied him the opportunity, although he did offer Ruth a minor-league managing job. On February 26, 1935, he was traded to the Boston Braves. Emil Fuchs, owner of the Braves, had promised Ruth a team vice presidency, an assistant manager position, and some equity in the Braves. Ruth soon discovered that Fuchs had no intention of keeping any of those promises. After playing in just 28 games, the 40-year-old Ruth retired on May 30, 1935. He then played golf, made public appearances, and coached for the Brooklyn Dodgers for a brief time. Ruth was honored the next year as part of the first induction class of the Hall of Fame, receiving over 95% of the votes.

out of the stands and rushed the field to see their hero. It stopped the game, but Ruth was loving it, laughing, and enjoying the sea of children. With a new contract valued at $80,000, Ruth and the Yankees entered the 1930 season with high expectations, but the pinstripes finished third and the Athletics won yet another World Series. Ruth had another great season though, batting .359 with 49 homers and 153 RBI.

The next season, under new manager Joe McCarthy, the Yankees could not catch the powerful A's. Ruth continued to dominate offensively, leading the league with 46 home runs. In 1932, things turned around for the Yankees. They won 107 games to take the American League pennant. Ruth's performance in the 1932 World Series only enhanced the legend of the Bambino. In Game Three in Chicago, the Cubs fans were relentlessly hostile, screaming insults

During World War II, Ruth raised funds for the war effort by playing in exhibition games and making appearances,

but in 1946, he began to experience discomfort in his eye and throat. He entered French Hospital in New York City for tests, where it was determined that Ruth had an inoperable malignant tumor. Losing weight rapidly as well as his voice, Ruth recuperated in Florida after radiation and chemotherapy treatments. On April 27, 1947, nearly 60,000 fans attended Babe Ruth Day at Yankee Stadium to honor the struggling Ruth who spoke briefly to thank the fans. During a remission period, Ruth made public speaking appearances around the country and even did some work for the Ford Motor Company. He also made good his promise to "Do something for the kids of America" by establishing the Babe Ruth Foundation to give financial support to needy children.

Ruth was able to attend the ceremony in Yankee Stadium on June 13, 1948, when his number "3" was retired but, sadly, his condition soon took a turn for the worse. On

August 16, 1948, the Bambino passed away at the age of 53. When Ruth was waked at Yankee Stadium with an open casket, 77,000 mourning fans filed past to pay their respects. He was laid to rest at the Gate of Heaven Cemetery in Hawthorne, New York. In 1949, a granite monument honoring Ruth was placed in Yankee Stadium's Monument Park. It is not necessary to list Babe Ruth's individual achievements and career statistics as every baseball fan knows his accomplishments go way beyond home runs, batting average, and pitching greatness. The Sultan of Swat is bigger than life, even today. Ruth has had a lasting impact on the game of baseball and on American society in general. In 2018, he was posthumously awarded the Presidential Medal of Freedom. A final award for the greatest player who ever lived.

Willie Mays 1969 signed game-used jersey, Mays game-used batting helmet circa 1960s, and Mays game-used bat circa 1962. *The Mike Heffner Collection.*

5

The Golden Boys (1935–1953)

★ ★ ★ ★ ★ ★ ★ ★ ★ ★ ★ ★ ★ ★ ★

This grouping of iconic baseball cards gives us a visual look at the time period from the last days of the Great Depression, through World War II, and into the Golden Age

of Baseball and the Korean War days. Players like Williams and DiMaggio moved from talented rookies to firmly established superstars. Jackie Robinson opened the doors for Black players, and a new young star, Willie Mays, was emerging. The pristine

1952 Topps Wille Mays #261 and 1953 Topps Willie Mays # 244 included in this grouping are the only known examples to achieve the PSA 10 Gem Mint grading level. Meet the players featured on the exceptional cards showcased in this chapter.

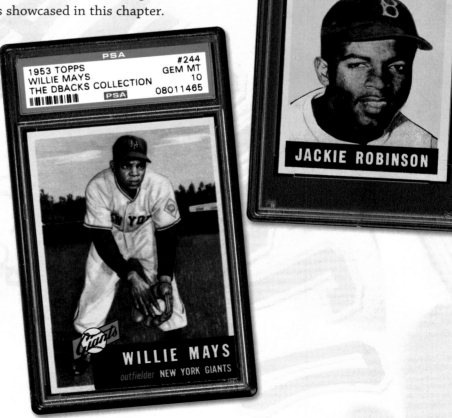

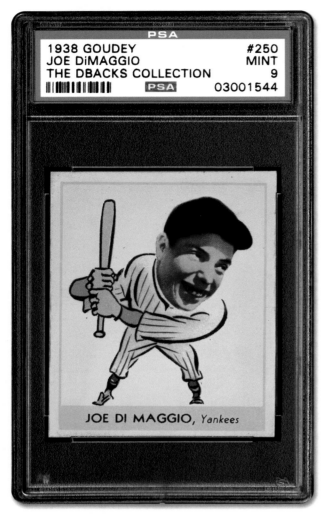

This PSA Mint 9 is one of two examples graded at that tier, with none higher in the PSA Population Report.

BEFORE THE DISTINCTIVE 1938 GOUDEY SET was released, Joe DiMaggio appeared in a handful of other issues. DiMaggio can be found in the 1936 World Wide Gum and 1937 O-Pee-Chee sets, which are both Canadian issues, to name a few. In fact, DiMaggio appeared in the 1933–1936 Zeenut series, which captured "Joltin' Joe" when he was playing in the Pacific Coast League before he joined the New York Yankees. Each of these cards are tough and desirable in their own right, but the two DiMaggio cards that reside in the 1938 Goudey set are considered by many hobbyists to be the first to gain mainstream acceptance.

This relatively small but incredibly condition-sensitive set is comprised of 48 total cards. Oddly, the set begins with card

#241. Why, you might ask? Even though Goudey released baseball card sets from 1934–1936, the company decided to pick up where the 1933 set, which contained 240 cards, left off. The 1938 set features 24 different subjects, with each one appearing in the set twice. All the cards in the set show a superimposed headshot of each player attached to a caricature of their body. Cards 241–264 offer a plain, off-white background behind the cartoon, while cards 265–288 include small illustrations and text around the figure. At one time, it was believed that the high-number series was more difficult than the low-number run, but there seems to be no discernable difference between the two groups when it comes to population numbers today.

In addition to print defects and poor centering/image tilts being common to the issue, border toning is more pronounced on this Goudey release than any other in their

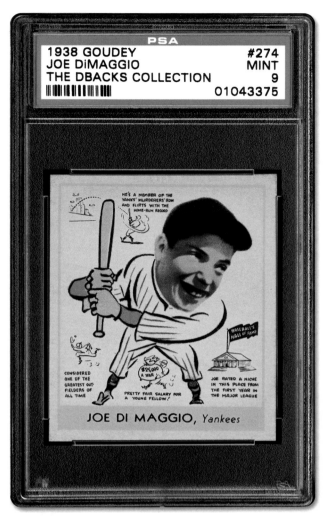

This PSA Mint 9 is one of three examples graded at that tier, with none higher in the PSA Population Report.

history. Collectors will notice a wide variance in color and consistency when it comes to the frame on these cards. Ironically, they are the exact opposite of what DiMaggio was as a player throughout his career, a man who was as consistent at the plate as they come, year after year. In addition to various shades of color, the borders will often have a blotchy look to them, similar to what you might encounter on the 1948/1949 Leaf set. This characteristic is so common to the issue that it seldom impacts the grade.

The set, which is believed to have been produced in far fewer numbers than Goudey's 1933 and 1934 sets, combines scarcity with the kind of childlike fun that reminds us all why we collect in the first place. It takes us back to a more innocent time in our lives when things were seemingly

simple. There was nothing simple, however, about DiMaggio...who might have been the most complicated man to ever don pinstripes.

The Yankee Clipper

Continued from page 51.

A fan favorite from his rookie season on, Joe DiMaggio helped the Yankees to the 1936, 1937, 1938, and 1939 world championships. By 1941, at age 26, he had won two American League batting titles and an MVP, but the best was yet to come.

Joe DiMaggio

The Streak. On May 15, 1941, DiMaggio stepped up to the plate and hit a single in his first at-bat in a game against the Chicago White Sox. Little did he, his teammates, or fans know this would be the beginning of a streak that may never be broken. "The Yankee Clipper" would get at least one hit in the next 55 consecutive games. Initially, not much was made of DiMaggio's streak, but as the games passed and the streak continued, both the press and the fans began to take notice. The American League record of 41 games was held by Hall of Famer George Sisler. First, "Joltin' Joe" broke the Yankee record of 29 consecutive games held by both Roger Peckinpaugh and Earle Combs and as DiMaggio approached Sisler's 41 consecutive game hits record, it became a national story. On June 29, 1941, DiMaggio tied Sisler's record in the first game of a doubleheader between the Yankees and the Washington Senators. In the second game, DiMaggio hit a double to break the record.

"The Streak" was on the front page of every newspaper in America. Fans across the country tuned in on their radios to get the most up-to-date information on DiMaggio's progress.

Next on the radar was the major-league record of 44 consecutive games held by "Wee Willie" Keeler. At Yankee Stadium on July 1, DiMaggio tied Keeler's record and on July 2 against the Red Sox, he blasted a two-run homer extending the streak to 45 to break the record. However, DiMaggio was not finished. By this time, "The Streak" was on the front page of every newspaper in America. Fans across the country tuned in on their radios to get the most up-to-date information on DiMaggio's progress. To capitalize on the national interest during his streak, the Les Brown Orchestra recorded a hit tune, "Joltin' Joe DiMaggio." The "Yankee Clipper" had become a national phenomenon. Finally, on July 17, 1941, it all came to an end in a game at Cleveland. Baseball historians, statisticians, and fans all believe DiMaggio's 56-game hitting streak will never be broken. DiMaggio won the 1941 Most Valuable Player Award, beating out Ted Williams who also made history that summer with his .406 batting average.

The Yankees went on to win the pennant and defeat the Brooklyn Dodgers in five games for the 1941 World Series championship. Sadly, life in America changed on December 7, 1941, when the Japanese bombed Pearl Harbor. As a result, the 1942 season would be the last for DiMaggio and many other ballplayers for the next three years. It was not one of DiMaggio's best. He batted just .305, very good for most players, but not Joe DiMaggio. That year, the Yankees won the AL pennant but lost the Series to the St. Louis Cardinals in five games. In 1943, DiMaggio enlisted in the US Army Air Force, and for three seasons he played exhibition baseball to entertain the troops. DiMaggio and his wife were divorced when he came home during war leave. When he returned to the Yankees in 1946, the rusty DiMaggio batted a career low of .290.

The 1947 season started slowly after DiMaggio had surgery for a bone spur in his heel and he did not heat up until May. Although his numbers that season were not typical for him (.315 average, 20 home runs, 97 RBI), DiMaggio played flawless defense to lead the Yankees to the AL pennant and a seven-game defeat of the Brooklyn Dodgers in the World Series. The highlight of the Series was an over-the-head catch made by Dodgers utility man Al Gionfriddo in Game Six, which robbed DiMaggio of what could have been either an extra base hit or a home run. Although his 1947 offensive numbers were not spectacular, DiMaggio continued to shine in the outfield to win his third MVP Award.

In 1948, the 33-year-old DiMaggio came back strong, batting .320 and leading the league with 39 bombs and 155 RBI. He finished second in the MVP voting, but the Yankees finished in third place. Entering the 1949 season with a new $100,000 contract, DiMaggio missed the first 65 games due to a foot injury but came back to bat .346 that season. He was honored in October in front of 69,500 fans at Yankee Stadium for "Joe DiMaggio Day," and the Yankees defeated the Brooklyn Dodgers in five games for the 1949 World Series title. Heading into the new decade, the Yankees swept the Philadelphia Phillies to win yet another World Series championship, but age was starting to catch up to DiMaggio. In 1950, he played in 139 games, batting a respectable .301 with 32 home runs and 122 RBI. However, the 1951 season would be his last. Batting just .263, the 36-year-old DiMaggio understood his skills were diminishing and he decided to call it quits in December. Just like Ruth

handed the torch to Gehrig, and Gehrig handed the torch to DiMaggio, it was time for "Joltin' Joe" to hand the torch to the next young Yankees superstar, a rookie named Mickey Mantle.

After a few uneventful years, the shy, reserved baseball icon rocked the entertainment and baseball world in 1954 by marrying Marilyn Monroe, the most famous actress in the world. The marriage lasted only nine months because DiMaggio became very jealous and controlling. Although the marriage ended, he remained devoted to Monroe and never remarried. In 1962, Monroe died from an overdose, and for the next 20 years, DiMaggio had flowers delivered to her grave twice a week. DiMaggio worked in and out of baseball and appeared at select celebrity events. In the

1970s, he regained national attention as spokesperson for "Mr. Coffee" coffee makers. A whole young generation of television viewers knew DiMaggio only as "Mr. Coffee." Like many athletes back then, DiMaggio was a heavy smoker. In October 1998, he was diagnosed with lung cancer, and sadly, on March 8, 1999, "The Yankee Clipper" passed away at age 84. DiMaggio's monument was installed in Monument Park at Yankee Stadium in April 1999 alongside the other Yankees greats. Although he lost three prime seasons to military service, DiMaggio's .325 lifetime average, 56-game hitting streak, 13 All-Star appearances, three MVPs, and nine world championships combine to make him more than special. "The Yankee Clipper" was elected to the Hall of Fame in 1955. The last great baseball icon of the radio era, DiMaggio's legend continues to this day.

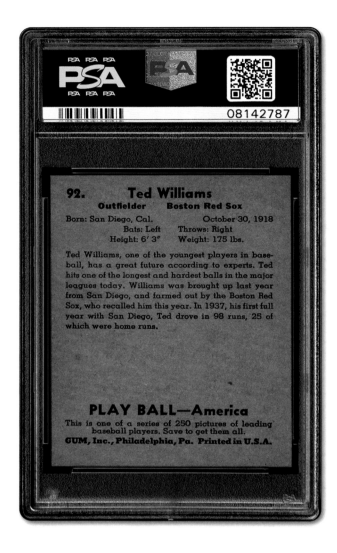

This PSA Mint 9 is one of 12 examples graded at that tier, with one higher in the PSA Population Report.

THROUGHOUT SPORTS CARD HISTORY, there are many examples of colorful artwork and masterful designs that draw the collector in, from the radiant 1933 Goudeys to the beaming 1955 Topps set in the vintage era. This is, of course, especially true in the modern era of card manufacturing, where some cards are so reflective in nature that you'd swear they came with a battery. In other cases, the simplicity of a card harkens back to another time and helps add to the nostalgic feel of a vintage treasure. That is certainly the case with the 1939 Play Ball Ted Williams rookie.

Fittingly, the slender, young Williams is pictured finishing his legendary swing, a swing that would give him the label

of the greatest hitter who ever lived by many. Whether you choose Williams or Babe Ruth in the debate, their hitting prowess is virtually interchangeable when it comes to their effectiveness at the plate. Like Ruth, the tales of Williams and his bat make him more than a mere mortal. Just watch footage from the 1999 MLB All-Star Game at Fenway Park and observe the reactions from the best players in the game when the legendary Williams took center stage. The 1939 Play Ball set has never been incredibly popular due to the black-and-white design; however, the lack of color adds to the charm of the iconic rookie card. Along with the Joe DiMaggio (#26), the Williams rookie is the clear star of the 161-card issue. Other than subpar centering and occasional print defects, the card is not as condition-sensitive as other noteworthy issues of the period.

This card represents the beginning of a career, and life, like no other. It was also the start of Williams' first run as a player before his career was interrupted by military service. For Williams, this happened on more than one occasion and robbed him of some prime years. While Williams lost hundreds of plate appearances as a result, his personal legend grew serving our country. There is something so captivating about a person who can do something better than anyone else, whether it is in sports, business, science, or art. Williams perfected the craft of hitting, at least as much as it can be perfected, better than anyone else. Williams obsessed about his craft, and that's what the great ones do. This card, which was issued during his first trip around the league, represents the birth of the master.

IN THE WORLD OF COLLECTING, THERE ARE TIMES

when so many positive things converge to make a card a product of a perfect storm. The 1941 Play Ball Ted Williams is a prime example. In the case of Williams, one could argue nearly every card the hitting titan was pictured on would fit that description, but this card offers a special kind of significance. It brings together a fable-like character with a classic set that was released during a year that, arguably, captures what "Teddy Ballgame" was about more than any other card issue as a player. It was a season that defined his grit and his greatness. Whether he was at the plate or flying combat missions in the sky, Williams feared nothing.

Going into the final day of the 1941 season, Williams made a decision that some athletes would not have the courage to make. The Red Sox legend decided to play in a doubleheader against the Philadelphia Athletics, thus jeopardizing his chance to finish the season with a .400 batting average. If Williams would have simply sat out that last day, he would have done something only one other player (Bill Terry) had done since 1930...but that wasn't Williams. His competitive nature and quest for perfection at the plate wouldn't allow him to sit. Instead, Williams ended up going 6-for-8, raising his average to .406. Even though he finished second in the MVP voting to Joe DiMaggio, Williams finished the season with 37 homers, 120 RBI, 147 walks and a .553 OBP. For Williams, it was just another day at the office.

The 1941 Play Ball set is comprised of 72 total cards and it contains a host of top names of the day, including the likes of Joe DiMaggio, Jimmie Foxx, Hank Greenberg, and Mel

This PSA Mint 9 is one of nine examples graded at that tier, with none higher in the PSA Population Report.

Ott. The Play Ball brand (1939–1941) began with a black-and-white design in 1939, which then moved to a sepia-toned look in 1940, before ending the three-year run with a full-color product in 1941. For that reason, and despite being the smallest of the three releases by far in terms of card count, the 1941 Play Ball set has long been the collector favorite of the trio. The Williams card, which offers a colorized version of his 1940 Play Ball image, is often found off–center, with border toning and variances in the color of the background acting as common condition obstacles as well.

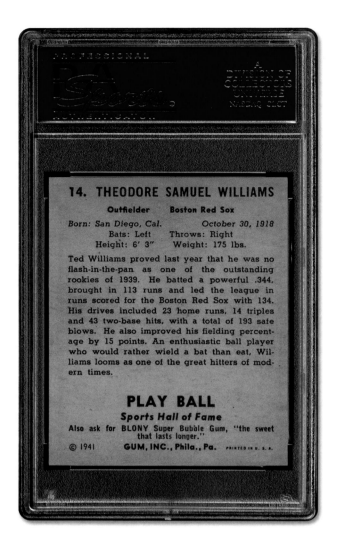

Teddy Ballgame

Continued from page 57.

A young phenom, Ted Williams wowed Boston fans as a rookie in 1939 and continued his excellent performance in his second MLB season, but for "Teddy Ballgame," the 1941 season proved to be one for the ages. He won the All-Star Game for the American League by hitting a game-winning three-run home run in the ninth inning. The second half of the season captured the imagination of the baseball world on two fronts. Yankees great Joe DiMaggio was on a mission to break the record for consecutive game hits and Williams was on track to bat .400 for the season. On the final day of the season, Ted Williams was right at the .400

mark entering into a doubleheader against the Philadelphia Athletics. Manager Joe Cronin offered to sit Williams so he could end the season with the .400 average, but he declined, wanting to do it the right way. Williams went on to have a 6-for-8 day at the plate and ended the season batting .406. At the time of this writing, no other player has reached the .400 milestone since Williams achieved it. That year Williams also topped the league with 37 home runs and 135 runs, while banging in 120 runs to help the Red Sox to a second-place finish. Although Williams' offensive performance is considered one of the best, if not the overall best, of all time, DiMaggio won the 1941 MVP Award with his 56-game hitting streak.

The world changed on December 7, 1941. The Japanese bombed Pearl Harbor and launched our country into World War II. Like many other major-league players, Ted Williams was drafted in 1942, but was granted a deferment because he was the sole supporter of his mother at that point. There was a backlash from both the media and fans who thought Williams should serve immediately. Instead, he joined the US Navy Reserve in May of 1942. During the 1942 season he batted .356 with 36 home runs and 137 RBI, to win the Triple Crown. He was called to active duty in November 1943 and in 1944, Williams was commissioned to second lieutenant in the US Marines as a naval aviator. He became a proficient aviator and gunner, and soon became a pilot training instructor. That year, Williams married Doris Soule, which would be his first of three marriages.

Williams returned to the Red Sox in 1946, at age 27, having missed three critical seasons during his prime. The 1946 Red Sox, with the likes of Williams, Johnny Pesky, Bobby Doerr, Dom DiMaggio and twenty-game winners Tex Hughson and Dave Feriss, won the American League pennant but lost the World Series to the St. Louis Cardinals in seven games. After suffering an elbow injury, Williams had a tough World Series and would never have the opportunity to play in another Fall Classic. In 1947, with a new $70,000 contract in hand, "Teddy Ballgame" won his second Triple Crown, blasted 32 home runs, batted .343, and drove in 114 runs. He continued his offensive onslaught in 1948, hitting his 222nd home run to tie Jimmie Foxx for the Red Sox record. The Sox and Cleveland Indians ended the season in a wild finish with identical records. In the one-game playoff to get into the World Series, the Sox lost to the Indians 8–3. Named the 1949 American League MVP, Williams had one of his greatest years, breaking Jimmie Foxx's home run record. The 30-year-old Williams batted .343, smacked 43 home runs to lead the league, and topped the AL with his 159 RBI. Again, the season got down to the final day, this time between the Sox and the Yankees, but the pinstripes prevailed, denying the Red Sox another shot at the World Series.

In the first televised All-Star Game, Williams injured his elbow in a leaping catch off the wall. Although that shortened the 1950 season for Williams, he hit over .300 in both 1950 and 1951 and averaged 27 home runs. Unfortunately, the Korean War put his career on hold for a second time. Captain Williams was called back to active military duty in May 1952, this time not as an instructor but as a combat pilot flying a F9F Panther Jet Fighter. As a member of the First Marine Air Wing, he flew a total of 39 missions. On one mission, his jet took on enemy fire, and burst into flames. Williams managed to get back to the base and made a belly landing. He jumped out of the cockpit and ran far enough to be out of danger before watching his plane burn on the runway. The next day he flew another mission. He also flew as a wingman for the future astronaut and senator, John Glenn, who later remarked that Ted Williams was one of the best pilots he ever worked with. In his book *John Glenn: A Memoir*, Glenn stated "There was certainly nothing 'bush' about him as a Marine combat pilot; he gave flying the same perfectionist's attention he

gave to his hitting." For his combat service, Williams earned several awards including the Air Medal with two Gold Stars. As the war neared its end, he was sent back to the States after developing pneumonia and an inner ear problem. Ted Williams received a hero's welcome when he returned to baseball.

Continued on page 133.

1948/1949 Leaf Jackie Robinson #79

IN RECENT TIMES, THERE IS ONE SPORTS FIGURE whose status has risen considerably in the hobby, perhaps more than any other name—Jackie Robinson. While it's true that Robinson has long been retired and deceased, his legend is growing. With so much focus on social justice issues, especially in the past couple of years, Robinson's contribution to the sport and society has been placed in an even more profound light. Of course, it's not that collectors didn't already know the story and appreciate what Robinson did to pave the way for so many who came after him. The new perspective has simply elevated Robinson to the Mount Olympus of icons.

The card, which was designated as a 1948 issue for decades, is now believed to have been released sometime in 1949. The specific dating of the cards is irrelevant as it pertains to market value, but it should be noted for accuracy. The 98-card, skip-numbered Leaf set is one of the most desirable productions of the era. It combines outstanding player selection with top-shelf difficulty when it comes to condition sensitivity. From Babe Ruth (post-playing days) to Satchel Paige to Ted Williams, the issue is absolutely loaded with stars, not to mention some very tough short prints throughout the set.

The Robinson card, like most cards in the set, can be challenging to locate in top grades due to the clear quality control deficiencies that plague the issue. Poor centering, inconsistent registration, color variances, paper stock problems, and print defects are commonly associated with the Leaf product. The Robinson card, which has always been regarded as one of *THE* cards to own in the hobby, has a background that ranges from very pale yellow to an almost yellow/orange color. The light-colored background, regardless of shade, makes it hard for dark print specks to hide. Robinson is pictured on a number of important issues, like the Bond Bread cards of the late-1940s and the more aesthetically attractive 1952 Topps, but the Leaf card is the one that possesses the most symbolic value of them all.

The Robinson card has always been regarded as one of THE cards to own in the hobby.

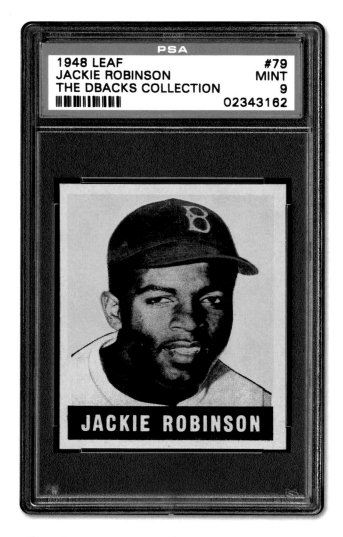

This PSA Mint 9 is one of seven examples graded at that tier, with none higher in the PSA Population Report.

Jackie

Considered one of the outstanding second baseman of all time, Jackie Robinson was a great Hall of Fame ballplayer. Taking it a step further, Jackie Robinson was the man who helped change the face of baseball and helped bridge the gap between Black and white. He was a real American hero.

Jack Roosevelt Robinson was born on January 31, 1919, in Cairo, Georgia. One of five children, Robinson had a difficult childhood. His father left when he was a baby, so his mother became the breadwinner of the struggling family.

Mallie Robinson decided to move her family to California, where she found work as a maid. She was able to purchase a home in Pasadena with the aid of government subsidies, but the family was harassed by neighbors just because they were Black. Jackie and his brothers got into many a fight to protect themselves, and they were usually on the winning side. Robinson was determined to rise above the racial bias by immersing himself in athletics. He attended Muir Technical High School and Pasadena Junior College, where he dominated in football, basketball, and baseball. Jackie went on to attend UCLA and became a star running back for the football team. Some considered him the best college running back in the country. He also starred on the basketball team, leading the conference in scoring during his junior and senior year but, due to financial issues, he dropped out before he graduated. Robinson went on to play semi-pro football in Hawaii before he was drafted in 1942. While in the army, he continued to contend with racial bias.

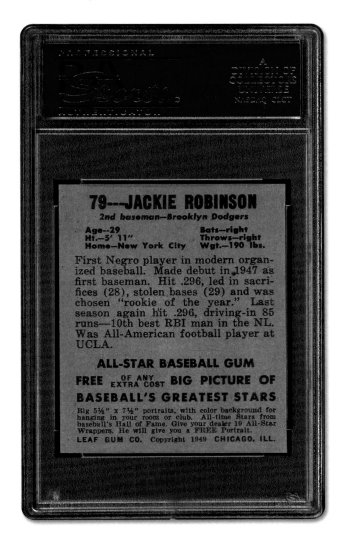

Robinson is pictured on a number of important issues, like the Bond Bread cards of the late-1940s and the more aesthetically attractive 1952 Topps, but the Leaf card is the one that possesses the most symbolic value of them all.

Jackie Robinson

Black player because he felt the time had come to include the great Negro League players in the all-white major leagues. The player Rickey chose would need to be capable of turning the other cheek when barraged with racial taunts by fans and opposing players. After a frank conversation between Rickey and Robinson, the young infielder was signed to a contract and assigned to the Dodgers' minor-league affiliate, the Montreal Royals. In 1946, Robinson reported for spring training in Daytona, Florida. Laws at the time would not allow him to stay with his teammates in the white-only team motel, so he found housing with a local Black couple. Robinson made his minor-league debut, going 4-for-5 against the Jersey City Giants. Surprisingly, the Royals fans showed great support for Robinson, who not only batted .349 with 40 stolen bases but led the Royals to the International League pennant.

In 1947, Robinson moved up to the big-league club, making his much-anticipated debut on April 11, 1947, playing first base in a pre-season game. Four days later, on April 15, he made his official debut, going hitless, but scoring a run, to become the first man to break MLB's color barrier. Robinson did experience pockets of discrimination from opposing players and even some of his own teammates. Some Dodgers players refused to play until manager Leo Durocher threatened to trade them. Some teams also threatened to strike until National League president Ford Frick made it clear that any player who refused to play would be suspended. The St. Louis Cardinals and Philadelphia Phillies players were particularly hostile, hurling racial slurs and even trying to

First, he was denied entrance into Officer Candidate School, and then he was not allowed to play on the camp baseball team. In 1944, Robinson infuriated his commanders by refusing to sit in the back of an army bus. They tried to court martial Robinson, but he was acquitted. He was honorably discharged, more or less just to get rid of him.

Following his military career, Robinson joined the Negro League's Kansas City Monarchs, where he batted .375 in 34 games in 1945 and was named an All-Star. While this was going on, the president and general manager of the Brooklyn Dodgers, Branch Rickey, was about to change Robinson's life and change the game of baseball forever. Rickey was looking to sign a talented injure Robinson. Yet, players like teammate Pee Wee Reese and opponent Hank Greenberg, among others, went out of their way to protect Robinson. Keeping his promise to Rickey, Robinson let his play on the field do the talking, batting .297 and winning Rookie of the Year honors. The Dodgers went on to capture the NL pennant but lost to the Yankees in seven games.

In 1948, Robinson had another good season batting .296 with 170 hits. The Dodgers drew enormous crowds both at home and on the road. Other Black payers began entering the league, easing the racial burden on Robinson. From that point on, he focused on improving his play, and by 1949, with the help of Hall of Famer, George Sisler, Robinson had the best year of his career, leading the league with his .342 batting average and 37 stolen bases while driving in 124 runs. That season, Robinson became the first Black player ever voted to the All-Star Team, and he was also named the National League MVP. By 1950, Robinson was the highest-paid player on the Dodgers team and justified the salary by batting .328. The 1951 season was one of the most exciting in baseball history. With his .338 average, Robinson led the Dodgers to a three-game tie breaker with the New York Giants. After Bobby Thomson's dramatic home run, the Giants won the pennant but lost the World Series to the Yankees.

In 1952, the Dodgers bounced back to win the National League pennant only to lose to the Yankees in seven games. Robinson had a decent season, batting .308 with 24 stolen bases. The next year, he moved from second base to play other infield positions, to make room for young second baseman Jim Gilliam. The 34-year-old Robinson posted another fine season, batting .329 in 1953, and he averaged .311 in 1954, his last of six-consecutive All-Star seasons. Finally in 1955, the Dodgers won their first world championship, although the aging Robinson played in only 105 games and batted a mediocre .256 as a part-time player. In his final season, 1956, he produced a .275 average with 98 hits and 10 home runs in 117 games. The Dodgers made it to the World Series to face the Yankees again but lost the seven-game contest. Although Robinson had a decent Series, he struck out in his last at-bat. It would be the last at-bat of his career. In January 1957, Jackie Robinson announced his retirement in a *Look Magazine* article. There was talk of the Dodgers trading him to the Giants to play alongside Willie Mays, but Robinson declined and remained retired.

The two-time stolen-base leader finished with a .313 lifetime batting average, 1,563 hits, six All-Star appearances, a Rookie of the Year Award, a NL Most Valuable Player Award, and a National League batting title.

Robinson moved on to corporate America, joining the Chock Full of Nuts coffee company as a vice president. He also went into the banking business, dabbled as a talk-show host, and remained a spokesperson for the civil rights movement. Robinson was elected to the Hall of Fame in 1962. Although he remained active, Robinson was diabetic, and his health began to decline. On October 24, 1972, Jackie Robinson passed away at the age of 53 after suffering a heart attack. His number 42 was permanently retired by every team in the major leagues 50 years after Robinson made his MLB debut. A courageous trailblazer, Jackie Robinson changed baseball, but more importantly, he helped change American history.

AFTER JACKIE ROBINSON BROKE THE MLB COLOR

barrier in 1947, a handful of other talented players from the Negro Leagues soon followed suit. One of those players was a stocky backstop by the name of Roy Campanella. Like Robinson, Campanella's career was relatively short, but the impact he had on the game was significant. All he needed was an opportunity, and Campanella received it in 1949, his first full season behind the plate. From 1949 through 1956, "Campy" was an All–Star. He won three NL MVPs (1951, 1953, and 1955) and was a fan favorite. With a simple smile from the gregarious catcher, you could sense the joy he brought to the sport.

After their initial release in 1948, when Bowman employed a black-and-white design, the company decided to incorporate some color in order to improve the issue's visual appeal. Bowman also increased the set's size, moving from 48 total cards to 240. It was a step in the right direction, as the 1949 set acted as a bridge to the next phase of development, a distinct look that lasted for three years (1950–1952). In 1949, the addition of color affected several historically important cards. In addition to official rookie cards of Campanella, Duke Snider, and Richie Ashburn; Robinson and Satchel Paige made their first Bowman appearances after being included in the contemporary Leaf product. The Campanella card, like others in the set, is often found with poor centering and border toning. Keep in mind that rough-cuts are common and not considered a detractor from a grading perspective, but the degree of roughness can vary.

Campanella, like other gifted players of the Negro Leagues, waited patiently for a chance in the major leagues. Unfortunately for Campanella, not only was his career cut short on the front end, but a brutal car accident brought his career to an abrupt close on the back end. In 1958, after Campanella was paralyzed from the crash, the tragic event was commemorated in the 1959 Topps set on card #550 entitled "Symbol Of Courage." Fans and collectors loved him. No greater evidence of that was shown than during an exhibition game in 1959, one that was scheduled in part to honor the beloved member of the Brooklyn Dodgers. Over 93,000 fans attended to cheer for him one last time as former teammate Pee Wee Reese pushed the wheelchair Campanella was seated in onto the field. It was the largest crowd ever assembled for a baseball game. This says more about the man than any words ever could.

This PSA Gem Mint 10 is one of only two examples to reach PSA's highest grading tier.

Campy

It is a melancholy fact that, in some cases, the end of a great baseball player's career is more remembered than the career itself. This can be said for the legendary Lou Gehrig and another rugged ballplayer whose career was cut short by tragedy. Roy Campanella began his professional baseball career in the Negro Leagues. Following the barrier-breaking lead of fellow Negro League star Jackie Robinson, he signed with the Brooklyn Dodgers and became the backstop and backbone of one of baseball's all-time greatest teams.

A sturdy and solid catcher, Campanella was as tough as they come, Brooklyn's version of the similarly stout Yankee Yogi Berra. Both of these men were born to be catchers. They were strong, built low to the ground, smart, and ferociously competitive. Campanella was amazingly adept at handling the talented Brooklyn pitching staffs with players like Johnny Podres, Sandy Koufax, Don Newcombe, Carl Erskine, Clem Labine, Don Drysdale, and Preacher Roe. Those men had no hesitation in taking the ball, but their success was buoyed by the man to whom they were throwing the ball. Born in Philadelphia, Pennsylvania, the 5-foot-9, 190-pound Campanella broke into the professional ranks in 1937 with the Washington Elite Giants. After six plus seasons with Washington/Baltimore, the two-time All-Star moved on to the Philadelphia Stars. In 1945, he returned to Baltimore and was again an All-Star, posting his best Negro League season to date with a league-leading 52

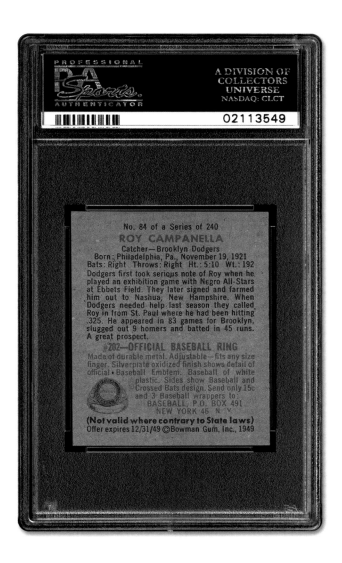

games, 48 runs scored, .385 batting average, and .479 OBP. In 1948, one year after Branch Rickey gave Jackie Robinson the opportunity to become Major League Baseball's first African American player, Campanella joined Number 42 at Ebbets Field. Campanella posted rather pedestrian numbers in 83 games with the Dodgers—a .258 batting average, nine homers, and 45 RBI, but those stats would serve as a prelude to greatness.

In 1949, the 27-year-old Campanella blossomed in what would be the first of eight consecutive All-Star seasons. He smashed 22 home runs, knocked in 82 runs, and batted .287 in 130 games. Moreover, he solidified the catcher's position for manager Burt Shotton, and the erstwhile loveable loser Dodgers won the National League pennant. In the World Series against the powerful New York Yankees, Brooklyn fell in five games. The club that was referred to both adoringly and derisively as "Dem Bums," had arrived. In 1951, Campanella took home the National League Most Valuable Player Award with a sterling season: 33 home runs, 108 RBI, and a .325 batting average. In addition, he remained a solid rock behind the plate, leading a pitching staff that included two 20-game winners, Newcombe and Roe. Brooklyn lost the pennant to their bitter rivals, the Giants, on Bobby Thomson's "Shot Heard 'Round the World" homer. Still, the man they called "Campy" had established himself as the best all-around catcher in the National League, on a definite par with his pinstriped rival Berra.

With players like Campanella, Robinson, Pee Wee Reese, Gil Hodges, Carl Furillo, and the sublime Duke Snider, Brooklyn would return to the World Series in 1952 and 1953, falling to the hated Yanks both times. In Brooklyn's 1952 World Series loss, Campy had one of his most disappointing efforts, batting just .214 in a seven-game heartbreaker. In 1953, his Series average improved to .273, with six hits including a home run as "Dem Bums" lost in six games. While the season did not end happily for a Dodgers team that won 105 games, 1953 was Campanella's best year ever. The 31-year-old star earned his second NL MVP Award with a career-high and league-leading 142 RBI, a career-high 41 dingers, and his .312 batting average.

Injuries curtailed his availability and production in 1954, but both Campanella and the Dodgers came to spring training in 1955 with renewed hope and determination to finally bring a World Series title to Brooklyn. Manager Walter Alston's

Roy Campanella

team ravaged the National League with 98 wins for the pennant. However, the specter of the Yankees awaited them in the Fall Classic. Campy had a comeback season in 1955, playing in 123 games and swatting 32 homers with 107 RBI at a .318 batting clip— good for his third MVP Award. Still, the Yankees, with a lineup that included Berra, Mickey Mantle, and Hank Bauer, along with pitchers Whitey Ford, Bob Turley, and Tommy Byrne, were expected to vanquish their cursed foes from Flatbush once again. Campanella and the Dodgers would have none of that. In an epic seven-game Series, Brooklyn finally defeated the Bombers to make history. Campanella had two home runs in the Series, but perhaps his greatest contribution was calling a great game and controlling the youthful excitement of Game Seven winner Johnny Podres. The borough of Brooklyn was delirious after winning the championship, and the Dodgers were the toasts of the town.

In 1956, Campanella would again achieve All-Star status, slugging 20 home runs along the way. A little more than a year later, the quiet leader of a National League dynasty would see his career end and life forever altered. It was January 1958 when Campanella lost control of his vehicle while driving to his Long Island home. The icy accident left Campanella with a broken neck and damaged spinal cord. At age 36, he was paralyzed from the chest down. In May 1959, more than 93,000 fans attended a tribute to Campanella at the Los Angeles Coliseum. Although wheelchair bound, Campanella scouted, was a special instructor in spring training, and worked in public relations for the Dodgers. He remained a dignified symbol of all that is good about baseball. Campanella was inducted into the Hall of Fame in 1969 and his number "39" is retired by the Dodgers. In 2006, the Dodgers established the Roy Campanella Award, which is given each year to the player who best exemplifies Campy's spirit and leadership. He passed away of a heart attack in 1993 at the age of 71.

IN THE TRADING CARD WORLD, collectors only have a handful of choices when it comes to the legendary Leroy "Satchel" Paige. Experienced hobbyists know that Paige's most desirable card is his 1948/1949 Leaf issue, a card that offers a superior level of scarcity versus the 1949 Bowman card. That said, a greater appreciation for the Bowman issue has developed in recent times. Why? In the past, the prevailing belief was that the Leaf cards were released in 1948 and therefore predated the Bowman set by enough time to separate the Leaf as his sole rookie. Today, a strong case has been made for the Leaf set first reaching the public in 1949, which means the approximate release date between the two sets is much closer than previously thought. In other words, the Bowman Paige is every bit the rookie card as the Leaf issue.

The 1949 Bowman set contains 240 cards, versus the 98 that comprise the smaller Leaf baseball issue. Despite its clear size advantage, the Bowman set doesn't include some of the star power found in the Leaf product, such as Joe DiMaggio, Ted Williams, and a post-career card of Babe Ruth. Along with the Jackie Robinson, the Paige card is one of two clear anchors to the Bowman issue. The Paige card mistakenly added an extra "l" to his nickname on the front, which reads "Satchell," but the error was never corrected. Interestingly, Paige would occasionally sign his name with two l's at the end versus one, which adds to the confusion. Not only was the 1949 Bowman release a huge step up in size over its 48-card predecessor, the injection of color also made for a significant improvement in visual appeal. While it wasn't technically a full-color design, Bowman added team colors to black-and-white photos and placed those modified images against a color background.

Like most cards in the set, the 1949 Bowman Paige is not viewed as overly condition-sensitive, but there are some potential obstacles to note. The card resides in the high-

> *The Paige card mistakenly added an extra "l" to his nickname on the front, which reads "Satchell," but the error was never corrected.*

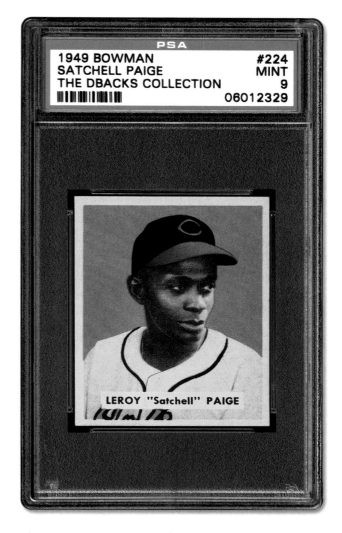

This PSA Mint 9 is one of nine examples graded at that tier, with none higher in the PSA Population Report.

number series, which is considered slightly tougher than those printed earlier. As with many vintage issues, centering can be a problem, as well as the strength of color in the blue/green background. The Bowman cards will occasionally exhibit varying degrees of toning and rough cuts along the edges. Rough cuts do not generally impact the grade, but toning can hinder the eye appeal if severe. At the age of 42, Paige won four games and saved five more to go along with his 3.04 ERA. Amazingly, three years later in 1952, Paige won 12 games and saved 10 at the age of 45! Major League Baseball fans were robbed of his prime, but collectors today have the 1949 Bowman Paige, one of the few cards that pay homage to this incredible talent.

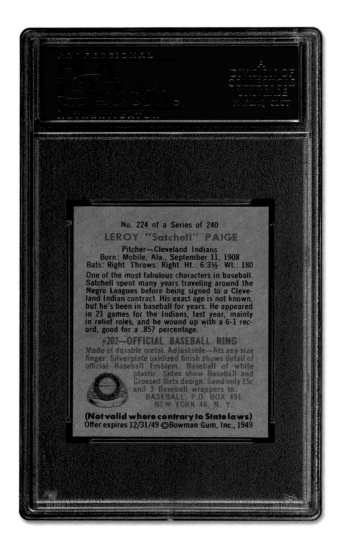

Negro Leagues data is not complete, and these stats do not include winter leagues, barnstorming, or exhibition games. Paige kept his own records in a notebook and claimed to pitch in 2,500 games, win 2,000 games, pitch for 250 different teams, and pitch 250 shutouts. Naturally, these numbers are impossible, but they do represent Paige's flare for promoting himself.

A real showman, his sizzling fastball seemed to disappear before it reached the plate. In addition to his fastball, Paige had an arsenal of pitches, which he had names for: "I got bloopers, loopers and droppers. I got a jump ball, a be ball, a screw ball, a wobbly ball, a whipsey-dipsy-do, a hurry-up ball, a nothin' ball, and a bat dodger. My be ball is a be ball 'cause it 'be' right where I want it, high and inside. It wiggles like a worm. Some I throw with my knuckles, some with two fingers. My whipsy-dipsy-do is a special fork ball I throw underhand and sidearm that slithers and sinks."

After dominating the Negro Leagues for more than 20 years, on July 7, 1948, at age 42, Satchel Paige became the first Black pitcher in American League history when the Cleveland Indians owner Bill Veeck signed him to a contract. It is said that in his audition for the team, Paige threw four out of five pitches directly over a cigarette he used for home plate. If true, that would have appealed to Veeck, who was himself a master of promotions. Paige had some success with Cleveland, at first using his hesitation delivery as his out pitch. However, the pitch was later declared illegal because many considered it a balk. On August 20, 1948, over 78,000 fans turned out in Cleveland to watch Paige pitch a 1–0 shutout victory against the White Sox. Satchel earned that win in front of the largest crowd ever to see a major-league night game. Even at his advanced age, with his personality, style, and talent, Paige became a tremendous drawing card for the Indians. That season, he posted a 6–1 record and helped the Indians to the World Series. The Indians beat the Boston Braves in six games for the title and Paige became the first African American to pitch in a World Series when he pitched part of an inning in Game Five. The next year was not nearly as successful for Paige. He posted a 4–7 record, and because of his age, he was released. Paige returned to the Negro Leagues, playing for the Kansas City Monarchs in 1950 and the Chicago American Giants in 1951, before he was signed by Bill Veeck's St. Louis Browns in 1951. Although he had some mediocre seasons in St. Louis, Paige was named to the All-Star team in both

Satchel

Continued from page 48.

Unlike most other ballplayers, Satchel Paige played year-round, barnstorming and playing winter ball in the offseason. On many occasions, he would come in and pitch three or four innings, register his six to ten strikeouts, and move on to another team. It is very difficult to determine how many games Paige played in and how many games he won over the course of his career, as official records were not kept for all of his games. Between his recorded Negro League games, and his major-league and minor-league seasons, the record books currently credit Paige with a career 118-80 record, 2.70 ERA, and 1,438 strikeouts, but the

1952 and 1953. After the Browns were sold that season, Paige was released.

Paige took up barnstorming again and rejoined the Monarchs in 1955 until he was signed to a minor-league contract in the Carolina League. The Miami Marlins Executive VP, Bill Veeck, brought Paige to the International League, where he played from 1956 through 1958 and posted an 11–4 record in 1956. He continued to pitch throughout the country and surfaced in 1961 in Portland, Oregon, pitching 25 innings in five games over three weeks for the Portland Beavers in the Pacific Coast League at age 54. After finally calling it quits as a player, Paige dabbled in movies and politics, but he did have one more outing. On September 25, 1965, in owner Charles O. Finley's publicity stunt to boost attendance, Paige was the starting pitcher for the Kansas City Athletics in a game against the Boston Red Sox. Paige was a fan favorite in the area because of his time with the Negro Leagues Kansas City Monarchs. Before the game, as a show for the fans, Finley had the 59-year-old pitching legend seated in a rocking chair in the bullpen with a nurse at his side, massaging liniment on his arm. Paige proceeded to pitch three shutout innings and future Hall of Famer, Carl Yastrzemski, was the only Boston player to get a hit. When Paige left the game after the third inning, he tipped his cap and bowed to the fans. The stadium lights were flashed off and on, and the crowd sang *The Old Gray Mare* in salute to the seemingly ageless Paige.

In 1968, when the Atlanta Braves heard that Satchel Paige was 158 days short of the five-year tenure needed for his MLB pension, they hired him as assistant

trainer and pitching coach. While with Atlanta, Paige pitched in several of their AAA affiliate's exhibition games in 1969 and retired after that season. He then held several honorary positions in baseball, making appearances at ballparks and banquets. Paige was elected to the Hall of Fame in 1971 by the Negro League Committee. On June 8, 1982, Leroy "Satchel" Paige died of a heart attack at age 75 in Kansas City, Missouri. Although his recorded stats may be incomplete, stats do not tell the whole story. He was a six-time

Negro Leagues All-Star and two-time American League All-Star, six-time Negro Leagues strikeouts leader, three-time shutouts leader, and winner of the 1944 Negro Leagues pitching Triple Crown. We will never know how great his numbers would have been had he pitched in the majors his entire career. In any event, Leroy "Satchel" Paige helped to change the face of baseball forever and will always be mentioned in the same breath as Gibson, Leonard, Mays, Robinson, and the rest.

COLLECTOR SENTIMENT IS SOMETHING that can change as time goes on, even when it comes to the players and cards of the distant past. The perception of the player's contribution or performance can evolve, as can the way collectors view the cards themselves. The 1952 Topps Willie Mays is a great example. The Mays card has always been desirable and for obvious reasons. The card resides in a set that is widely viewed as the hobby's most important postwar baseball issue, and, by the way, he's Willie Mays. This first Mays Topps card captures the young prospect before he became one of the best to ever do it in all facets of the game. While the demand has always been strong, the card has ascended to an entirely different level as of late. After all these years, the question is, "Why?"

There are two main factors that have been responsible for this new level of market demand. First, there seems to be a greater appreciation for the man himself. It's hard to imagine someone who accomplished so much being underrated, but it's true in the case of Mays. Perhaps the best way to put it is that most people already knew Mays was an exceptional player, but they may not have truly realized just how special he was until now. Second, the card is being viewed in an entirely different light now than it once was. It is following in the footsteps of the Mickey Mantle card. To explain, even though the 1952 Topps Mantle is not his rookie card, a title that belongs to his 1951 Bowman issue, it always had a special place with collectors and its market value reflected that feeling.

Now, to the Mays card. Until just a few years ago, the 1952 Topps Mays was never looked at in the same way. In the past, collectors made a greater distinction between the 1951 Bowman rookie and his 1952 Topps card. Times have changed and the gap has closed significantly. To be perfectly clear, experienced collectors know there will always be something extra special about the 1952 Topps Mantle, an X-factor that is hard to quantify. The Mays card might never possess that kind of cache, but it is finally getting the due it deserved a long time ago. Nestled in Series 5 (251–310), the Mays card is often found with a titled

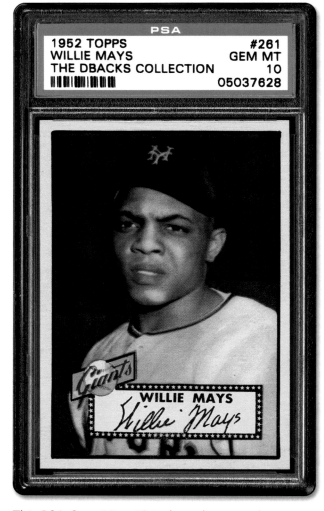

This PSA Gem Mint 10 is the sole example to reach PSA's highest grading tier.

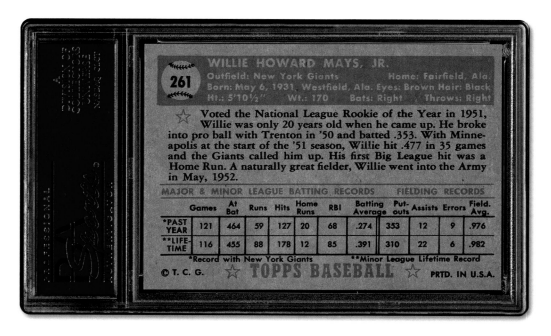

image or diamond cut, which can create centering issues if extreme. In 1952, Mays would have his season interrupted by military service, but he would come back stronger than ever in 1954, winning the NL MVP and the World Series.

WHEN TOPPS DECIDED TO MAKE A BOLD MOVE

in 1952 by issuing their first, major baseball card set to the public, little did the company know that their effort would stand the test of time as the most important postwar set in our hobby. One year later, Topps followed their previous release with one that some collectors believe is superior in aesthetic appeal compared to its predecessor. Like the 1952 issue, the keys to the 1953 Topps set are similar, with one noteworthy newcomer. Jackie Robinson leads off at #1, while Mickey Mantle, Willie Mays, and Satchel Paige (his first and last Topps appearance) act as additional pillars. The Mays and Paige cards can be found in the high-number series, which is regarded as the toughest print run in the set.

In 1953, Topps reduced the size of their set from 407 in 1952 to an intended 280 total cards, but the set actually contains 274 instead. Six cards in Series 4 (221–280) were never made due to contractual issues. Bowman, their chief rival, decided to move away from the artwork used from 1950 through 1952 and instead went with full-color photos that same year. Bowman also failed to include Mays in their 1953 set. Conversely, Topps modified their design, transitioning from color-tinted photos in 1952 to original artwork in 1953.

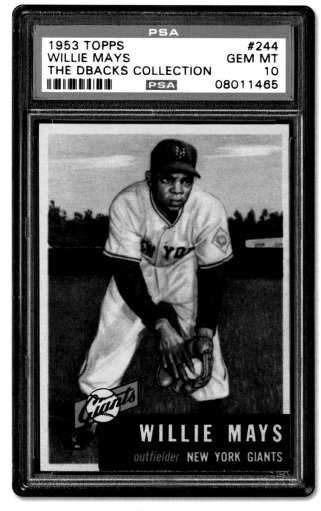

This PSA Gem Mint 10 is the sole example to reach PSA's highest grading tier.

The company retained the services of Gerry Dvorak, a renowned artist from New England, to generate the oil paintings used for some of the cards. It remains a mystery as to who was responsible for the remainder of the artwork, which allegedly includes the Mays and Mantle images, as Dvorak himself admitted he wasn't responsible for those two in a 1984 *Baseball Cards* magazine interview. For most of his career in cardboard, Mays is captured via portrait or shown with his lethal bat, but this fantastic card shows the great centerfielder in a basket-catch position. The ultimate complete player, Mays would earn the Gold Glove Award 12 consecutive times (1957–1968) for his fine defense.

Each card in the set is surrounded almost entirely by white borders but also features a colored portion of the bottom border, which is easily chipped and reveals the slightest

degree of wear. The colored edge on the Mays card, which is solid black, covers the majority of the center and lower-right portion of the bottom border. Furthermore, finding well-centered copies of this card can be challenging.

In the 1980s and 1990s, there were a couple of small discoveries of high-grade 1953 Topps cards dubbed "The Canadian Finds," yet no Mays cards were found in the groups. It remains one of the most attractive and challenging Mays cards to locate in top condition. Mays would miss the entire 1953 season serving in the military, but Topps gave the public a card to remind them of what they were missing on the field.

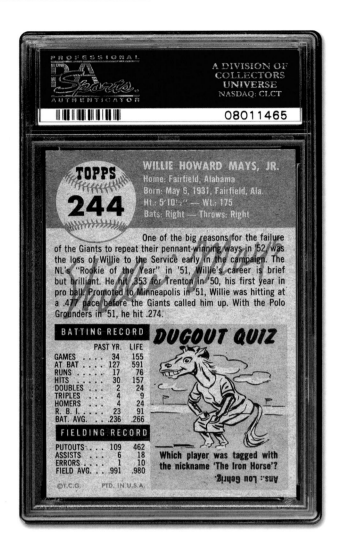

Say Hey Kid

Continued from page 73.

After playing in just 34 games in 1952, Willie Mays, like many other ballplayers, was drafted into Uncle Sam's army. Stationed at Fort Eustis, Virginia, he mostly played baseball while in the service, and remained under Durocher's watchful eye. Mays came back with a vengeance in 1954, batting .345 to win the league batting title, and slammed 41 home runs to go along with 195 hits, establishing himself as one of the new stars of the game. Mays was named to the All-Star team for the first time and was also named the National League MVP. Led by Mays, Don Mueller, and 21-game winner Johnny Antonelli, the Giants won the National League pennant and swept the Cleveland Indians in the

World Series. The highlight of the Series was the spectacular over-the-shoulder eighth inning Game One catch by Mays off the bat of Cleveland's Vic Wertz. The catch is considered the greatest of all time.

During the offseason, Mays played winter ball in Puerto Rico, and he showed up for spring training with the hopes of putting together another great season in 1955. Mays did not disappoint, walloping 51 home runs to go along with his .319 batting average, 127 RBI and 24 stolen bases. However, the Giants fell to third place in the National League. Outspoken manager Leo Durocher was replaced by Bill Rigney, and by 1956, Willie Mays was considered the best player in the National League. Along with great offensive numbers, he led the league with 40 stolen bases and continued to do so over the next three seasons. In another amazing season for Mays, he won the first of 12 consecutive Gold Gloves, batted .333, hit 35 home runs, and led the league with 38 stolen bases in 1957. For the Giants, that was a season of transition. Attendance at the Polo Grounds had been steadily decreasing, and the Giants wanted new stadium, which drove the club's decision to relocate to San Francisco. They played at Seals Stadium until a new stadium was built for them. Living in California took some adjustment for Mays. He had productive seasons in both 1958 and 1959, yet his power numbers were down. The team began to rebuild, bringing in the talented 20-year-old Orlando Cepeda, who won the NL Rookie of the Year in 1958.

After two years at Seals Stadium, the Giants moved to Candlestick Park in 1960. Mays found hitting in the new ballpark tricky because its proximity to the water created unpredictable, swirling winds. The season was a disappointment for the Giants, who finished in fifth place. However, more pieces of the puzzle were assembled with the emergence of 22-year-old first baseman and future Hall of Famer Willie McCovey and future Hall of Fame pitcher Juan Marichal. After hiring new manager Alvin Dark in 1961, the Giants finished in third place. Mays had another terrific season, batting .308 with 40 home runs. The decade of the sixties was bittersweet for Mays and the Giants. Mays put up extraordinary numbers and the Giants won more games than anyone except the Baltimore Orioles, but they only got into the World Series once during the 1960s. That was in 1962, when the Giants lost the Series to the Yankees in a seven-game heartbreaker. Mays had another terrific year, batting .304 and leading the league with 49 home runs, but he batted just .250 in that World Series.

Although he was the highest-paid player in baseball from 1963 through 1965, Mays experienced financial and personal problems off the field. Professionally, Mays was on the All-Star team every year, and led the league in home runs in both 1964 and 1965. He won his second MVP Award in 1965 and delivered a career-high 52 home runs. On September 13, 1965, Mays hit his 500th home run, becoming only the fifth player to do so. That season, the Giants replaced manager Alvin Dark with Herman Franks. The new manager's relationship with Mays was extremely beneficial because, as a successful investor himself, he gave financial advice to Mays which helped him turn things around. In 1966, the 35-year-old Mays batted .288 with 37 homers and 103 RBI, but age was starting to take its toll. By the end of the 1966 season, Mays trailed only Babe Ruth for the home run record and by 1969, he surpassed the 600 home run and 300 stolen bases mark. In May 1972, the aging Mays requested a trade to the New York Mets. Mays was rewarded by playing in the 1973 World Series as a part-time player, batting .286. The 24-time All-Star retired at the end of the 1973 season at age 42, with a career .301 average, 660 home runs, and 12 Gold Gloves.

Mays did public relations work for the Mets and was also a spokesperson for Colgate Palmolive. However, his work for Bally Casinos caused Mays to be banned from working for Major League Baseball. That ruling was reversed in 1985 and Mays was reinstated. In his first year of eligibility, the "Say Hey Kid" was elected to the Hall of Fame in

1979 with 94.7% of the vote. Among numerous honors, he was awarded the Presidential Medal of Freedom by President Obama in 2015, and in 2017 MLB renamed the World Series MVP Award as the Willie Mays Award. At the time of this writing, the 90-year-old Mays resides in California. A tremendous athlete, Willie Mays played with dedication and enthusiasm throughout his exceptional 23-year career. His unbelievable plays in center field and his tremendous blasts at the plate elevated the game and created excitement for fans throughout the country.

1973 Al Kaline signed game-used bat and Kaline game-used batting helmet circa 1960s, Ozzie Smith signed game-used cap circa 1987 and 1990 signed game-used jersey. *The Mike Heffner Collection.*

Mr. Tiger to the Wizard of Oz (1954–1980)

★ ★ ★ ★ ★ ★ ★ ★ ★ ★ ★ ★ ★ ★ ★

This grouping of fantastic cards brings us from the end of the Korean War through the culture-changing 1960s and 1970s.

From an aging Teddy Ballgame to a young, exuberant, and athletic Ozzie Smith, this grouping from the collection features some of the great players that many of us grew up with. This chapter features high-grade examples of the rookie cards of several outstanding Hall of Famers, including Al Kaline,

Sandy Koufax, Brooks Robinson, Bob Gibson, Nolan Ryan, and Ozzie Smith. These magnificent cards are some of the most sought-after in the hobby and include the only known examples of the 1954 Topps Kaline #201, 1957 Topps Robinson #328, and 1968 Topps Koosman/Ryan #177 to achieve the PSA Gem Mint 10 grading level.

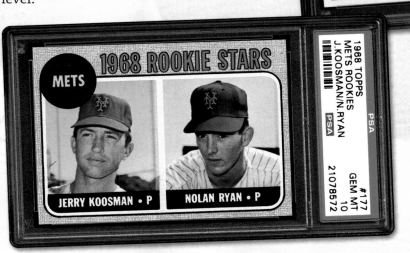

1954 Topps Al Kaline #201

THE STORY OF THIS MAN AS A PLAYER and the story of his rookie card almost mirror each other. Kaline played in what many baseball historians consider one of the most talent-rich eras the game has ever seen. There were so many outstanding players, especially in the outfield, from the 1950s to the 1970s. Hank Aaron, Roberto Clemente, Mickey Mantle, Willie Mays, and Frank Robinson were just some of the names that roamed the outfield grass during that period. It was a special time to be a fan and a collector. One of the stars of the period, who ultimately became a legend of the game by the time his career was over, was Al Kaline. Despite everything Kaline did on the field, the tale of the Detroit Tigers icon and his rookie card are still those of a somewhat unsung hero.

In 1954, Topps issued a 250-card set that combined large colorized portraits with black-and-white action shots on the face of each card. Collectors have long revered the design of the issue, which is one reason why it is so popular today. There are a couple of big names missing from the set, such as Mickey Mantle and Stan Musial, but their absence has not diminished demand in the slightest. In addition to the Ted Williams cards that begin and end the set at #1 and #250, three key rookie cards define 1954 Topps. In addition to the Kaline, cardboard debuts of Hank Aaron and Ernie Banks are included. The Kaline rookie, while highly desirable in its own right, is a more affordable option compared to the Aaron and Banks when it comes to market value.

Featuring a bold background, the primary color on the Kaline card can vary a bit. Sometimes, the rookie card will feature of heavier dose of cherry red behind his two images, while a color closer to orange appears on others. As is the case with all other 1954 Topps cards, green-colored edges are located on the reverse. From a grading perspective, high grades are attainable with some degree of chipping or wear from the cut, but it's important to remember the back when evaluating condition. It's hard to imagine a perennial All-Star with over 3,000 career hits, nearly 400 homers, 10 Gold Gloves, and a World Series title could be overshadowed, but Kaline was a victim of the times. In some ways, his rookie card suffers the same fate, but its importance to the set is as indisputable as Kaline's place is in the hallowed halls of Cooperstown.

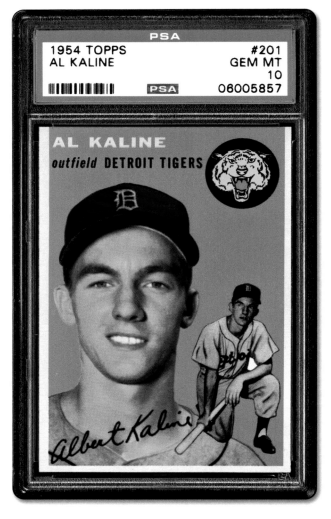

This PSA Gem Mint 10 is the sole example to reach PSA's highest grading tier.

Mr. Tiger

The face of the Detroit Tigers during the Golden Age of Baseball, Al "Mr. Tiger" Kaline, had an extraordinary 22-year career, spent entirely with the Tigers.

A two-sport star at Southern High School in Baltimore, Maryland, Albert William Kaline was signed by the Detroit Tigers the day after he graduated in 1953 for a three-year $35,000 package. The 18-year-old "bonus baby" outfielder made his professional debut on June 25, 1953, in an uneventful ninth inning against the Philadelphia Athletics. In that initial season, Kaline batted .250 with one home run in 28 at-bats, the highlight being a three-hit game in September against the Red Sox. Although his power was still developing, he became the regular right fielder for the Tigers in 1954. In his first full season, Kaline batted .276 with 139 hits in 504 plate appearances. His postseason work on strength conditioning and hitting paid off in 1955. Not only was Kaline voted to the All-Star team, but he upped his power numbers to 27 home runs with 102 RBI and topped the league with 200 hits. Moreover, he led the league with his .340 batting average, becoming the youngest player to win the American League batting title, a distinction previously held by Ty Cobb. Kaline also finished second in the 1955 MVP voting. The Tigers had a new star on their hands.

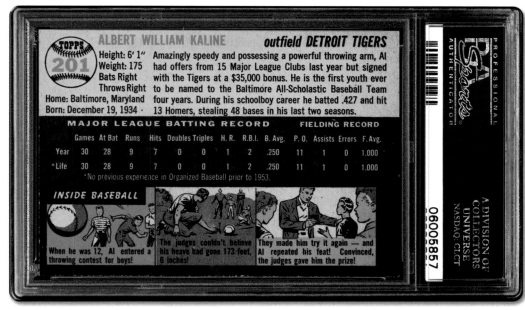

In 1956, Kaline and teammate Harvey Kuenn packed a punch for the Tiger offense. Kuenn led the AL in hits, while Kaline batted .314, blasted 27 homers, was again voted an All-Star, and led all American League outfielders with his 18 assists. Although Kaline trained diligently in the offseason, his 1957 numbers did not match the previous season, yet he made another All-Star team and won his first Gold Glove. Up to this point, Kaline excelled while the Tigers were not very competitive. From 1958 through 1960, he continued to be one of the best players in the American League, but the Tigers were mediocre at best. An All-Star each year during that period, he won two more Gold Gloves, and was in the hunt for the AL batting title. In a very successful 1959 season, Kaline batted .327 with 167 hits, but finished second in the AL batting race to teammate Harvey Kuenn.

The Tigers made key offseason moves after the 1959 season by acquiring slugging first baseman Norm Cash for light-hitting Steve Demeter, and power-hitting outfielder Rocky Colavito for Harvey Kuenn. With the batting trio of Kaline, Cash, and Colavito, the Tigers won 101 games in 1961, only to finish second to the powerhouse New York Yankees. Kaline batted .324 but again lost the batting race to a teammate. This time it was Norm Cash. The 1962 season was a mixed bag for Kaline. Although he missed 54 games after breaking his collarbone while making a diving catch,

Kaline batted .304, slammed 29 home runs, won another Gold Glove, and was an All-Star again, but the Tigers were never really in the hunt for the pennant. Once again, the Tigers were not pennant contenders in 1963, but Kaline had another solid offensive year batting .312 with 27 homers and 172 hits. He won another Gold Glove, finished second to Carl Yastrzemski in the AL batting race, and was second to Elston Howard in MVP voting.

The Tigers assembled a mix of veterans that would define the next several seasons. Besides the anchors, Kaline and Cash, the team brought in Dick McAuliffe, Willie Horton, catcher Bill Freehan, and Jim Northrop to bolster the offense. A couple of young pitchers, Denny McClain and Mickey Lolich, would make a tremendous impact on the mound. Most people had no idea that, as a child, Kaline had osteomyelitis, a bone disease that affected his left foot. When this resurfaced in 1964, he missed playing time. Although he made the All-Star team again, Kaline was not able to play in the Midsummer Classic. Still, he batted a respectable .293 and won his seventh Gold Glove. After batting .281 in 1965 and earning his eighth Gold Glove, Kaline decided to have foot surgery in the offseason, hoping extend his career. He came back in 1966 to blast 29 homers, bat .288, win his ninth Gold Glove, and enjoy his twelfth consecutive All-Star season.

The 1967 American League pennant race was one of the most exciting in the history of baseball. A four-way fight

Al Kaline

between the Tigers, Red Sox, Twins, and White Sox went down to the last week of the season with the Tigers, Sox, and Twins battling to the last day. Unfortunately, the Tigers finished second to the Red Sox by splitting a doubleheader with the California Angels. After missing 26 games with a broken hand, Kaline had another All-Star and Gold Glove season, batting .308 and swatting 25 home runs. The Tigers were poised to battle for the pennant in 1968 with a powerful lineup and pitching staff. Just days after he blasted home run number 307 in May to beat Hank Greenberg's Tigers team record, Kaline broke his arm and was lost to the team until July. For the rest of that season, he played some first base and was used as a pinch-hitter. The Tigers did not miss a beat though, winning 103 games for the pennant and defeating the powerful St. Louis Cardinals in an exciting seven-game contest to win the 1968 World Series championship. With his arm fully healed, Kaline played in the outfield in the Series, batting an excellent .379 with 11 hits and two home runs.

Although his batting average and power numbers slipped a bit, the next three seasons were productive for Kaline. In 1971, he batted .294 and made the All-Star team again. His playing time was diminished in 1972 but he helped the Tigers to the playoffs batting .313 with 10 home runs in 278 at-bats. At 39 years old, Kaline reached the 3,000 hits milestone in September 1974.

He retired at the end of that season to launch a 25-year career as a Tigers broadcaster before becoming an advisor to Tigers ownership and a special

assistant to the Tigers GM. With 10 Gold Gloves, 18 All-Star appearances, 399 home runs, 3,007 hits, the 1968 Lou Gehrig Memorial Award, 1969 Hutch Award, the 1973 Roberto Clemente Award, and over 45 years in the Detroit Tigers organization, Al Kaline truly earned the moniker "Mr. Tiger." In 1980, his number "6"

was retired, making Kaline the first player in Detroit Tigers' history to be so honored. That year he enjoyed the ultimate honor when he was inducted into the Hall of Fame. "Mr. Tiger" passed away on April 6, 2020, at 85 years old.

THROUGHOUT HIS PLAYING DAYS, TED WILLIAMS was featured on some of the most memorable cards the hobby has ever produced. We all know that Williams put up incredible offensive numbers year after year as a player, but perhaps his best year for cards was 1954. Williams was chosen to act as the "bookend" for the ultra-popular 1954 Topps set, appearing on cards #1 and #250. Both colorful cards are collector favorites. Outside of the mainstream, the 1954 Wilson Franks Williams card is still considered by many to be the most important regional card ever made. From a hobby perspective, the Topps and Wilson Franks cards by themselves would make 1954 a standout year for Williams, but his 1954 Bowman issue seals the deal.

In 1954, Bowman issued a 224-card set, which contained some of the great stars of the day. While it was missing the three key rookie cards found in the Topps issue, those of Hank Aaron, Ernie Banks, and Al Kaline, it did have the advantage when it came to Mickey Mantle. Along with Mantle, a card of Williams acts as one of the keys to the Bowman issue. The Williams card, however, is tougher to find than the Mantle and there's an interesting explanation behind it. Williams had an exclusive deal with Topps at the time, yet he appeared on card #66 in the Bowman set during initial print runs. The card was eventually pulled from production as a result of that contract dispute and it was replaced with one of Jim Piersall, even though the fellow Red Sox outfielder could already be found on card #210. Piersall was the only player in the set to appear twice.

There was a time when the Williams card was viewed as a much greater rarity than it turned out to be, but it is still considerably more challenging to find than the Mantle. At the time of this writing, four times more Mantle cards had been graded by PSA than the Williams, which indicates the discrepancy in surviving copies. In addition to its relative scarcity, the card can be tough to find well-centered. There are also dark print defects in the light background and color variances to contend with, which can impact eye appeal. In 1954, Williams did what Williams always seemed to do. The legendary hitter played in only 117 games that year, but hit .345 with 29 homers, 136 walks, a .513 OBP, and slugged .635. His year in cardboard was just as good, and the Bowman card offers the best tale of them all.

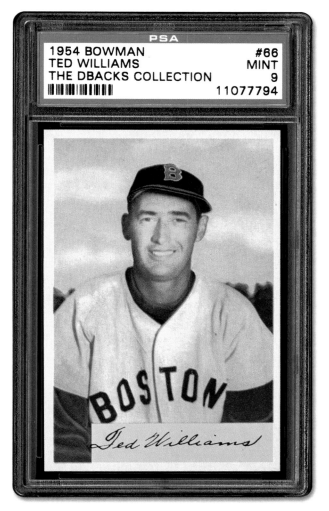

This PSA Mint 9 is one of three examples graded at that tier, with none higher in the PSA Population Report.

The Splendid Splinter

Continued from page 113.

After serving in the Korean War as a combat pilot with 39 missions under his belt, Ted Williams came back to the Boston Red Sox in 1953 at age 34. The decorated war hero threw out the first pitch at the 1953 All-Star Game and quickly got back into baseball shape, batting .407 in 91 at-bats. In 1954, he batted .345 but because of a broken collarbone, Williams did not have enough at-bats to qualify for the title. That same year, he and his wife Doris divorced. In an injury-shortened 1955 season, Williams batted .356 and knocked in 83 runs, but in 1957, at the age of 38, he

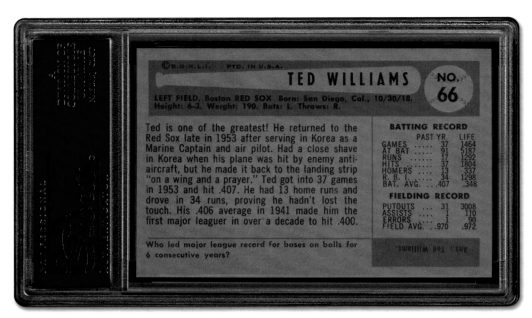

On the personal front, Williams married socialite and model Lee Howard in 1961, but they divorced six years later. He married *Vogue* model Dolores Wettach in 1968. The couple had two children, John-Henry and Claudia, but the marriage ended in divorce in 1972. Williams then met the love of his life, Louise Kaufman, and they lived together for 20 years until her death in 1993. After retiring as a player, Williams focused on his other love, fishing. One of the best fly fishermen in the country, he was elected to the Fishing Hall of Fame in 2000. As a Red Sox spring-training hitting instructor, Williams worked with the young Carl Yastrzemski, among others. He also

produced one of the greatest seasons of his career. Williams batted an amazing .388 to win the American League batting title while blasting 38 home runs and 163 hits. Incredibly, he won the title again in 1958 at the age of 39, with a .328 batting average.

From a hobby perspective, the Topps and Wilson Franks cards by themselves would make 1954 a standout year for Williams, but his 1954 Bowman issue seals the deal.

Age began to catch up with Ted Williams. He batted a pedestrian .254 in 1959 and was so upset with his performance that he asked the Red Sox to cut his pay. By this time, the Red Sox were not drawing many fans, and although Williams bounced back somewhat in 1960 to bat .316 as a part-time player, he finally called it quits. In his last at-bat in front of a sparse Fenway crowd of 10,000 fans, he cracked a 1–1 pitch off Baltimore Orioles pitcher Jack Fischer into the bullpen, and in typical Williams' fashion, after rounding the bases he neither acknowledged nor tipped his cap to the fans. The career of Ted Williams had come to a bittersweet end.

spent time at the pediatric cancer treatment hospital, The Jimmy Fund Clinic. The old Boston Braves lit the torch to support The Jimmy Fund, and after they left Boston, the Red Sox, and especially Ted Williams, took up the cause. He would periodically slip into the clinic with little fanfare and spend hours with the kids.

Williams endorsed his own line of fishing equipment for Sears and endorsed products for other companies as well. As Washington Senators manager in 1969, he was voted Manager of the Year. A renowned hitting guru, Williams penned *The Science of Hitting* in 1970. In his later years, managed by his son John-Henry, Williams became a fixture at card and memorabilia shows across the country. One moment that best describes what Ted Williams meant to baseball took place at the 1999 All-Star Game at Fenway Park, when the 80-year-old Williams came onto the field in a golf cart to the wild cheers of a sold-out crowd. In a very poignant, unscripted moment, the players from both the American League and National League, surrounded the cart, hoping to shake the hand of "The Splendid Splinter."

In a February 2000 interview with the Hall of Fame, Williams discussed his thoughts on hitting. "You've got to have some ability, have good eyes, and you have to have athletic ability where you can swing coordinated and quick. Making good contact with a round ball and a round bat even if you know what's coming is hard to do. That seems to be the one major thing that all young players have difficulty

"You've got to have some ability, have good eyes, and you have to have athletic ability where you can swing coordinated and quick. Making good contact with a round ball and a round bat even if you know what's coming is hard to do..." —Ted Williams

with. Why? It's the hardest thing to do in baseball. Maybe it's the hardest thing to do in sports."

Two years later, on July 5, 2002, Ted Williams passed away. Sadly, controversy surrounded his death. His children claimed that Williams wanted his body to be cryonically preserved in hopes that science would unlock the key to immortality. After lawsuits by other family members who tried to prevent this, the court ruled in favor of his children. Today the body of Ted Williams is frozen in a cryonics lab in Arizona—a bizarre ending to a controversial life.

Williams was elected to The Hall of Fame in 1966, and along with numerous awards, he received the Medal of Freedom. To put things in perspective regarding the career of Ted Williams, let's look at his body of work, and then at what could have been. With his .344 lifetime batting average, 2,654 hits, 521 home runs, 1,839 RBI, 19 All-Star appearances, six batting titles, two MVP Awards, two Triple Crowns, his all-time great .482 on-base percentage, and that one stellar .406 season, Ted Williams is certainly in the conversation as the greatest hitter of all-time. Based on statistical analysis on what may have happened had he not missed five years in the prime of his career, Williams could have hovered around 3,400 hits, over 2,300 RBI and hit about 663 home runs. The greatest hitter who ever lived? The discussion continues to this day.

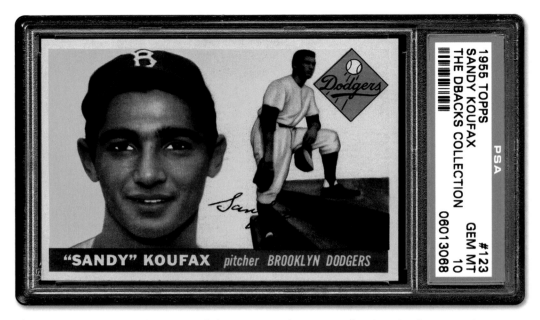

This PSA Gem Mint 10 is one of three examples to reach PSA's highest grading tier.

The beautiful design reminds us of another time. By 1957, Topps would change the look of their product in dramatic fashion by focusing on original photography, without the additional artistic flair. For collectors, there is something extra captivating about those early Topps issues (1952–1956), and the Koufax rookie is one that rockets to the head of the class, like one of his sizzling fastballs. The card captures Koufax as a young talent who hadn't found his stride yet. It would take several years, but once he did, Koufax became a juggernaut on the mound. The only thing that could stop him was his own decision to walk away. Koufax chose his long-term health over money and fame.

SANDY KOUFAX CAME THROUGH THE LEAGUE like a comet. As the old saying goes, something that burns so bright is never destined to last a long time, but the mark Koufax left on the game was eternal. Despite retiring at the young age of 30, just after recording one of the greatest individual pitching seasons ever in 1966, the electric lefty was able to dominate in a way that keeps him in the conversation when debating the best hurlers of all time. Still, to this day, there aren't many baseball historians who wouldn't pick Koufax to start a Game Seven in the World Series above all the legends who have stepped on the bump.

The 1955 Topps production, which is one of the most attractive-looking designs in hobby history, is home to Koufax's only recognized rookie card. With the absence of Mickey Mantle, due to a contractual obligation with Bowman in 1955, the Koufax rookie takes on even greater importance within the 206-card set. The Koufax rookie joins two other keys in the set, those of slugger Harmon Killebrew and superstar Roberto Clemente. The combination of colors, from green to Dodger blue to the bright yellow background, can give the Koufax rookie elite eye appeal if the card was well preserved. Speaking of the yellow backdrop, it can be a haven for dark print defects, which are easily seen due to the extreme contrast. The card, like most made during the era, can suffer from inconsistent centering as well.

The Left Arm of God

Sandy Koufax really had two distinct careers with the Dodgers. First, we had Koufax, the lefty pitcher who from 1955 through 1960 struggled because of control problems and almost quit baseball. Then there was Koufax the lefty pitcher who from 1961 through 1966 was not only the best pitcher on the planet, but one of the greatest pitchers of his era.

On December 30, 1935, Sanford "Sandy" Koufax was born in Brooklyn, New York. A standout basketball player at Lafayette High School, he received a partial basketball scholarship to attend the University of Cincinnati. Because of his athletic prowess and his powerful left arm, Koufax was encouraged to pitch for the baseball team during his senior year. That is when he caught the eye of several major-league scouts. Koufax began to get feelers from major-league teams, and a bidding war started with the Yankees, Giants, Braves, Pirates, and Dodgers all making offers. Although the Braves offered more, Koufax chose his hometown Brooklyn Dodgers and got a $14,000 signing bonus to go along with a $6,000 salary. The "bonus baby" Koufax began his career with the Dodgers in 1955. Because of the bonus money, he was automatically added to the major-league roster. Major League Baseball rules stated that bonus babies had to remain on the big-league roster for a minimum of two years before they could be sent down to the minors for more seasoning. In Koufax's case, that never happened.

In his pitching debut on June 24, 1955, against the Milwaukee Braves, the 19-year-old Koufax came into the game in the fifth inning, fanned two batters, and did not give up a run. Koufax struggled in his first career start on July 6, 1955, against the Pittsburgh Pirates. He walked eight batters and lasted only 4½ innings. He fared much better in August, getting his first win by striking out 14 Cincinnati Redlegs batters and pitching a two-hitter. Between injuries and his lack of pitch command, the first six years of the future Hall of Famer's career were unimpressive and more of a roller-coaster ride than anything. Brooklyn manager, Walter Alston, would not give Koufax a regular turn in the rotation until he could prove he had command of his pitches.

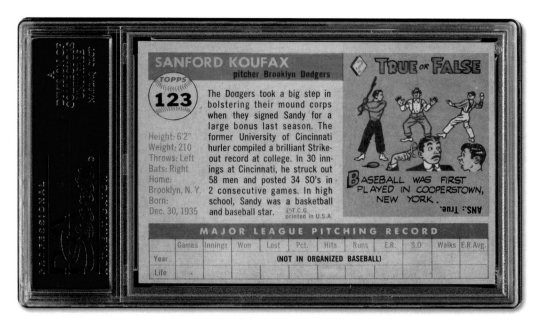

For collectors, there is something extra captivating about those early Topps issues (1952–1956), and the Koufax rookie is one that rockets to the head of the class, like one of his sizzling fastballs.

In 1955, the Dodgers won their first ever World Series, defeating the New York Yankees, but Koufax did not get into a game. Occasionally, Koufax showed his amazing ability, but he just could not harness it consistently. Over the next three seasons, he was in and out of the rotation and sometimes showed flashes of brilliance, but he continued to have difficulty finding the strike zone. After the 1956 season, Koufax honed his skills by playing winter ball in Puerto Rico. In 1957, Koufax was 5–4 with a 3.88 ERA. The high point of his season was striking out thirteen Chicago Cubs in a game.

Following the 1957 season, the Dodgers relocated to Los Angeles, which did not sit well with Brooklyn fans. Owner Walter O'Malley had been haggling with city officials over a new ballpark in Brooklyn, but it never materialized. This move would eventually benefit Koufax. Between 1958 and 1960, Koufax continued to work in and out of the Dodger rotation. Frustrated with his lack of progress, he thought about quitting baseball but instead he stuck around for the 1959 season. Although Koufax only posted an 8–6 record that year, two games stood out that would define what the future held for him. After a dismal start to the season, Koufax struck out 16 batters in a June game against the Philadelphia Phillies, and in an August 31 game against the San Francisco Giants, his 18 strikeouts matched Bob Feller's major-league single-game strikeout record set in 1938. The Dodgers won the 1959 National League pennant and Koufax got to play in the World Series. They won the six-game contest against the White Sox, with Koufax pitching in relief in Game One and starting in Game Five. The 1960 season was not successful for Koufax whose record of 8–13 with a 3.91 ERA prompted him to once again consider giving up baseball. Thankfully, things began to come together after the 1960 season, and the second half of Koufax's career was set to begin.

Two things made the difference. One of the Dodgers scouts suggested to Koufax that he was losing sight of the plate because he was rearing back too far with his delivery.

Sandy Koufax

On September 9, 1965, Koufax pitched a perfect game, becoming the first pitcher to attain the four no-hitter milestone.

upstart New York Mets on June 30, 1962. That season, the Dodgers moved from the Los Angeles Coliseum to Dodger Stadium, a very pitcher-friendly facility, which helped Koufax as well.

Sandy Koufax and the Dodgers were expecting a huge season in 1963. Koufax did not disappoint, winning a league-leading 25 games and losing only five. He also led the league with 11 shutouts, 306 strikeouts, and his 1.88 ERA. On May 11, Koufax no-hit the San Francisco Giants, besting future Hall of Famer Juan Marichal. Koufax won the Cy Young Award, was the NL MVP, and was named to his third All-Star team. That season the Dodgers swept the Yankees in the World Series and Koufax was named Series MVP. Unbeknownst to many people, Koufax was experiencing elbow pain which was diagnosed as arthritis. He went through a rigorous treatment program of icing, heat treatments, and nonsteroidal drugs between starts. This condition would burden him for the next three

Catcher Norm Sherry also suggested that he take a little off his fastball because he was overthrowing. Those two suggestions plus a rigorous conditioning program made the difference. Besides posting a record of 18–13 in 1961, Koufax was an All-Star for the first time, and led the National League with 269 strikeouts, which broke the single-season record of 267 Ks set by Hall of Famer Christy Mathewson in 1903. Koufax also worked on mixing up his pitches with certain hitters rather than just throwing fastballs. Although he had a second All-Star season in 1962, a 14–7 record, and a league-leading 2.54 ERA, Koufax missed several starts due to lingering issues from an April hand injury. The highlights of that season for Koufax were his 18-strikeouts performance in an April game against the Chicago Cubs and throwing his first no-hitter against the

years. In a season plagued with elbow issues, Koufax won 19 games in 1964. He led the league with a 1.74 ERA and seven shutouts, and pitched his third no-hitter on June 4 against the Phillies. At this point, Koufax was treated on a regular basis with cortisone shots, and he stayed away from throwing much on off days. Amazingly, though Koufax had fewer starts, he still had 223 strikeouts.

The 1965 season was extremely successful for Koufax, but behind the scenes he suffered terribly with his sore arm. Doctors had him on a series of medications and supplements to get him through the season. Koufax led the league with his 26 wins, 2.04 ERA, and 27 complete games. His 382 strikeouts broke Hall of Famer Rube Waddell's single-season major-league record of 349 Ks by a left-hander. On

September 9, Koufax pitched a perfect game, becoming the first pitcher to attain the four no-hitter milestone. He won another Cy Young Award and led the Dodgers to the World Series where they defeated the Minnesota Twins in seven games. Interestingly, Koufax pitched Game Two of the Series because he refused to pitch on Yom Kippur which fell on the same day as Game One. He lost his first start but won Game Five and Game Seven and was named the Series MVP.

Going into the 1966 season, Koufax and pitching mate Don Drysdale held out together for a raise. After they sat out most of spring training, negotiations became heated, but both were finally signed. Before the season started, doctors told Koufax that 1966 would probably be his last season because his elbow was deteriorating. Koufax kept that under wraps, played through the pain, and posted a league-leading 27–9 record. He also topped the league with 1.73 ERA, 41 games started, 27 complete games, and 317 strikeouts. The Dodgers won the 1966 pennant but were swept in the Series by a very good Baltimore Orioles team. About a month later, the 30-year-old Koufax announced his retirement. He went on to work in broadcasting on the NBC *Game of the Week* and has worked periodically as a coach in the Dodgers organization. Nicknamed "The Left Arm of God," Sandy Koufax ended his distinguished career with a 165–87 record, a career 2.76 ERA, and an average of more than 9 Ks a game. Among other awards and records, he was a seven-time All-Star, NL MVP, three-time Cy Young Award winner, three-

time pitching Triple Crown winner, two-time World Series MVP, and the first to pitch four no-hitters. Sandy Koufax was inducted into the Hall of Fame in 1972 at age 36, and he was later named the left-handed starting pitcher on the MLB All-Time team. At the time of this writing, Sandy Koufax is 85 years old and resides in Florida. The greatest lefty of all time? Sandy Koufax may be that guy.

IN 1957, TOPPS DECIDED TO CHANGE THE LOOK of their baseball cards altogether. They moved away from the colorized photo or hand painted artwork look and instead simplified their design by making color photographs the focal point. Furthermore, they reduced the size of their cards from 2⅝″ by 3⅝″ to 2½″ by 3½″, which would become the standard for trading cards of all types going forward. The simplicity of the design has made the set, which took a similar approach to the 1953 Bowman issue, a collector favorite over the years. Speaking of collector favorites, one of its keys is the Brooks Robinson rookie card, which features the man who is regarded as the best defensive third baseman of all time.

Along with the only recognized rookie of the "Human Vacuum Cleaner," inaugural cards of fellow Hall of Famers Jim Bunning, Don Drysdale, Bill Mazeroski, and Frank Robinson also reside in the set. The Brooks Robinson card is arguably one of the most eye-catching in 1957 Topps. It features a bright background, unlike many of the other cards in the set, which show the players positioned against a dark or gray-toned backdrop. The Robinson was also part of the toughest series in the issue. Cards 265–352 are considered more challenging than those printed in any other, including the high-number series. The two most noteworthy condition obstacles for 1957 Topps cards are centering and what is referred to as print "snow."

This term is often used to describe lighter-colored defects that appear scattered in the background. Since the Robinson card exhibits an orange/pink background, darker print specks will contrast greatly with it, but more traditional "snow" might still be visible in his dark cap area. A few years after this card was released, Robinson would start an unthinkable streak, earning 16 consecutive Gold Glove Awards (1960–1975). Beyond his 1964 AL MVP and two World Series championships (1966, 1970), this exceptional player is widely considered one of the most personable and likable stars of his era. Being beloved by fans and collectors matters, and Robinson is admired just as much for his character as he is for his performance on the field.

This PSA Gem Mint 10 is the sole example to reach PSA's highest grading tier.

Human Vacuum Cleaner

When it comes to the best defensive third baseman of all time, Brooks Robinson the "Human Vacuum Cleaner" leads the pack. The slick-fielding Robinson made it look effortless with his grace, glove work, and range.

A gifted athlete at Central High School in Little Rock, Arkansas, Robinson captured the interest of scouts with his defensive wizardry while playing Legion ball. Baltimore Orioles scout Arthur Ehlers convinced the club to sign Robinson after he graduated in 1955. Assigned to the Class B York White Roses in the Piedmont League, Robinson batted .331, earning a call up to the Orioles in

September 1955, but the 18-year-old infielder batted only .091 in 22 plate appearances. Considered a mediocre hitter initially, Robinson's defensive skills were never questioned. He bounced between the minors and the parent club for a few seasons while developing his offensive skills. With Vancouver in the Pacific Coast League in 1959, Robinson batted .331 to earn a call back to Baltimore for good in July. He responded by batting .284 in 313 at-bats.

Every great player has a breakout year, and for Robinson it was 1960, when the 23-year-old third sacker batted .294 with 14 home runs. Now the face of the Orioles, Robinson made two All-Star appearances, won his first of 16 Gold Gloves, and finished third in the American League MVP voting, while the Orioles finished second in the American League to the powerful New York Yankees. An All-Star in 1961 and 1962, Robinson batted .287 and .303 respectively and won Gold Gloves both seasons. By this time, Robinson's reputation as a fielder was the talk of baseball. His fluid style, extraordinary range, and soft hands were the envy of every infielder in the league. After another Gold Glove and All-Star season in 1963, Robinson had a tremendous season in 1964, batting .317 while smacking 28 home runs with 194 hits and leading the league with 118 RBI. An All-Star again, he won another Gold Glove, was voted the 1964 AL MVP, and led the Orioles to a third-place finish. Robinson hit a respectable .297 in 1965, even though he missed some time due to a broken thumb. The Orioles won 94 games that season to finish in third place.

It all came together for the Orioles in 1966. The new general manager, Harry Dalton, made a blockbuster deal to acquire Cincinnati Reds superstar outfielder Frank Robinson. The two Robinsons, along with power-hitting first baseman Boog Powell, future Hall of Famer Luis Aparicio, and young pitching prospects Jim Palmer and Dave McNally, were the nucleus of an excellent team. The third sacker batted .269 with 23 home runs and 167 hits, was named the 1966 All-Star Game MVP, and finished second to teammate Frank Robinson in the AL MVP voting. The Orioles won the 1966 pennant and swept the Los Angeles Dodgers

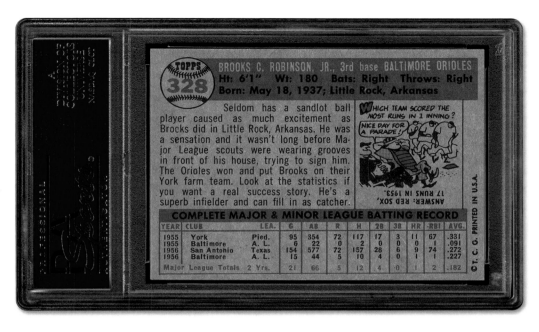

for their first-ever World Series championship. Although Robinson made another All-Star appearance in 1967 and batted a respectable .269 with 22 home runs, the Orioles had a dismal season, finishing in sixth place. Robinson had another All-Star and Gold Glove season in 1968, a season that proved to be a building block milestone for the team. When the Orioles fired manager Hank Bauer in mid-season and brought in fiery Earl Weaver to right the ship, they laid the groundwork for success. With an impressive 109–53 record in 1969, the Orioles crushed the opposition. Robinson had a subpar season batting just .234 with 23 home runs and 84 RBI, but he was exceptional defensively, earning another Gold Glove and All-Star selection. Although the Orioles won the pennant and were heavily favored to win the Series, they lost to the Miracle Mets four games to one.

Robinson was outstanding defensively in 1970, one of the best seasons in the history of the franchise. That year, he hit two personal milestones, slamming his 200th home run in May and logging his 2,000th hit in June. He had a fine regular season, batting .276 with 18 homers and 168 hits, but Robinson really turned on the gas in the postseason. The Orioles faced the Minnesota Twins in the ALCS with the winner advancing to face the Cincinnati Reds. Robinson not only batted .583 in the ALCS, but he solidified his reputation as the best defensive third sacker of his generation. Against the Reds, Robinson batted a spectacular .429, but his third base play became the talk of the Series. In Game One,

Brooks Robinson

Robinson made a spectacular play, throwing out Cincinnati's Lee May. In Game Two and Game Three, the 33-year-old third baseman continued to play flawless defense. The Orioles beat the Reds four games to one to win their second world championship, and Robinson was voted MVP of the World Series. In 1971, Robinson had another consistent season, batting .272 with 20 home runs. The Orioles swept the Oakland Athletics in the ALCS but lost the World Series in seven games to future Hall of Famer Roberto Clemente and the Pittsburgh Pirates.

After the Orioles traded Frank Robinson in the postseason, they found themselves finishing in third place in 1972. At 35 years old, Brooks Robinson had slipped offensively but he still won a Gold Glove and made an All-Star appearance. The Orioles came back strong the next couple of seasons but could not get past the Oakland Athletics to get into the World Series. As age began to catch up with Robinson, his offense suffered but he remained the best defensive third baseman in the league. The highlight for Robinson offensively in 1973 was registering his 2,417th career hit, breaking Pie Traynor's record for most hits by a third baseman. In 1974, his last decent offensive season, Robinson batted .288, received another Gold Glove, and was an All-Star for the 15th consecutive season. In 1975, Robinson was awarded his 16th consecutive, and final, Gold Glove. He decided to call it quits in August of 1977, retiring at age 40 after 23 years with 2,848 hits and 268 home runs. The Orioles honored their longtime third baseman at Memorial Stadium in September, presenting him with third base, and his number "5" jersey was retired soon after.

Robinson moved to the broadcast booth as color analyst for the Orioles and remained in that capacity for 15 years. He also endorsed a variety of products, appeared at card shows, and became part-owner of four minor-league teams. In 1983, Brooks Robinson was elected to the Hall of Fame on the first ballot. At the time of this writing, the esteemed 84-year-old Oriole resides in Maryland. How good was Robinson? In 9,165 chances, he made only 263 errors, and he still holds third baseman records for games defended (2,870), putouts (2,697), assists (6,205), and double plays (618). One of the most beloved athletes to come out of Baltimore, Brooks Robinson was all class—no controversy, no drama. Simply put, he was an exceptional third baseman.

THERE ARE CERTAIN PITCHERS WHO, at their best, were so dominant and locked in that it's hard to imagine anyone making solid contact against them. Some of the names that inevitably come up in the discussion are Randy Johnson, Sandy Koufax, and Pedro Martinez. At their peak, they possessed hellacious movement with uncanny control. There was another pitcher, however, that combined wicked stuff with a menacing presence that made him the most feared pitcher in the league—Bob Gibson. At a time when pitching inside was an art form, no pitcher owned the inner half of the plate the way Gibson did. His hobby debut was captured in the 1959 Topps set, on a card that contrasts his intimidating image.

The 572-card set contains most of the big stars of the day, from Roberto Clemente to Mickey Mantle to Stan Musial. The one big name missing was Ted Williams, who had an exclusive deal with Fleer at the time, but the set has always been a collector favorite regardless. An All-Star run that appears in the final series, a trend that Topps started a year earlier in 1958, adds to the appeal of this colorful issue. In addition, some intriguing multi-player cards make the set even more desirable. The Gibson card, which pictures the young pitcher with a joyous smile in the high-number series, is one of the more eye-catching cards in the set. The image of Gibson is surrounded by a bubble gum-tinted frame, which can really pop if the print quality remains vibrant. The light-colored background, however, can be a haven for dark print defects.

Gibson reeled off five 20-win seasons, including two additional 19-win performances, during his incredible career. Gibson's devastating slider never looked better than it did in 1968, when the St. Louis legend posted his best year on the mound, a year that might never be matched in the modern era. That season, Gibson finished with an ERA of 1.12 and 13 shutouts, which earned him both the NL Cy Young and MVP awards. The following season, MLB lowered the mound and shrank the strike zone in response to offense being down throughout the league. While the Hall of Famer isn't entirely responsible for the change, the adjustments became known as the "Gibson Rules." Like his pitching, Gibson's inaugural 1959 Topps card overpowers the rest of the rookie class.

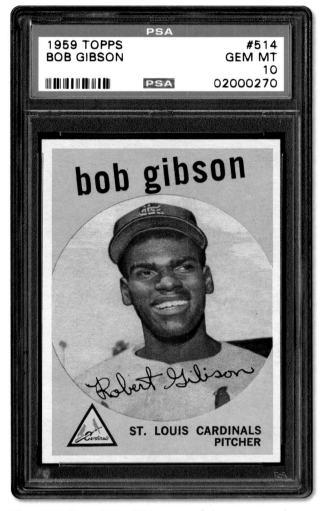

This PSA Gem Mint 10 is one of three examples to reach PSA's highest grading tier.

Gibby

When you think of the most intimidating pitchers in baseball history, names like Walter Johnson, Bob Feller, Nolan Ryan, and Randy Johnson come to mind. These men not only had tremendous talent, but they had a steely stare and powerful presence that triggered trepidation in the hearts of hitters. There was, however, one man whose frightening veneer topped all others.

Robert Gibson was born on November 9, 1935, in Omaha, Nebraska. The youngest of seven children, Gibson's early years were filled with organized youth sports. At Omaha Technical High School, he played both basketball

166 batters. On the flip side, the still wild youngster led the National League in walks with 119. Gibson's control struggles strangely added to his growing reputation as one of the hardest throwing and feared young pitchers in the game. He made his first of eight All-Star appearances in 1962, winning 15 games for the Redbirds and leading the National League with five shutouts while posting an ERA of 2.85. Still, for Gibson, the best was yet to come. He followed up an 18-win 1963 season with 19 victories in 1964. More importantly, he had worked hard to harness his control. In 1964, Gibson fanned 245 batters while walking only 86 in just over 287 innings pitched. The Cards were developing into a powerhouse. In 1964, they won the National League pennant and faced the Yankees in the World Series. In his first Fall Classic appearance, the 28-year-old Gibson came of age, winning Series MVP honors. He went 2–1 in the Series, striking out 31 Bronx Bombers in just 27 innings with two complete games. The 1964 season propelled Gibson into what would become a legendary Hall of Fame career.

Gibson was downright terrifying to face as a hitter. His eternal scowl, will to win, blazing fastball, and complete ownership of the mound and plate put hitters on notice and on edge.

and baseball. Along the way, he encountered his share of prejudice and outright racism that sadly was part of amateur and professional sports at that time. While he would eventually achieve immortality on the diamond, it was in basketball that Gibson initially excelled. He followed his brother Josh to play hoops at Creighton University and even had a brief stint playing with the famed Harlem Globetrotters. Eventually, baseball won out. Gibson was signed by the St. Louis Cardinals as a free agent before the 1957 season and joined their Triple A team in his hometown of Omaha. This action of pen to paper began one of the most sterling pitching careers in major-league history.

Gibson debuted with the Cards in 1959, winning three games. He tallied the same number of victories in 1960. While not spectacular, 1961 was a breakout season for the young hurler. He posted a 13–12 record and struck out

He was an All-Star in seven of the next eight seasons and would also capture Gold Gloves every season from 1965 through 1973. In 1967, Gibson led the Cardinals back to the World Series, this time against the upstart Boston Red Sox. He again won Series MVP honors, shattering Boston's Impossible Dream with a remarkable performance. The Red Sox had Triple Crown winner and American League MVP Carl Yastrzemski on their side, but Yaz's heroics were not enough to overcome the domination of Gibson, who won three games and outdueled AL Cy Young Award-winner Jim Lonborg in Game Seven. In that Series, the 31-year-old Gibson had 26 strikeouts and walked just five batters. He pitched three complete games, allowing 14 hits and only three runs. Just when baseball aficionados thought they had seen Gibson in his most dominant form, he took it one step further with a watershed season in 1968. This was the iconic "Year of the Pitcher," where Detroit's Denny McLain became baseball's last 30-game winner. Gibson did not eclipse that fabled mark, but he won both the National League Cy Young and Most Valuable Player awards with a 22–9 record. He topped the NL in ERA with an amazing 1.12 mark. Gibson's 13 shutouts and 268 Ks also paced the senior circuit.

St. Louis returned to the World Series in 1968 to defend their title, this time against the Detroit Tigers. In the ultimate battle of baseball's best pitchers, the Tigers won the World Championship in seven games. Still, Gibson shone brightly, winning two games, posting an ERA of 1.67 and fanning 35 Tigers in 27 innings pitched. He vastly outclassed McLain, who lost two games in the Series for Detroit. Beyond the stats, Gibson was downright terrifying to face as a hitter. His eternal scowl, will to win, blazing fastball, and complete ownership of the mound and plate put hitters on notice and on edge. Gibson established his presence immediately and was not afraid to brush back or throw at hitters who crowded his plate.

Gibson continued to add to his stats and legacy. In 1969, he again won 20 games and pitched a league-high 28 complete games, even though MLB had lowered the mound by five inches and tightened the strike zone in response to the pitching dominance in 1968. These changes are known as the Gibson Rules. The following season, at age 34, he won a career-high 23 games, losing just seven, to take home his second

Cy Young Award. In 1972, at 36 years old, Gibson went 19–11 with a 2.46 ERA and 208 Ks in his last All-Star season. His stellar 17-year Cardinal and big-league career ended after the 1975 season. Overall, he won 251 games with a career ERA of 2.91 and 3,117 strikeouts. Gibson played with some outstanding teammates in his career including Stan Musial, Lou Brock, Curt Flood, Roger Maris, and Orlando Cepeda, but make no mistake, it was the flame-throwing man from Omaha who sent the Cardinals soaring. After retiring as a player, Gibson

was pitching coach for the Mets, Braves, and Cardinals. He was also a broadcaster and had various business interests. In 1981, Gibson took his rightful place among baseball's best in the Hall of Fame. He was later elected to the Missouri Valley Conference and the Omaha Sports Halls of Fame and was named to the MLB All-Century Team. Bob "Gibby" Gibson passed away from pancreatic cancer in 2020 at 84 years old, leaving a legacy of pride, poise, and power.

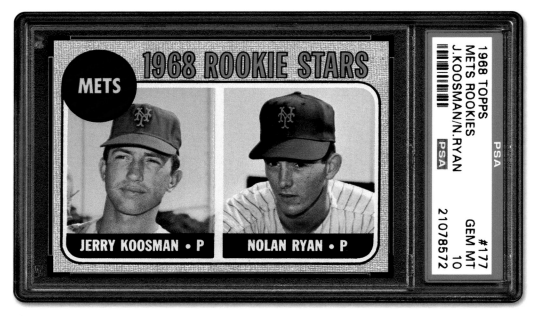

This PSA Gem Mint 10 is the sole example to reach PSA's highest grading tier.

had a time machine they would steer Topps away from that approach, as most prefer rookie cards dedicated to one player. As they say, it's just the way it was.

While the Ryan card is by no means a rarity and not overly tough to find in high grades, centering can be an issue on the front. The somewhat thin left and right borders leave little room for error if a shift in either direction is present. Furthermore, the colored reverse is somewhat susceptible to chipping along the edges, but it's not viewed as a major issue. Finally, the design of the borders can often mask corner and edge wear, so make sure you look closely with the help of a loupe to properly determine its condition. Make no mistake about it; Ryan belongs with the baseball immortals, which means his only recognized rookie card matters even more from a historical standpoint. Ryan's persona and popularity ensure long-lasting appeal for his inaugural issue.

NO OTHER PITCHER WAS MORE EMULATED BY

children over the course of his career than Nolan Ryan. "The Ryan Express" was not only effective, he was entertaining, and the flame-throwing righty had an offensive mindset on the mound. Ryan and his incredible stuff were coming after the batter, not the other way around. Baseball bats were turned into firewood on a routine basis when facing Ryan, who arguably embodied the "Don't mess with Texas" mentality better than anyone on the planet. Beyond all the accomplishments and records, some of which seem unreachable the way the game has changed, Ryan is one of the rare players whose performance would be rated higher if he were active today than when he actually played. Ryan was even better than previously thought based on current analytics.

The 1968 Topps baseball set is a collector favorite. At 598 total cards, the set is filled with stars, multi-player cards, and two incredibly important rookies. Ryan is joined by his former teammate Jerry Koosman on this 1968 Topps card, and for the record, Koosman was the superior pitcher out of the gate in New York, but we all know why collectors clamor for this card today. The other rookie card features fellow legend Johnny Bench, along with pitcher Ron Tompkins. From the 1960s through the 1970s, many of the most significant baseball rookie cards in the hobby contained anywhere from two to four players. Of course, if collectors

The Ryan Express

With a curveball so devastating that it came at you like a fastball and then dropped off the table, "The Ryan Express" was one of the toughest pitchers of his era. Some called it a 12-to-6 fastball, although it was a curve. Nolan Ryan's fastball regularly reached 95 miles per hour and sometimes topped off at 100 mph. Many baseball experts say that had Ryan not pitched on so many mediocre teams, he probably would have surpassed 400 wins.

A product of Refugio and Alvin, Texas, Lynn Nolan Ryan was dominant right from the start as a Little Leaguer. By the time he got to high school, batters were afraid to hit against him. Ryan led his Alvin High School team to the state finals, compiling a 19–3 record his senior year. Averaging two strikeouts an inning as a junior, Ryan caught the eye of New York Mets scout, Red Murff, and in 1965 he was drafted by the Mets in the 12th round. The 18-year-old phenom started his professional career with the

Appalachian League's Marion Mets in 1965. Promoted in 1966, Ryan dominated the Class A and AA leagues, striking out 307 batters in 202 innings. Except for a brief three-inning appearance for the Mets in 1966, the young right-hander continued in the minors through 1967, averaging 14 strikeouts per nine innings. Called up to New York in 1968, he pitched a shutout for six innings in his April 14 debut before he developed a blister. Opposing players took notice during that first campaign and many declared Ryan the most overpowering pitcher in the league, although his record was only 6–9. To say the least, the ninth-place 1968 Mets were

> *"The Ryan Express" was not only effective, he was entertaining, and the flame-throwing righty had an offensive mindset on the mound.*

not a very good team, but 1969 would be a different story.

Despite some military obligations, Nolan went 6–3 in 1969. The "Miracle Mets" won the National League pennant and defeated the heavily favored Baltimore Orioles to win the world championship. This was the only World Series appearance in Ryan's 27-year career. In 1970, he posted a 7–11 record with a 3.42 ERA, and the Mets finished in third place. The 23-year-old hurler was dealing with control problems, yet his fastball was the best in the league. Ryan was frustrated, believing the Mets did not help him develop because he was the third or fourth starter behind Tom Seaver and Jerry Koosman.

Ryan's fortunes changed in 1971 when he was traded with three teammates to the California Angels for Jim Fregosi. This proved to be one of the most lopsided trades in baseball history. Under the tutelage of pitching coach Tom Morgan, Ryan started a conditioning program, developed better command of his fastball, and learned to throw that nasty 12-to-6 curveball with extraordinary velocity. Ryan's years in California were his most productive. He averaged 17 wins a season and dominated American League batters for eight years, although some of his Angels teams were fair at best. In 1972, Ryan won 19 games and led the league with 329 strikeouts. In 1973, his 383 strikeouts broke the single-

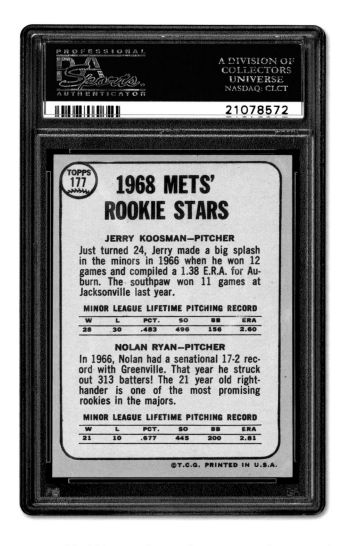

season record held by Sandy Koufax. He tossed not one, but two, no-hitters that season against Kansas City and Detroit. Ryan again topped the league with 367 strikeouts in 1974 and threw his third no-hitter against the Twins in his last start of the season. That year he also had three 19-strikeout games. Ryan was so good, he would occasionally tell an opposing batter what pitch to expect, and the batter still could not hit it. In June 1975, he threw his fourth no-hitter against the Orioles. From 1976 through 1979, Ryan led the league in strikeouts although he had a losing record two of those seasons because of the woeful Angels offense. The 1979 season was a turning point for the Angels, who finally won a division title. Although he was hurt for part of the season, Ryan started in the first playoff game in Angels' history against Baltimore's Jim Palmer.

Granted free agency after the 1979 season, Ryan signed with the NL Houston Astros, becoming the first $1 million

Nolan Ryan

athlete in MLB history. He compiled an 11–5 record and topped the league with his 1.69 ERA in 1981. That September, he broke Sandy Koufax's MLB record when he threw his fifth no-hitter against the Los Angeles Dodgers. Ryan recorded his 3,000th career strikeout in 1980, broke Walter Johnson's 3,509 strikeouts record in 1983, logged his 4,000th strikeout in 1985, and his 4,500th strikeout in 1987. The greatest hitters in baseball dreaded facing Nolan Ryan. Some even developed "Ryanitis," a one-day illness that kept them out of the lineup. Following the 1988 season, the Astros asked the 41-year-old Ryan to take a pay cut because they thought his better days were behind him. Believing that he still had a lot left in his tank, Ryan decided to sign with the Texas Rangers and stay close to home.

His initial season with the Rangers proved Ryan correct when he posted a 16–10 record, 3.20 ERA, led the American League with 301 Ks, and logged his 5,000th strikeout. In June 1990, Ryan pitched his sixth no-hitter, beating the Oakland A's, and in May 1991, at age 44, he hurled his seventh and final no-hitter against the Toronto Blue Jays. Ryan's career began to ramp down, but not before one of the most famous altercations in baseball history. In an August 1993 game against the White Sox, Ryan hit Chicago player Robin Ventura in the arm with a fastball. Ventura stormed the mound to go after Ryan, who was 20 years his senior. Ryan proceeded to get Ventura in a headlock and pummeled him unmercifully until the fight was broken up. During a late-season game that year, Ryan tore a ligament in his elbow, which ended his storied career. He was a first ballot inductee into the Baseball Hall of Fame in 1999.

While playing for the Rangers, Ryan established the Nolan Ryan Foundation to provide resources for youth, education, and community development. After retiring, Ryan and partner Don Sanders started Ryan Sanders Baseball. This organization founded two successful minor-league teams in Texas and built stadiums for them—the Class AAA Round Rock Express, and the Class AA Corpus Christi Hooks. Ryan was president of the Texas Rangers from 2008 to 2013 and later was special consultant to the Houston Astros. At the time of this writing the 75-year-old Ryan resides in Texas.

Had Nolan Ryan played on competitive teams for most of his career, his numbers would certainly have equaled or surpassed the stats of many of the greatest pitchers in the game. An eight-time All-Star, two-time National League ERA leader, and 11-time strikeout leader, Ryan holds the all-time record for strikeouts, with 5,714, and the all-time record for no-hitters, with seven. He holds the all-time record for lowest hits per nine innings pitched ratio, with 6.56, and his 773 career starts are second only to Cy Young. Nolan Ryan is certainly in a class of his own.

IF YOU LOOK BACK AT THE WAY FANS and even baseball writers evaluated players, especially when it came time for Hall of Fame voting, offensive prowess was always given the majority of the weight. Of course, the players with thunder in their bats are still the ones who tend to grab the headlines and excite crowds across the league. A much greater appreciation for defense, however, has emerged. It's hard to imagine a player who embodied the importance of the glove better than Ozzie Smith. "The Wizard of Oz" was just that, a mere mortal who transformed into something supernatural once leather was placed on his hand. He made highlight-reel plays and routinely took the field with a backflip. Smith's 1979 Topps rookie card is a symbol of his athleticism and defensive genius.

The 1979 Topps baseball set does not receive the fanfare like some of the other major issues of the decade. It doesn't quite have the eye-catching design of the 1972 Topps set, the Hall of Famer rookie selection of the 1975 Topps issue, or the monumental condition challenge of the black-bordered 1971 Topps production. That said, in the Smith card, the 726-card set does contain one of the most difficult Hall of Fame rookies from the 1970s to find in top condition. The Wizard's rookie is often found with poor centering, especially top-to-bottom, which can prevent even the sharpest of examples from achieving an unqualified grade of "Mint" or better. Relatively soft paper stock and print defects, which often come in the form of stray lines, can also contribute to the problem.

To illustrate the point, with nearly 10,000 Smith cards graded to date according to the PSA Population Report, only five examples have achieved Gem Mint 10 status at the time of this writing. Today, with increasing importance placed on defense, Smith's legacy has actually improved long after his retirement, as his achievements have been cast in a new light. With 13 Gold Glove Awards, 15 All-Star selections, 580 stolen bases, nearly 2,500 hits, and a World Series title to his credit, Smith's resume checks a variety of boxes. In the last Topps set of the decade, the Smith rookie card has emerged as its uncontested key. As a shortstop, Smith became the gold standard for defense during his prime.

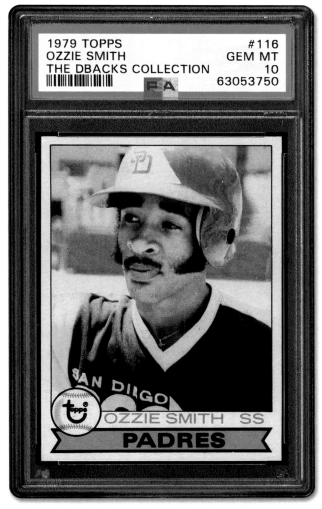

This PSA Gem Mint 10 is one of five examples to reach PSA's highest grading tier.

The Wizard of Oz

A ballplayer nicknamed "The Wizard of Oz" carries with him endless opportunities for movie-related puns and wordplay. So, let's get started. Ozzie Smith's Yellow Brick Road of a Major League Baseball career took him from San Diego to St. Louis. Along the way, he played the game with a brain, a heart, and courage. The brain—Smith was one of the most intelligent players of his generation—studying opponents and using both knowledge and instinct to position himself perfectly at shortstop to make reality-defying plays. The heart—no one played baseball with more joy, love, passion, and enthusiasm than Smith. From opening games with his patented backflips to scaling ungodly heights in catching

1979 Topps Ozzie Smith #116

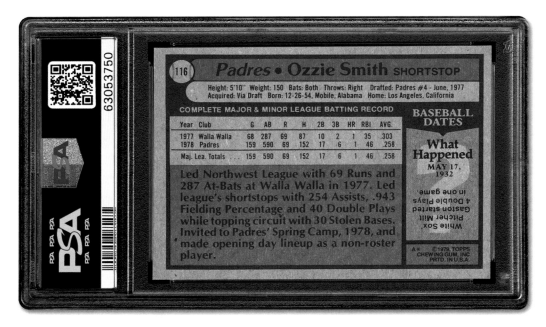

With nearly 10,000 Smith cards graded to date according to the PSA Population Report, only five examples have achieved Gem Mint 10 status at the time of this writing.

line drives to acrobatic fielding plays that would make the Wallenda family blush, when you watched Smith play, you were undoubtedly smiling. The courage—Smith stood at 5-foot-11, 150 pounds, yet he would take that throw from the second baseman and tag that second base bag fearlessly with powerful players sliding at his knees, often spikes high. In addition, Smith was unafraid of big moments, often delivering the key hit or decisive defensive gem with the game on the line.

Born in 1954 in Mobile, Alabama, Osborne Earl Smith was first drafted by the Detroit Tigers in 1976 while attending California Polytechnic State University, but he chose to stay in school instead of signing. He was eventually picked by the San Diego Padres in 1977. Upon reaching the big leagues, Smith delivered a solid debut season in 1978, one in which he finished second in National League Rookie of the Year voting, but he batted a paltry .211 in 1979. It was clear, however, that this cyclone of a shortstop would earn his keep in the field. Ozzie Smith would crush the hopes of all other National League shortstops, winning the Gold Glove Award for 13 straight seasons beginning in 1980. His mind-bending plays afield had not been seen at any point in baseball history. Smith led the NL in games played, plate appearances, and at-bats in the strike-shortened 1981 season, his first as an All-Star. Despite his growing talent, the Padres traded Smith to the Cardinals after that season. Among other players in the deal, San Diego received Garry

Templeton, an emerging star at shortstop. Templeton would go on to play ten years in San Diego, fashioning a solid MLB career. Smith would go on to Cooperstown.

Upon his arrival in St. Louis in 1982, the Cardinal faithful embraced Smith's dynamic play. Known for his defense, it was the switch-hitting Smith that propelled the Cards to the 1982 Series, batting .556 in the NL Championship Series vs. Atlanta. In the World Series, manager Whitey Herzog's crew used speed, defense, and pitching to beat the powerful Milwaukee Brewers known as Harvey's Wallbangers in a nod to Manager Harvey Kuenn. In 1985, Smith would again star at the plate, batting .435 against the Dodgers in the NLCS, with a memorable walk-off home run in Game Five, and was named NLCS MVP. Smith hit that legendary blast batting lefty. He had batted from the left side 3,009 times in the majors to that point without a single round-tripper. Smith was an All-Star every year from 1981 to 1992 and again from 1994 to his final season of 1996. His fielding percentages, at perhaps the most challenging position on the field, were eye-popping: .984 in 1982, .982 in 1984, .987 in 1987 and again in 1991, just to name a few. Defensively, his name is aptly mentioned with the game's all-time great shortstops from Honus Wagner to Ernie Banks to Luke Appling to Derek Jeter to Luis Aparacio to Cal Ripken Jr. Ozzie Smith had become one of baseball's biggest box office attractions. His voice and animated likeness even appeared on *The Simpsons* TV show in 1992. Smith spent the final

15 seasons of his career in St. Louis and became as cherished a figure in that baseball-loving community as Stan Musial, Rogers Hornsby, Bob Gibson, and Albert Pujols.

While Smith made hair-raising defensive plays and clutch hits look easy, his journey to the big leagues had its challenges. At Cal Poly Tech, he was a partial scholarship, walk-on in baseball, not recruited or offered a full scholarship by any other school. Even when Smith eventually signed with the Padres, he went to spring training in 1978 as a non-roster invitee. It was his hustle, determination, and drive that helped him make the team. In 1979, Smith started the season 0 for 32, and in 1982, he was heartbroken at the trade that would force him to leave his adopted home state of California. Whitey Herzog, the Cardinals manager, assured Smith that the move to St. Louis would be beneficial, and he was prophetic. These challenges only served to fuel Smith's fire and passion to succeed.

Ozzie Smith would crush the hopes of all other National League shortstops, winning the Gold Glove Award for 13 straight seasons beginning in 1980.

Smith retired as a player after the 1996 season at the age of 41. The Cardinals retired his number "1" uniform that September, and in 2002, his first year of eligibility, Smith was inducted into the Baseball Hall of Fame. It is ironic that after his playing career ended, Smith hosted the popular *This Week in Baseball* television program originally hosted by legendary broadcaster Mel Allen. It was largely Smith's on-field exploits that helped to popularize the show in the 1980s and 1990s. He also worked as a broadcaster in St. Louis and for CNN before returning to the Cardinals as a special instructor. At the time of this writing, Ozzie Smith is 67 years old and resides in Missouri. In addition to Cooperstown, Smith has also been immortalized in the Missouri, Alabama, and St. Louis Cardinals Halls of Fame. It is safe to say that no one will ever forget those magical years when baseball fans everywhere delighted in watching the wonderful Wizard of Oz.

1960 Ted Williams game-used jersey,
Williams game-used cap circa 1941,
Williams 1950 game-used bat, and
US Marine Corps ID card. *The Mike
Heffner Collection.*

A Look at an Evolving Hobby

★ ★ ★ ★ ★ ★ ★ ★ ★ ★ ★ ★ ★ ★

In these pages, longtime collector and hobby expert Joe Orlando takes a look at how the sports card collecting hobby has evolved over the years.

From the explosive growth of the 1980s through to the hobby's recent dramatic growth, Orlando breaks it all down for us and makes it easy to understand that this hobby is as strong as it has ever been, and the future is bright. Along the way, he touches on pre-war, Golden Era, modern, and ultra-modern cards and details the evolution of the hobby decade by decade.

Introduction _____

Before we begin, there are two things readers should keep in mind as they move through the text.

First, there are many noteworthy and impactful events that took place during the more than 40 years covered in this chapter. Some of the most influential aspects of each decade are touched on in the paragraphs ahead, though not all are included. A lot has changed in that time frame, which means a lot of details led to that change and not all of it could fit neatly into the next few pages.

Second, this chapter is written from the perspective of one collector who happened to live through it all. As a child, I started collecting in the 1970s. I took my personal hobby to another level the following decade when the entire collectibles market made the same move. Unlike many of my friends, however, I stayed active through all the ups and downs to follow. Eventually, I joined PSA in 1999 and remained connected to the hobby, personally *and* professionally, from that point forward.

For those of you who stayed the course and lived through all of it with me, perhaps the timeline and corresponding events will bring back memories that helped shape your collecting journey. For those of you who were around but lost touch with the collecting world at different points, or for those who joined along the way and stayed active but weren't around for all of it, here's one collector's view from ringside.

The 1980s _____

A Niche Hobby Becomes a Nationwide Industry

The 1980s. Sports card collecting had been around for a century before Journey and Van Halen were coming into their own, so why begin here?

While it's true that the hobby was alive and well for many years up to this point, the relatively small collectibles field blossomed into a coast-to-coast phenomenon during the 1980s. Before the decade began, hardcore collectors dominated the industry. After it started, the masses gradually joined the party as collecting cards became more of a mainstream pastime.

In addition, the 1980–present time will always represent the break between modern and vintage, no matter how many years pass. In my view, defining what should be considered modern or vintage is not about the sheer age of the card. It has to do with how the hobby changed. You see the same type of differentiation in other collectibles fields such as coins and stamps. Everything, from the perception of the hobby, to the way collectors began to protect their cards in a more meaningful way, to its structure, changed during the decade.

Price guides played a big role in the changing structure of the market. While there were basic, annual guides that you could purchase at local bookstores, the monthly guides had more meaningful impact. Of course, they were all delivered in hard-copy form only. Beckett released their first monthly price guide in 1984, which became a staple during the robust run. Other guides such as *Current Card Prices* (CCP) and *Card Prices Update* (CPU), which predated Beckett's monthly effort, also had success at the time. There was an appetite for data and the up and down action in these guides gave collectors something to look forward to each month. Today, it's hard to imagine having to be that patient in the age of immediate gratification, but we all had to cope with it when it came to box scores, too.

Furthermore, publications like *Sports Collectors Digest* (SCD), and *The Trader Speaks* helped facilitate a robust mail-order business in the pre-internet era. If you were an active collector during this period, then you probably remember how there seemed to be a baseball card shop every square mile and a show every weekend once the business started to boom, and that boom was driven by baby boomers. This group grew up during the 1950s and 1960s, when Topps dominated the scene. At the end of the day, the collectibles world is selling things like history and scarcity, but nostalgia is arguably part of its most powerful pitch. A whole generation of people who now had disposable income were looking to reconnect with their inner child, and the hobby offered that opportunity.

Long-retired baseball icons like Joe DiMaggio, Mickey Mantle, and Ted Williams suddenly found that they could earn far more money by signing their name than they ever did playing the game that made them famous. I can remember, however, paying a paltry sum of $10 for an in-person Mantle signature at a Los Angeles Airport show. Where is a time machine when you need it? In fact, pitching legend Bob Feller would often secure his own table at shows with a handwritten sign that offered his signature for a mere $3. For those of you who weren't around at the time, I know how hard all of this is to believe, but it's true.

Before the big boom occurred, things were relatively simple from a card manufacturer perspective. Donruss and Fleer joined Topps in baseball at the start of the decade, and baseball was easily the most widely collected sport in the hobby. Error cards were all the rage, and people were starting to hoard complete sets and unopened cases. Even though Topps had been the tried-and-true brand for seemingly eons, each brand had its moments by the middle

In the spring of 1986, approximately 5,500 uncirculated 1952 Topps baseball cards were unearthed and brought to market.

of the decade. For example, who can forget the excitement around the 1984 Donruss or 1984 Fleer Update sets? Within a few years, however, the field of card brands would get crowded.

Some were resurrected names such as Bowman, through Topps, while others were entirely new players like Score. There were also short-lived products like Sportflics, which promoted their "Triple Action Magic Motion" design. By tilting the cards, the image of the player would change on the front. The beauty of these incredibly sturdy cards is that you could hurl them against the wall or use them like a ninja throwing star against your siblings and they would remain in strict mint condition.

Unfortunately, I traded a high-grade 1960 Topps baseball card set for a case of these reflective weapons at a convention. Financially, it would prove to be a terrible move in the long term, but how do you place a value on your brother screaming, "Pete Incaviglia is stuck in my leg!" Boys will be boys.

Around the same time, perhaps the greatest discovery of vintage sports cards took the collectibles world by storm. In the spring of 1986, approximately 5,500 uncirculated 1952 Topps baseball cards were unearthed and brought to market. For the baby boomers that were at the heart of the industry eruption, the "1952 Topps Find" was something dreams were made of. It was *THE* post-WWII set and it contained *THE* card in Mantle, the holiest of holy grails in their eyes. The miraculous event not only excited collectors across the country, but it also helped raise even more awareness about the hobby we all love.

The 1989 Upper Deck Griffey is the most iconic card of its generation.

In 1989, the company that made the biggest impact in the card market was Upper Deck. The look and feel of their cards was simply different and more advanced than what collectors were accustomed to for most of the decade. Their inaugural release was a cut above in terms of quality and it contained hologram technology on the reverse to help prevent counterfeiting. Over time, we all learned that no decade's card products were counterfeited more than those from the 1980s. From the 1985 Topps Mark McGwire to the 1986 Fleer Michael Jordan, the simplicity of the card designs made them enticing targets for criminals.

Upper Deck changed the game and their first card, in their first set, became the most recognizable image of the new hobby wave—the #1 Ken Griffey Jr. rookie card. The card may not have a market value that properly reflects its symbolic value, but the 1989 Upper Deck Griffey is the most iconic card of its generation. It also set the tone for the following decade, one that produced the good, the bad, and the ugly before it came to an end.

The boom had legs, but it was about to bust...at least temporarily.

The 1990s

Ups and Downs During a Turbulent Decade

On the heels of Upper Deck announcing their presence with authority a year earlier, Nuke Laloosh style, the decade got off to a great start.

The energy created in the 1980s was spilling over into 1990s, and business continued to be good. In 1991, our industry experienced the most well-attended National Sports Collectors Convention (NSCC) the hobby has ever witnessed. The unprecedented show took place in Anaheim, California, and it was pure chaos. As strong as the NSCC was in 2021, the 1991 show was next-level nutty. Sotheby's, an auction company used to offering Picassos and chateaus in France, sold the incredible Copeland Collection, which garnered next-level bidding.

Just a short time earlier, Professional Sports Authenticator (PSA) opened its doors. PSA was not the first card-grading service on the block, but they were the first to gain serious traction. That said, it took time for that to happen. The concept of third-party grading was still new, but once the hobby saw how it could help the market advance, it

became a fixture. In 1998, PSA would grade its one-millionth card after being in business for several years. From 1998 to 2020, PSA graded a minimum of one million cards each year. At the time of this writing, PSA was grading more than two million cards per quarter.

In 1994, the event that caused the most harm to our hobby in the decade took place. During one of the most exciting baseball seasons I have ever watched, the players went on strike on August 12 and the league didn't resume play until April 2, 1995. It was the longest work stoppage in baseball history, and it acted as the pin in the balloon for collectors. All of the positive energy generated from the previous 10-plus years had been eviscerated. Hobby participation, which was still largely driven by baseball, declined rapidly. Stores and shows gradually became endangered species. It wasn't a death sentence, but it hurt for a while.

Parallel and insert/memorabilia cards became all the rage, especially by the second half of the decade. They are otherwise known as "chase" cards, the Willy Wonka Golden Tickets of the trading card world.

At the manufacturer level, we not only saw an increase in card brands, but we also witnessed a shift in focus. Parallel and insert/memorabilia cards became all the rage, especially by the second half of the decade, and they came in various forms. They are otherwise known as "chase" cards, the Willy Wonka Golden Tickets of the trading card world. Some of the most desirable chase cards ever made were produced in the 1990s, but their prominence would eventually cause some market issues. These limited-edition cards went from being a positive to somewhat of a negative, and back to being one of the key drivers of the modern market today.

I can vividly remember watching collectors of all ages opening packs, standing over a trashcan and tossing all the non-chase or base cards into it. The only cards they were interested in keeping were the cardboard lottery tickets. This was not a healthy practice, and while none of us have a crystal ball, you could see problems on the horizon. Base cards and sets were becoming less relevant and, in some cases, obsolete. The chase for the chase cards was on and everything else was just in the way, at least to those collectors who were making it rain into the garbage. The allure of swatches or patches, slivers of bats, autographs, and finite numbering was too great.

The scarcity of these cards was manufactured, which wasn't always embraced in the way it is today. Now, many modern-era collectors prefer it because you know *exactly* how many of each card was made. This is one advantage over vintage cards. Population reports are terrific and critical to becoming an informed buyer, but they are limited to what has been submitted to each grading service. We would all love to know exactly how many 1952 Topps Mickey Mantles were made and, more importantly, survived. With the help of population data and experience, we can piece estimates together, but it's not an exact science.

By the late-1990s, the stars aligned in an almost ideal way, which brought the industry out of a multi-year slump.

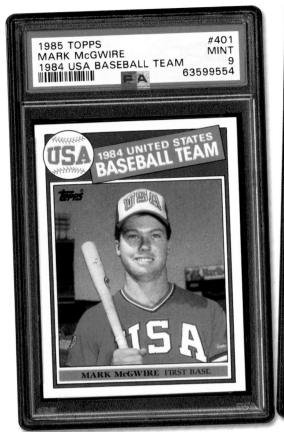

Baseball was back, opportunities to buy were increasing, and there was money on the sidelines waiting to get into the game. The hobby was on fire once again.

we lost Pinnacle as one of the big manufacturers, and auctions started to become more prevalent as the decade headed to a close. There was one sale, however, that changed the auction circuit forever. In 1999, Sotheby's was in the news again. The renowned auction house handled the Barry Halper collection, which was comprised mostly of vintage baseball memorabilia. This extraordinary event attracted new buyers and, when the final lot closed, the prices realized surpassed the $20 million mark. To put that groundbreaking tally into perspective, a PSA NM-MT 8 1952 Topps Mantle was worth about $25,000–$30,000 at the time. A PSA Poor 1 T206 Honus Wagner was worth about the same.

That same year, the industry's most high-profile bust—Operation Bullpen—was in its early stages. In the coming years, the FBI would bring a number of people involved in a prolific autograph forgery ring to justice. It not only sent a message to criminals far and wide, but it also reminded us just how big this business had become. The good news was that the federal government was not only watching, but they were willing to help. These convictions and others became part of the hobby's maturation process. Card manufacturers had begun to take a more active role in documenting their signed products, and credible authentication services were emerging, which helped provide a safer environment for collectors.

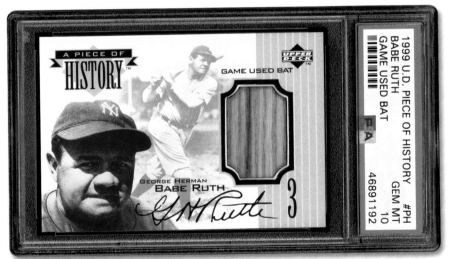

The combination of the 1998 home-run chase between Mark McGwire and Sammy Sosa, the emergence of internet platforms such as eBay, and the dot-com boom which suddenly created more disposable income for some folks all helped inject life into the business. Baseball was back, opportunities to buy were increasing, and there was money on the sidelines waiting to get into the game. The hobby was on fire once again.

Around the same time, a few more grading services sprouted,

It had been a 10-year rollercoaster ride, but the hobby was back on its feet.

The 2000s

Back to Basics

The next decade would have its share of ups and downs, just like the previous one, and major changes were on the horizon.

By the end of the 2000s, we lost two more card company staples in Donruss and Fleer. Their brands, like Pinnacle's, would be acquired by the likes of Upper Deck and newcomer Panini, a company that became a force in the coming years. For longtime collectors like myself, the loss of those companies was unsettling at the time, but manufacturer attrition would ultimately prove to be a good thing. The reduction in manufacturers meant fewer products to consider, which improved the structure of the marketplace.

In 2000, it was evident that the vintage market had moved to another level by the time of the NSCC in Anaheim, California, that summer. Record prices were being paid on the show floor, especially for 1950s and 1960s material.

The modern market was continuing to ride the McGwire/Sosa wave and price barriers were being broken. For the first time, PSA Gem Mint 10s of the 1986 Fleer Michael Jordan card were routinely selling well into five figures as the valuation wall between vintage and modern started to fall, at least a little. As the years passed, online auctions were not only producing more and more price records, but they also became *THE* preferred venue for buying and selling.

By the 2001 NSCC in Cleveland, Ohio, the modern market had reached a peak. The excitement around 2001 Upper Deck Golf and the sport's biggest star, Tiger Woods, was palpable. It had been a long time since a major manufacturer produced a golf card product and it had a transcendent superstar leading the way, which brought mainstream interest to the game in droves. Dozens of new grading services virtually popped up overnight to take advantage of the demand, but only a handful stood the test of time by weathering the incoming storm. After hitting such a high that summer, the

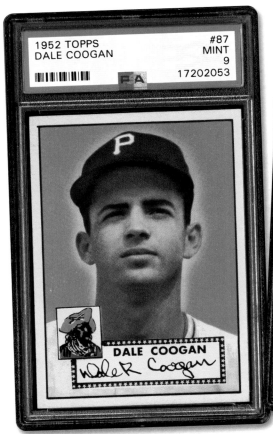

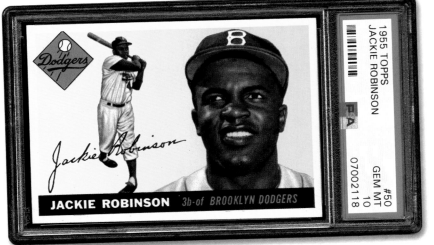

It was like looking at a Cheesecake Factory menu. Where do you even begin?

To make matters worse, for those whose collections were dedicated to their favorite players, the checklists for star players with long careers became obscenely long. To put things in perspective, Derek Jeter and Albert Pujols (who was still active when this was being written), each had over 10,000 different cards issued during their playing days. Let that sink in for a moment. Even if you had the financial wherewithal, completing a player run became a pipe dream, especially with the influx of limited-edition cards.

Speaking of completing sets, one very positive reaction to the new market dynamic was that it drove more people back to basics and traditional set building. By the middle of the 2000s, a resurgence in classic set collecting was evident. The non-star cards, or commons, were becoming increasingly relevant because you needed them all to finish the task. The PSA Set Registry was growing steadily, year after year, and still is today. This was a healthy practice and sign for the industry. Set building is a foundational piece of collecting and it helped prop the business up during some leaner times in the modern market.

As the decade came to a close, there were plenty of other noteworthy developments that impacted the collecting world, from Topps securing an exclusive MLB license, to PED scandals in baseball, to economic and societal events that changed the entire world. Amazingly, the hobby lowered its head and powered right through all of it like Marshawn Lynch in "Beast Mode." The 2008 financial crisis was felt far and wide, from 401(k) plans to real estate. It was swift and painful, but the hobby carried on. It would be disingenuous to describe it as "thriving" at the time, but the sports collectibles business wasn't affected like other markets.

Here's a great example. Early in the decade and during the week of 9/11, a modest-sized vintage card auction was scheduled to close, just days after the horrific events took place. The owner was struggling as to whether he should shut it down or let nature takes it course. He decided the

modern market would start suffering a decline by 2002. Around the midpoint of the decade, the vintage star card market was softening as well.

Something interesting was happening. Card collecting was changing. For most of the prior two decades, demand was more concentrated, especially when it came to current rookie cards. In the past, and at worst, collectors had to decide between a handful of different rookie cards to buy. As time went on, the number of choices became overwhelming. The market became fractured as a result. If you were new to the hobby, figuring out which cards to buy could be daunting.

show must go on. Amazingly, record prices were generated in the midst of this incredibly uncertain and emotional time. Why? The hobby is an escape. It's the place some collectors go to get away from the daily grind, and, in this case, the horrific side of humanity. It was proof that collectibles had an advantage over most other tangibles, one that can be difficult to articulate or quantify at times.

By the middle of the 2000s, a resurgence in classic set collecting was evident. The non-star cards, or commons, were becoming increasingly relevant because you needed them all to finish the task.

Unsettling events like these drove some collectors further into vintage collectibles. While collecting cards of active players is exciting as new pages of their stories are written each day, there is a comfort in collecting vintage material. It tends to be less volatile when the market turns. Downward trends, while they do occur, tend to be less severe. The

legacies of these players are already carved in stone. These collectibles have been battle tested in a way that those of most active athletes haven't. Collectors don't have to worry about Jackie Robinson and Ted Williams getting injured, suspended for PEDs, or involved in off-the-field controversies. It's a safer place to play for those who want to stay active but are concerned about the happenings in the world around them.

In the 2000s, our world was rocked, but collecting was comfort food for many Americans.

The 2010s
Don't Call It a Comeback

Near the outset of the 2010s, we started to see steady, albeit modest, growth in the space as the market began to gradually pick up during the period.

It began in vintage, but by the end of the decade, demand in the modern market started to pick up at a substantial rate before it exploded in 2020, which we will address a little later in this chapter. The card market started blossoming in the non-sports and TCG genres, too, as the typical generational cycle was taking place. The youngsters of the 1990s were now entering their 30s and becoming nostalgic like previous generations did before them.

At the manufacturer level, Topps remained the only game in town for licensed MLB cards, while Panini became the

exclusive provider of both licensed basketball and football cards. Panini wrangled the NBA exclusive at the beginning of the decade and secured one with the NFL by 2016. Upper Deck, once on top of the mountain, started to fade into relative obscurity outside of hockey after losing their ability to produce licensed

cards for the big three American sports. For fans of their product, and there were many, it was a loss felt by many collectors but the further reduction in choices would prove to be a positive change for the hobby once again.

A noticeable increase in hobby content production was evident in the 2010s. More available information often leads to increased commerce because it improves buyer confidence. This is a trend that continues today as established and emerging companies seek to provide essential intelligence to consumers. The advancement of mobile devices, namely smartphones, made that content more attainable during the decade. Like the underlying Internet itself, these ever-improving data vehicles helped facilitate increased activity. As a collector, you could suddenly access or do almost anything, at any time, from anywhere, with your fingertips.

As this 10-year stretch continued, we began to see more global interest in trading card collecting, and some of it coincided with greater international interest in sports, with basketball leading the way. There was also something brewing in the non-sports genre, with Pokémon cards leading the way. It was the perfect example of the generational cycle in full effect. The Pokémon trading card game became a nationwide phenomenon in the late 1990s and now the kids that once drove sales for the product were reconnecting with their youth as adults. Like the gradual growth in the NBA card market across the world, Pokémon cards were being submitted for grading, from the UK to Japan.

The baseball card market, which was strong throughout the decade and still is today, finally had some challengers for hobby supremacy. Well, at least as it related to submissions-by-type. By the end of the decade, and for the first time in PSA's long history, more basketball cards were submitted

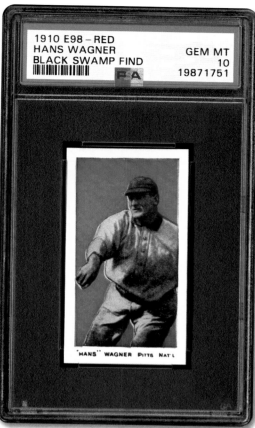

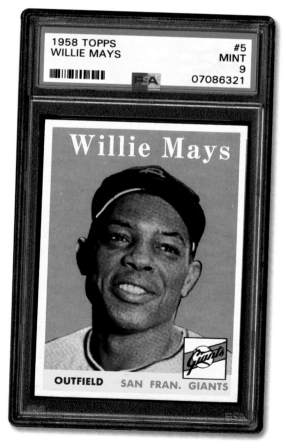

annually for grading than any other sport. To be fair, more baseball cards were being sent to PSA for grading than ever before as well, but basketball cards had a slight edge in volume by 2020. It's not that baseball card interest was declining. Basketball demand was just exploding. The global advantage of the sport was evident as it helped cultivate more international collectors.

As the years passed, it was becoming increasingly difficult to find great vintage collections. Since third-party grading had caught on in such a big way, it wasn't long before fantastic ungraded cards found their way into a plastic holder of the submitter's choice. Amazingly, two shocking finds made national news in the 2010s. The 2012 "Black Swamp Find," where hundreds of high-grade 1910 E98 baseball cards were discovered, and the 2016 "Lucky Seven Find," which contained several examples of the 1909–1911 T206 Ty Cobb back rarity, went viral. Both finds, as well as others, reminded us that buried treasure still exists.

By the middle of the decade, there appeared to be a shift in collector focus, which started to impact the vintage card market more significantly. In the prior decade, when set building gained momentum, the star card market cooled a little. I wouldn't describe it as soft, but there were plenty of cases where prices for tough commons were the record

setters everyone was talking about after an auction would close. In the 2010s, the stars were not only back in the spotlight, but they were also pulling away from the rest of the pack in dramatic fashion. The cards that are best described as "beachfront property" were being treated as such. This trend continues and it's one that will remain, in my opinion.

By definition, the stars have always received the lion's share of collector attention, but this market move was

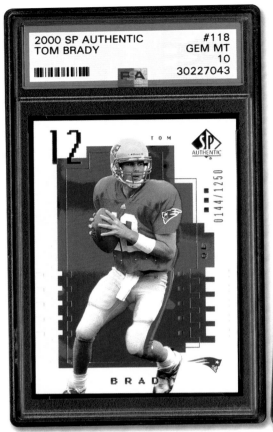

During the last few years of the 2010s, the modern card segment of the business started making a significant move. There were signs that market conditions were improving before 2020 and the pandemic, which we will get to in a bit. Younger people were getting involved and modern card issues were being given greater respect by some veteran collectors. There is a percentage of collectors out there who tend to scoff at modern card activity and prices, especially when those prices start competing with the classics, like some that are featured in this book. It is simply hard for those collectors to get their minds wrapped around it.

For the record, while the modern card market has surged to unprecedented levels, the dynamic isn't exactly new. Let me explain. When large numbers of new people start entering the market, they tend to start with modern cards. There are different reasons for this, which range from the vast opportunities to open packs of new product, to the relatively inexpensive options available in modern cards, but the driving force is something altogether different.

different. There are stars, and then there are superstars. There are Hall of Famers, and then there are legends. There is a difference and more collectors seemed to be focusing their dollars on the A-list names and their most important cards. The gap was always wide between Ty Cobb and Elmer Flick, or Willie Mays and Orlando Cepeda, but it was getting wider. It was also widening between the card issues that were considered pillars of the hobby, like Cracker Jacks and Goudeys, versus more esoteric issues. Card brand, and player brand, matters. That is what most new buyers want.

Modern collecting, specifically of active athletes, can offer something that even the greatest vintage cards can't. It's a reality show versus an account, memory, or tale. With current sports stars, the story is unfolding right in front of you. It's real-time action. Much like the appeal of playing fantasy sports, the ups and downs are felt as they happen. This actually elevates the emotional component of collecting. Being able to witness the player's career helps improve the connection to them and the events that define their legacies. When these moments come to end, they become memories...and those memories become nostalgia.

In some ways, the 2010s represented the calm before the storm, but you could feel the train moving down the tracks before it became a runaway in 2020.

Modern collecting, specifically of active athletes, can offer something that even the greatest vintage cards can't. It's a reality show versus an account, memory, or tale. With current sports stars, the story is unfolding right in front of you. It's real-time action.

2020 to the Present

Forces of Nature Collide – COVID-19

In a year none of us will ever forget, when our livelihoods were challenged in a way we never anticipated or imagined, the hobby somehow rose above.

So much has been written about this unlikely outcome, but it happened. For many, it was as unfathomable as George Foreman knocking out Michael Moorer for the heavyweight title in 1994, or even Tom Brady winning a Super Bowl in his first year with Tampa Bay in 2021. The hobby didn't just survive 2020 and the pandemic, it knocked COVID-19 out and raised the trophy.

In many cases, mainstream media made it seem as if the hobby was dead prior to this resurgence and it rose from the grave in 2020, which is completely untrue. The hobby was healthy, and growing steadily, before the pandemic hit us. In my view, a more accurate description of what took place is that the fire was already burning, but the circumstances at the time were akin to gas being thrown on the fire, which turned the flames into an inferno. People had more time on their hands. They had an opportunity to reconnect with old hobbies or seek out new ones to pass the time.

A host of individuals found collectibles in 2020, a market that combines the freedom of tangible assets with an outlet for the human condition. For some, collectibles are an emotional investment, both literally and figuratively. These objects we pursue resonate in ways no stock or bond could ever dream of doing. Collectibles have an advantage over just about any traditional form of investment you can think of because we want them in a way that goes far beyond the strict

financial component. Collectibles can provide more to the owner than just monetary returns.

People disappear into their hobbies in times of stress, and the pandemic gave us a need to seek refuge in other things. Some may call it a distraction, others might think of it more as a process, but like most other endeavors of its kind, collecting can take your mind off the things you prefer not to dwell on all day. Human beings need a place to go, mentally, and the hobby provided it to hordes of people who craved it in 2020. Some of the new participants, whether they were complete novices or inactive collectors trying to rekindle an old flame, started tapping into the inherent gene all hobbyists share.

The influx of buyers spawned a level of growth never seen before. As is often the case in the hobby, the surge started and was perhaps most dramatic in trading cards. Why do cards usually lead the charge in the sports collectibles world when new consumers arrive on the scene? Cards are simple, and I mean that in the most positive way. They are easy to

understand. They are part of sets. They are graded on a scale of one-to-ten and are separated only by condition. Cards are the closest things our market has to commodities. They are also more likely to connect us to our youth versus memorabilia. Most current hobbyists, even ones who presently collect other things, started in cards.

Furthermore, there is more free content and historical data available about cards than any other segment of the sports collectibles industry. The card market has support, and, more importantly, the kind of underlying structure that makes collecting easier. Memorabilia, which comes in many forms, from game-used items to display pieces, requires more research and a better understanding of how one item measures up against another even when the technical grade is exactly the same. If we are talking about the same card, then a card is a card is a card, with the exception of its physical attributes. That simplicity helps facilitate a robust market.

During this transformative run, from 2020 to well into 2022, trading cards have garnered the most attention. Cards have always been the foundation of our hobby. They have the power to pull other segments of the industry up with them because cards have the ability to attract such large numbers of new players, some of whom will expand their horizons as they gain more experience. Rising cards tend to raise all collectibles, but cards have been the talk of the town since the pandemic began.

Cardboard has been the fuel behind our hobby's most recent rally, one that has no peer in our hobby's long history.

The Future of the Hobby

Like the rest of the world, the hobby is changing quickly. New money is coming in, and it's not just limited to buyers.

Interested individuals and entities have provided an injection of resources into the collectibles space. In the summer of 2021, Fanatics shook things up at the manufacturer level. In the coming years, innovation is sure to accelerate with more investments in technology. Fractional ownership, vaulting services, advanced pricing data, collection management tools, and more are changing the way we view the hobby altogether. The items we cherish are being given the red-carpet treatment, and they deserve it. Truth be told, it's long overdue. Collecting is fun, but it's also serious business because of the money at stake.

We are all watching the second noteworthy market surge since the 1998–2001 growth period, but this

one is much, much more significant. There are some pure speculators out there who have joined the fray, there is no doubt about it. There are also, however, plenty of people who have fallen in love with the action. The hunting, gathering, sharing, trading, bidding, and building side

of what collecting is all about can provide a thoroughly rewarding experience. Once that happens and those who enter begin tasting the potential fruits of their labor, it gives the hobby a great opportunity for collector retention. Money aside, with the proper guidance and education, collecting can be really fun.

Speaking of money, there was a time when a six- or seven-figure sale was a rare occurrence. Over the past year or so, sales in this range have become common. High-quality examples of vintage classics like the 1952 Topps Mantle and T206 Wagner have broken the $5 million and $6 million barriers, respectively, while modern card marvels of Tom Brady, Michael Jordan, and Mike Trout have also joined the seven-figure club. Six-figure sales, which were far more infrequent just a few years ago, have become a dime a dozen. What has been driving values at this level? Quality and scarcity. Whether it's modern or vintage, acquiring something that few others can claim to own is as appealing as it has ever been. Rarity, in many cases, rules.

There are also, however, plenty of people who have fallen in love with the action. The hunting, gathering, sharing, trading, bidding, and building side of what collecting is all about can provide a thoroughly rewarding experience.

Who knows how long this current surge will last and where the market might settle to, if at all. Only time will tell, but collecting is part of who we are. It's not going anywhere and there's never been a better time to be involved. The world is our oyster when it comes to the hobby, and the future is getting brighter by the day. Over the past 40-plus years, our hobby has shown its resilience in the face of adversity and its ability to adjust when change is required. The next 40 years should be fascinating to watch, for those of us who are fortunate enough to see it.

At its core, no matter what lies ahead for the industry, collecting is part of our DNA and that primal driver should carry the hobby through whatever comes its way.

1966 Roberto Clemente game-used jersey, Clemente game-used bat circa 1969, Clemente game-used cleats circa 1969, and Clemente-signed baseball. *The Mike Heffner Collection.*

Index

About the Authors and Contributors

Tom Zappala is a businessman in the greater Boston area who is passionate about maintaining the traditions and historical significance of our National Pastime. He is co-author of the award-winning books *The T206 Collection: The Players & Their Stories*, *The Cracker Jack Collection: Baseball's Prized Players*, *The 100 Greatest Baseball Autographs*, *Legendary Lumber: The Top 100 Player Bats in Baseball History*, *An All-Star's Cardboard Memories*, and *Baseball & Bubble Gum: The 1952 Topps Collection*. In addition to co-hosting a popular Boston area radio talk show, Zappala co-hosts *The Great American Collectibles Show*, which airs nationally every week. As co-owner of ATS Communications, a multimedia and consulting company, he handles publicity and personal appearances for several authors and a variety of artists in the entertainment field. He enjoys collecting vintage baseball and boxing memorabilia, using the simple philosophy of collecting for the love of the sport. Proud of his Italian heritage, Zappala authored *Bless Me Sister*, a humorous book about his experience attending an Italian parochial school.

Ellen Zappala is president of ATS Communications, a multimedia marketing and consulting company. Co-author of the award-winning books *The T206 Collection: The Players & Their Stories*, *The Cracker Jack Collection: Baseball's Prized Players*, *The 100 Greatest Baseball Autographs*, *Legendary Lumber: The Top 100 Player Bats in Baseball History*, *An All-Star's Cardboard Memories*, and *Baseball & Bubble Gum: The 1952 Topps Collection*. Zappala also worked with former welterweight boxing champ and Boxing Hall of Famer, Tony DeMarco, on his autobiography *Nardo: Memoirs of a Boxing Champion*. The former publisher of a group of weekly newspapers in Massachusetts and New Hampshire, Zappala also served as president of the New England Press Association. She works closely with various publishing companies on behalf other authors and handles publicity in both print and electronic media. She especially enjoys bringing the stories of the Deadball Era and Golden Age baseball players to life.

Joe Orlando is one of the foremost experts in the sports card and memorabilia industry. As the former CEO of Collectors Universe, Inc. and president of Professional Sports Authenticator (PSA), Orlando was responsible for developing the authentication and grading standards used by the hobby's recognized leader. Orlando's diverse knowledge base helped PSA become the premier brand in the hobby. During his 22-year tenure, Orlando operated as editor of Sports Market Report (SMR), a nationally distributed, monthly publication and he wrote dozens of articles for PSA's website. Amongst other book projects, Orlando authored *Collecting Sports Legends* (2008), and he was the lead author of the award-winning *Legendary Lumber: The Top 100 Player Bats in Baseball History* (2017). Orlando contributed to the award-winning *The T206 Collection: The Players and Their Stories* (2010), *The Cracker Jack Collection: Baseball's Prized Players* (2013), *The 100 Greatest Baseball Autographs* (2016), an *All-Star's Cardboard Memories* (2018) and *Baseball & Bubble Gum: The 1952 Topps Collection* (2020). As a market expert, Orlando has appeared as a featured guest on numerous radio and television programs, including ESPN's *Outside the Line*s, HBO's *Real Sports*, and the Fox Business Network.

John Molori is a columnist/ writer for *Boston Baseball Magazine*, *Northeast Golf Monthly*, and EBSCO Publishing. He contributed to the award-winning books, *The Cracker Jack Collection: Baseball's Prized Players*, *The 100 Greatest Baseball Autographs*, *Legendary Lumber: The Top 100 Player Bats in Baseball History*, and *Baseball & Bubble Gum: The 1952 Topps Collection*. Molori has also written for ESPNW. com, *Patriots Football Weekly*, *Boston Metro*, *Providence Journal*, *Lowell Sun*, and the *Eagle-Tribune*. A rotating co-host on *The Great American Collectibles Show*, his radio and TV credits include: ESPN, SiriusXM, FOX, Comcast, NESN, and NECN. Molori has lectured on writing and media at Emerson College, Boston University, Lasell University, and Curry College. His awards include: New England Emmy Award, CableACE, Beacon Award, and the New Hampshire Association of Broadcasters Award. For his contributions as a sports journalist and commentator, Molori is an inductee into the Methuen, MA, Athletic Hall of Fame alongside 1987 Cy Young Award winner Steve Bedrosian.

Christina Good is a senior photographer for Collectors Universe, Inc. A Seattle native and 2005 graduate of Brooks Institute of Photography in Santa Barbara, Good initially honed her skills on portraiture and wedding photography. Since joining the company in 2013, she has become a key part of the photography team and especially enjoys the opportunity to use her photography skills to artistically document rare coins and collectibles. Her beautiful, artistically styled images have also appeared in the award-winning books, *An All-Star's Cardboard Memories* and *Baseball & Bubble Gum: The 1952 Topps Collection*.

Brooks Robinson Gold Glove commemorating 16 consecutive Gold Glove Awards from 1960–1974. *The Mike Heffner Collection.*